*You Aren't Alone
The Voices of Homosexuality*

You Aren't Alone

THE VOICES
OF HOMOSEXUALITY

PEGGY KIRK, M.A.

Blue Dolphin Publishing

Published by Blue Dolphin Publishing, Inc.
P.O. Box 8, Nevada City, CA 95959
Orders: 1-800-643-0765
Web: www.bluedolphinpublishing.com

ISBN: 1-57733-144-3

Library of Congress Cataloging-in-Publication Data

Kirk, Peggy, 1937-
  You aren't alone : the voices of homosexuality / Peggy Kirk.
    p. cm.
  Includes bibliographical references.
  ISBN 1-57733-144-3 (pbk. : alk. paper)
  1. Homosexuality. 2. Homosexuality—Psychological aspects.
3. Gays—Interviews. I. Title.

  HA76.25.K57 2004
  306.76'6'0922—dc22

2004000355

Cover art © 2004 Prestige Art Galleries, Inc.
for Tito Salomoni (1927-1987).
Mr. Salomoni was one of the last classical surrealists,
evocative of the works created by Escher, Dali, and Magritte.
Used by permission: www.prestigeart.com

First printing, February, 2004

Printed in the United States of America

10   9   8   7   6   5   4   3   2   1

You Aren't Alone: The Voices of Homosexuality
is dedicated to those living and those to be born
who are looking and will be searching for a pathway
out of brokenness, and to Nicky.

Contents

Preface

IF YOU ARE A HOMOSEXUAL or are considering becoming one you have opened the right page in the right book. *You Aren't Alone: The Voices of Homosexuality* is filled with stories of men and women who have perhaps walked in your path and even danced in your shoes. You may find a story somewhere in this book which will tug at your heart. You may also find yourself identifying with someone in the book and want to follow their path.

You Aren't Alone: The Voices of Homosexuality is not meant to bury you in a grave of guilt, inundate you with theological doctrine, or pass judgment on you. This book, the second in the *You Aren't Alone* series, is written for men and women who are presently living as homosexuals or are perhaps trying to decide if that way of living is best for them.

The men and women who shared their stories did so with a desire to help someone searching for happiness grasp their own golden ring. Each one requested that I share their names and addresses, but this is not possible. The names and locations in the book are not real; however, the stories are true, the people are real, the words are their own, and the circumstances are authentic.

Reading these stories will likely bring tears to your eyes, laughter to your lips, or even anger to your soul. In reading about the lives of these courageous people, you may decide on a path you wish to take, realizing it has been traveled before. Others have been where you are at this very moment. You are not alone.

Why have I written on this subject? I was asked to do so and was directed to follow the same format as in the first book, *You*

Aren't Alone: The Voices of Abortion. When the call went out that
I wished to interview men and women who were homosexuals or
ex-homosexuals I was amazed at the response. Much to my
delight each person who contacted me was extremely happy this
book was being written.

As I did for the first book I found it necessary to travel
extensively to contact individuals who wished their stories told.
My new friends live in many different areas of this country. The
silver cord which holds them together is their heartfelt desire to
show others a pathway to happiness.

I have received verbal and written permission to share these
stories with you. Each interview was taped. Each tape took more
than an hour; consequently the texts are condensed to comply
with space requirements. It was exciting listening to men and
women sharing their lives. I listened with my heart to the stories
of hope and despair as I watched the smiles, tears, and anger.
While I taped each story, I cried and laughed, hoped and de-
spaired along with my new friends. It was sad to hear the stories
of families who had cut the strings on their homosexual relatives,
and heart warming to hear of families who included and loved
their gay and lesbian members.

It has been my experience as a marriage and family counselor
that homosexuality touches the loved ones of those involved. It is
impossible for human behavior not to affect others either posi-
tively or negatively. The subject of homosexuality is controversial; there are those who accept it as normal, and those who feel
it is unacceptable. Many people believe homosexuality to be
wrong from a religious perspective. There are also those individuals who have determined it is not for them, but feel people should
have a right to choose. And then there are those with no opinion.
This book is written to help a reader decide, without pressure, his
or her own response to homosexuality.

In the chapter on the history of homosexuality I will go into
how this particular way of life has affected families, nations, and
religions. Over the past few years our society's feelings toward
homosexuality has changed. Several years ago the subject of
homosexuality was seldom versed openly in society. Many naïve

individuals, were unaware of its existence, or the number of those participating. Most individuals living in homosexual relation-ships were closeted, living that part of their lives in secrecy. Parents and family members ignored or shunned a relative who self-identified as gay or lesbian.

Today homosexuality is literally "out of the closet." The subject is approached in most social gatherings. Homosexual organizations have been established. Gay Pride parades dot the horizon. The media speaks with equanimity about homosexual life styles, plays are produced, movie and T.V. programs expound on the subject, and children are introduced to the topic in school.

Controversy over its correctness is causing considerable dif-ficulties in church denominations as to whether it is religiously correct to accept homosexual pastors or to offer membership to openly gay men and lesbian women. Some mainline churches now look on the subject with such affirmation that they rewrite a marriage-like ceremony for those who wish it. There are several countries which have made gay marriage legal, and some of the states are now also legalizing same-sex unions.

The book's chapters are titled with phrases from the men and women interviewed. The book also includes a chapter on medical problems related to homosexuality, the history of homosexuality, and religious differences with respect to this subject. A glossary of terms is supplied as is an extensive bibliography.

I have been asked, "Why did I write the book?" The answer is easy and also quite difficult. Being a mother of 6 children, a grandmother of 19, and a great grandmother of 13, this is a subject which should be addressed with compassion, under-standing, and above all else love and truth.

Why does a little boy or girl profess to be a homosexual? What causes them to turn to the same sex? Why do so many endure the displeasure of, if not rejection by, their families, their society, and their church? You will hear how the men and women in this book discovered their own answers to these questions.

The men and women in the book are sharing their feelings, experiences, thoughts, and reasons for staying gay and lesbian. Some want to share why they decided to give up this way of life.

By exposing their souls to friends and even strangers they want others to find the same path they did. They want others to know their present happiness. They want others to know their reality.

I wrote this book with a prayer asking the Lord to grant me a heart filled with love for people either homosexual or heterosexual; my desire that both would perceive it is not with judgment but with a desire to understand is why I began this inquiry. My prayer was for wisdom. My prayer is for sympathy. My prayer is that anyone who reads this book will find someone in it whose story will be of value.

I would ask everyone to read this book before he or she judges a homosexual person. Read it before you accept or reject a homosexual relative or friend. Most of all realize that homosexual people are breathing, loving, tax-paying, good people. And dear homosexual friend read the book and know that you are not alone.

Acknowledgments

IT IS DIFFICULT TO EXPRESS APPRECIATION with words to those people you are indebted to for going beyond the realm of friendship in their efforts to help with this book. Without the personal interest and extreme help of all involved this book would still be an outline on my desk. To the dear Lord I owe the debt of His patience and care, as well as several nudges when I tended to wander down different paths and needed my priorities to be redirected.

Also, if it were not for the many individuals who stepped forward to share their stories this book could not possibly have been written. It is their stories; I have only been the agent who placed it onto the paper. So many of them courageously wanted to use their names and addresses which was not possible. Changing only the names and the areas each story follows the person's life with vigilance and with caring awareness.

It is necessary to thank my husband for enduring cold food, answering the ever-ringing telephone, and finding something to do as I interviewed each individual who shared their life. Interviews almost always exceeded two or more hours. Some of the interviews were taken over the phone which meant quiet, no T.V. and no interruptions.

It was a privilege to dialogue with Dr. Colette Kato. I thank her for helping me with the medical chapter. She took time from her busy schedule to take a personal interest in the book and carefully edited its contents for medical correctness.

There is a need to thank individuals who contacted the participants informing them and urging them to contact me. It is sad the lack of enough space to share each and every story I received. Many are praying this book reaches out and shares the wonderful news that change is possible for those who wish to do so.

I also wish to thank family and friends for their understanding while I have been closeted in front of the computer. My children, grandchildren, and great grandchildren, have seen and heard little from their doting grandmother in the last several months. My friends have been extremely kind in taking over some of my many duties at church, organizations, and in the neighborhood. My neighbors have waved at the window as they passed hoping to catch a glimpse of their friend. And, painting orders, are still on a spindle in my art room.

I wrote this book because of the political pressure exploited for and against gays and lesbians. I wrote this book because I have listened with my heart to people who are gay and lesbian and who need to be heard. I wrote this book because I felt the Lord was directing me to do so. And, I wrote this book because my best friend, my son, is gay.

1

"I Tried but Failed"

EASTER WAS ALWAYS AN EXCITING TIME at our house. There were seven of us kids and I was exactly in the middle, three girls on both sides of me. It occurred to me I should be a little special because I was the only boy. Mother and Father saw to it that every one of us had a new outfit at Easter and that included shoes and, for the first time that year, long pants for me. I was eight and I even got a cap that matched my jacket.

We all piled into the station wagon to go to Mass, then home for baked ham, and to the park in the center of the town for the Easter egg hunt the city put on for us kids. There were candy eggs, little yellow marshmallow chickens and pink marshmallow rabbits. And if you won the prize for finding the most eggs you got a giant chocolate rabbit. I never got one but every year I tried and always failed. My two older sisters, Marianne and Jane, each had gotten one and even Calley, the one younger than me, got it last year but never me.

Living in a family where Father and I were the only men made it sort of difficult. Father had to be with the men who worked for him most of the time. We had a dairy farm but Father's heart was in the thoroughbred racing horses he raised, what he called, his hobby. None of us kids were ever allowed near the horse area or where the cows were. Father was afraid with so many children that one of us might get under the fence and get trampled. We had a bull down in the south pasture and if we even went near there out came the razor strap and we would think twice before we disobeyed again.

We had a big yard fenced and filled with slides and teeter-totters, swings and even a large play house. We had a nurse whom we called Granny and Mother had house help, a black lady from South Carolina. We had a hard time saying her name, Priscilla, so most of us got out Prissy and that was her name as far as all of us were concerned. We loved her dearly; she was always getting us out of scrapes. As far as Granny went we tried to stay out of her way as much as possible. She was the one that made us brush our teeth and bath and put on clean socks and all those things nobody wanted to do anyway.

We all adored our Father even though we didn't see much of him. Our farm was very big and he was often out with the horses or to some race somewhere. I guess he had a lot of money because none of us ever went without and seven kids is a lot. Our Mother was always sick or complaining. I can't remember a time she wasn't in her room with the blinds drawn and all of us having to be quiet because she was resting. It was those times that Prissy would take us out in the yard and play with us. Prissy was awfully pretty and I remember the men that came to the farm to see the horses would look at her funny. It wasn't until I got a little older that I knew what that look meant.

Mother was English and demanded we talk properly and always have clean hands. Even though she never helped us or did it herself she saw to it that Granny or Prissy wouldn't let us get by with anything. In the summer we had extra help but they weren't allowed in the house or near our play yard. We were never supposed to talk to "the help" because some of them weren't nice people. Every morning we had to go to her room or she would come to the nursery to see if we were doing things "properly." She was very tall and thin and had a large straight nose, and her hair was sort of yellow. I know I shouldn't have thought it, but I didn't think she was at all pretty.

I loved the horses and when I turned eight I begged Father to take me with him to the track. He promised that when I was just a little older he would. I tried to get him to tell me how old and he would just laugh and say when I came up to his chin I would be old enough. I was not very tall. Martin, the man who took the most care of our horses, lived in a small house on the other side of the corral with his wife, Betty, and their son, Justin.

Justin was seven and almost a head taller than I was. His father let him help feed the horses and even ride them from the pasture to the barn. I thought it very unfair and when I brought this to the attention of my Father he told me that Justin's Dad was a hired hand and had Justin help him. Father informed me I was his son and his heir and I needed to learn different kinds of things so that I could work with him as soon as I was old enough.

We lived quite a way from town and I didn't have anybody to play with except my sisters. I'd dress up in Mother's long dresses along with the girls and played house with them almost as if I were one of them. I remember putting on lipstick and fingernail polish and even letting Jane, my favorite sister, put some small metal curlers in my hair. She was thirteen and never teased me like Marianne who, the oldest, was fifteen and thought she was our boss. None of us really liked her. Even baby Abigail who we called Abby preferred me to pick her up instead of Marianne.

I never thought much about playing with the girls until I started school. We rode the bus into Heritage and went to a public school. My first grade teacher was a lady who hugged us and made us really want to learn. She'd been the first grade teacher of the three girls before me and when I came she thought it was wonderful they had a little brother. In the second grade things began to change. The boys would play marbles at recess and the girls were off to the school steps to play jacks. I'd played jacks with my sisters at home and was pretty good. When I pulled my jack-bag out of my pocket and sat down on the steps next to them to play they made faces and told me to leave them alone. They said I was a silly old boy and they didn't want me there.

It was a shock to me because I had been the prize possession of my sisters. The older ones petted me and the younger ones looked up to me as their big brother. I'd never been told I was a silly boy. In fact I had just never thought about the difference between boys and girls. I guess that isn't quite the way it was because at Easter all the girls had frilly dresses and I had long pants. I didn't know how to play marbles so I went and sat on the school swing and pouted.

That afternoon when I got home I asked Prissy why I couldn't play with the girls. I told her my sisters wanted me to play but the other girls didn't. She laughed and hugged me to her. I loved the way she smelled. Prissy smelled like the lilac bushes that bloomed every year in the spring. There were several bushes walling in a graveled path leading to the gate which kept us out of the pasture area. It was always locked. Father wore a large key ring that jingled on his belt when he walked. He had the gate key on it and Martin had the only other one. I always felt like it was spring whenever Prissy was near me.

Prissy got some marbles at K-Mart and a leather sack to put them in. For two or three afternoons she taught me how to hold my hand and pull in my thumb tight to hit the marbles in the ring in the dirt where all the marbles were. We were supposed to knock the marbles out of the circle she had drawn around them. I thought I was pretty good and one day tried to get in with the boys playing marbles. They laughed and called me a sissy and told me to go back and play with the girls. I swung at them and hit a couple before the play-yard teacher separated us. We all ended up in the office and had a good scolding. The next day when I joined the guys at recess they let me play. I guess I'd showed them I was no sissy. From then on I played marbles and did sort of O.K.

Going home on the bus I started sitting with the guys and let my sisters sit together with the other girls. I was doing guy things and it was great. The summer of that year I still only had my sisters to play with, but I wouldn't let them dress me with girls clothes or do my hair or nails. That was sissy stuff and I was too old to play baby things. I guess I was Prissy's pet as she always made certain I had an extra piece of cake, and she saw I got just about anything I wanted. She started to call me by my full name, Magnus, and not her little boy.

Things were pretty predictable. Going on ten I was in the fifth grade and almost to my Father's chin. I was growing and couldn't wait until I was tall enough. Every so often he would measure me and grin, pat me on the shoulder and tell me I was almost to his chin that it wouldn't be long now. I dreamed of being a real man and walking beside my Father to the corrals and into the dairy farm and going to the race-tracks with him. I'd show Justin who was the boss. He could ride the horses to the barn but I owned them, well sort of owned them.

I even began to try and walk like my Father did. He was over six feet, had sort of gray hair and was awfully big across the shoulders. When Father walked with other men he was taller than most of them and always walked with his head tilted up. He was always laughing. Arthur Tracy Holmes was his name. When they named me Magnus Tracy Holmes I was told Tracy was a family name and all the first sons had it.

My Father was liked by everybody except my Mother who seldom ate dinner with us and hardly ever spoke when he was in the room. She would constantly tell him how she was feeling and that having so many babies had caused it. Then she would add, "What did he care he hadn't had to birth any of us. He could come and go when he wanted to." She whined, "But she was locked in with having to take care of us." I never understood that because it was Granny and Prissy who did the "taking care of us." I couldn't remember my Mother ever doing anything with me except brushing the hair out of my eyes and scolding Granny for letting me look like a little pig all the time. She made Granny cry quite often and we kids would go and hug her even though she wasn't our favorite like Prissy.

When I was in the last half of the sixth grade I reached my Father's chin. All at once I had started growing and within about five or six months grew almost three inches. It was then I realized how different girls and boys were. I'd never thought anything of leaving the bathroom door open when I took a shower. My sisters were just that, my sisters. I'd never been shy in front of them until one Friday night Marianne was in the bathroom and I popped in to take a shower. She screamed and pulled a big towel around herself and told me to get out and stay out.

"What's the matter with Marianne?" I questioned Prissy who was coming up the stairs. She laughed and took me into the

kitchen for one of her famous cups of cocoa. I learned all about
the birds and the bees that night, not from my Father or Mother
but from hired help.

The girls were getting so silly. They would go into one of their
bedrooms and giggle and talk about certain boys. When I went in
they'd stop talking and tell me to get out. I drifted into making
excuses to go see Justin but he was busy helping his Dad so it
ended up I was by myself. Even Prissy seemed to be busy; she was
always with the new man Father had hired to help Martin. I
seldom saw her except when she was doing work in the house. My
three younger sisters were such babies I didn't have much in
common with them and Jane, my favorite, was getting as silly as
Marianne. Tammy, the sister just two years my senior, tagged
along with Marianne and Jane and preferred them to being with
me.

I'd thought when I was up to my Father's chin he would take
me everywhere, but he always made some excuse when he was
going out of town. "Next time son, can't this time, but for sure next
time." He was gone more than ever. He seldom was home and
when he was, he was in his office, on the phone, or in the corral
with Martin deciding which horse needed what. Even though I
went to the corral with him he spent his time talking with Martin.
I usually sat on a bale of hay and listened. I was starting to learn
about horses. When he was gone I didn't go to the corral because
Martin wouldn't let me do anything and Justin gloated over the
fact he could work with the horses and his Dad wouldn't let me.

Bored I thought I'd explore the attic. I hadn't been up there
for a long time; in fact I couldn't remember ever really looking
through everything. The girls and I had played hide and seek at
times and hid in the attic, but I'd never gone through any of the
boxes or old suitcases stored there. Behind an old dresser with a
broken mirror and one drawer missing I found an old trombone
that someone had left. It was in pretty good shape. There was
even a mouth piece with it in a little box that looked new. I spent
the whole afternoon experimenting and for days I would escape
to the attic and try and play it. There was some music in an old

trunk with a man's name on it, Glenn Miller. I had no idea how to read music but pretty soon I was making music that sounded like something. I became determined almost obsessed to learn how to play it correctly. That week-end, one of the few that Father was home, I asked him if I could have trombone lessons, he was reading the paper and grunted a yes. I was thrilled. Now all I had to do was to find a teacher and that is exactly what I did.

There was a music store in Heritage. I called and asked if they had a trombone teacher. Darrell Forman, a student at our state college, who was home from college, was teaching part time and, yes, he could come to the house. I was afraid when I told them where I lived he wouldn't come, it being so far out but he did. The very next Wednesday afternoon I took my first lesson. Darrell was a music major who was planning to teach band and orchestra in school. He played several instruments including the trombone. I spent that summer in heaven. Darrell purchased me some Glenn Miller records and I tried my best to copy them. I always practiced at the end of the attic where there was a window I could open when it got too hot.

I went to school because I had to but the minute I got home I was in the attic practicing. I tried out for the school orchestra and made it and before long was doing solo work. I knew what I wanted to do when I graduated, have my own orchestra and be another Glenn Miller.

Not only was Darrell teaching me how to play the trombone but he also taught me how to do other things. I wasn't about to tell anyone because I'd do anything to learn and it wasn't all that bad being with him. He really took an interest in me and before long I lived for two things, music and Darrell. I didn't bother Father anymore. It really wasn't worth it. I never went to the corrals with him. He didn't even ask me why. In fact I don't think he knew I was around, and Mother wasn't out of her room enough to know what any of us were doing. Granny and Prissy did what had to be done and the girls just grew.

I was practicing one afternoon after school when Marianne came to the attic and sat on an old suitcase with a rounded top and listened. I noticed she was crying so I put my horn down and sat beside her, the lid creaked but it held. I'd no idea what to say to her. She was graduating that June and planned to go into nurse's training. She'd already registered at State and Father promised her a car when she graduated. In fact he told all of us that a car would be his graduation present to us. I don't think he knew which girl was which. He mixed their names up all the time. The little ones thought it was funny. He knew who I was because I was the only boy, and I didn't think it was funny at all.

Marianne was pregnant and had no idea what to do. I didn't know about such things so couldn't help her. I was too busy with Darrell and my horn and trying to get good grades so I'd be accepted to college to worry about girl things. I just sat there with my arm around her and let her cry. I knew who could help, the only person in the house who cared, Prissy. We went to find her. Priscilla had her own apartment over the garages. She'd lived there ever since she started working for us. Granny had the bedroom next to the nursery.

Prissy was not at all surprised. She said these things happen and immediately put a call into Father and told him. That afternoon Prissy drove Marianne into Heritage to Father's office, he had one at the house and also one in town. I figured between Father and Prissy they could take care of everything and went back to practicing. It was late that night when I heard Prissy drive up. Father had purchased her a small Thunderbird one Christmas, it was red and Prissy was very proud of it. I went downstairs to see if Marianne was with her, she was. Marianne was white and leaning on Prissy. She looked sick and was terribly quiet.

"Prissy, what's wrong with Marianne?" I ran over to my sister and she practically fell into my arms.

"Magnus, it was terrible. Oh, Magnus, it was terrible." I held her close and took her up to her room with Prissy close behind us.

Prissy was quiet too and then almost in a whisper told me that Father had arranged for an abortion that afternoon and that Marianne was no longer pregnant. I wasn't quite certain about all this but I damn well was going to find out. I yelled at Prissy and demanded why she allowed such a thing, I knew enough to know from what the Priest had taught that you don't get abortions if you are a Catholic.

I guess Mother heard the commotion and came out into the hall leaning on Granny. When she found out what had happened she was so angry she stood straight and went down the stairs by herself and into Father's office. I heard her screaming at Father over the phone. Between her screaming, Marianne crying, the other girls crowding in from their rooms I felt I needed some help. Granny took over as she always had in the past. She sent the girls to their rooms, helped Marianne get into bed, and with Prissy's help restored some sort of order. When Mother came back upstairs without Granny's help I was amazed. I hadn't seen her walk anywhere without someone helping her for quite some time. She went into Marianne's room and I escaped into the attic, some peace, and my horn.

I had a small tape recorder and was taping some of the things I played. I would listen to it and find the mistakes and do it over until I thought it sounded good. I was trying for a music scholarship at State. I had to send them a portfolio of my playing. I was going to graduate the next year and wanted to be accepted as soon as possible. I wanted to go where Darrell was going so we could be together. I had my whole life planned out and I felt that nothing would happen that could change anything.

Darrell came to tell me he was on his way back to school and that he would see me during the summer and on holidays. He said he wasn't feeling too good. We thought he had the flu. I knew that I would miss him but I had the horn and my time would be spent practicing. I was going to be a contestant on a radio contest for young musicians the week before school started. I wanted my Mother and Father to go, but Father was on a buying trip in England and Mother didn't feel good Prissy said she would take me and was excited I was going to try out. I was never good at competition, never did get the chocolate bunny at Easter. It seemed whenever I tried for something I always failed.

I played my heart out and got second place. I figured that was good for a start. Darrell called that same evening to see how I'd done and told me he was thrilled, my first try and to get second place he thought was great. I asked how he was feeling and he said he was running a little fever but it was just the flu and he would be O.K.

I was graduating and the senior prom was coming up. We were supposed to ask a girl. I was going to play in the dance band for the prom but thought I'd better ask somebody. Most of the girls were silly and I didn't have time for them. Father and Mother were coming to graduation and my car arrived two days before the big event. Father asked who the lucky girl was who would be going to the prom with his handsome son. He handed me the keys to my new car, a hundred bucks and told me to have a good time.

I asked a girl in my chemistry class, Natalie, if she would go to the prom. We had talked a little during class. She wasn't all that good looking but we at least could talk and she didn't giggle every time I said something. She accepted and I picked her up early because I would be playing part of the night. She understood and said it was fine. She would enjoy the music. I picked her up around seven and she sat at one of the tables while the band warmed up. The dance didn't start until nine. I bought her a couple of cokes and then forgot her while I was playing. Things never were as important as my music and girls were way down on my list.

She was very nice and when I took her home she thanked me for a nice evening. I knew that I should kiss her good night so I did and was surprised at the feelings I got. We sat in the car and talked and then I kissed her again. She was nice much to my surprise and I liked being with her. I had listed myself as a musical gay and didn't think much about it; after all I had Darrell and my horn.

Summer came, school was out, and Darrell would be back the following week. Anxious to see him and have him hear some new arrangements made waiting through the week hard. I'd taken some of Miller's sounds and arranged a few of the popular tunes his style. When I called Mrs. Forman to tell her I'd be glad to pick Darrell up she thanked me as she wasn't a very good driver. The airport was quite a ways out of town and usually crowded. It served three small towns and one rather large one.

Darrell was waiting for me at the baggage pick-up and when he saw me he came running to meet me. He looked like he had lost a lot of weight and was very pale. As we got his bags off the conveyor and out to my new car, he said very little. While we were driving home he said he had to talk, so we stopped at a restaurant and took a booth near a window.

"Magnus, I've got AIDS," Darrell said after the waitress took our order for coffee.

"AIDS, good God, Darrell, what are you saying?"

He repeated the news, "I've got AIDS, Magnus, and I'm dying."

I don't remember having cried as I grew up but at that moment I lowered my head on the table and sobbed my heart out. My best friend was dying. Who would I have left in this world that cared for me? Hell, I knew that sounded about as selfish as you could get, but my horn and Darrell were all I had to cling to on this earth.

We talked for hours. The lights came on, and it grew black outside. Darrell told me that I would have to be tested too. Me, I thought. I felt fine. He told me how he had met a guy in college who got him going to a group of gay men who were trying to leave homosexuality. He said they talked about the Lord constantly and about three weeks ago he had given his heart to Jesus and knew where he was going when he died.

I went to Mass with the girls when they dragged me but I never really thought too much about it. My family had always been Catholics and the only time it ever seemed to get in the way was the time Marianne had the abortion and my Mother came alive for a few days.

I wasn't about to go and be tested. Especially not in Heritage and have somebody say something to my family, not me. Hell, I was nineteen and healthy and was going to college and eventually have my own group. I was doing some pretty smooth arrangements, even had one published. I'd never been with any guy but

Darrell. You get AIDS from gay bars and bath houses and I'd never stooped to that sort of stuff, not me. Besides it had been last summer when Darrell and I had been together. During school I never went with anybody else. In fact, no one knew I was gay, even the girls didn't suspect. I had taken Natalie out several times so no one would have any reason to assume I was a homosexual.

That summer I spent as much time as I could at Darrell's. He was too sick to drive out to my house so I always went there. All he could talk about was what he read in the Bible and how he was looking forward to seeing Jesus. I thought he was getting a little strange. His father had been killed by an accident where he worked; a crane had fallen and knocked him into a wall crushing him to death. His Mother was a devout Christian and was kind and loving, something I'd never had from a mother. I watched her and how she cared for Darrell and my heart ached. How I would have loved my mother to hold me the same way. Darrell's mother would sit on the side of his bed and pull him to her and hold him tight, and then they would pray together. I bowed my head out of respect but somehow it didn't really get to me.

I was used to going to Mass, but praying something particular wasn't what I was used to. Catholic prayers are pretty well universal and there isn't the freedom that Darrell and his mother seemed to have talking with God.

It was about two in the morning when I got a telephone call from Mrs. Forman to come at once. I raced to his house and ran upstairs to Darrell's bedroom; she was kneeling at the side of the bed praying. I went directly to Darrell. His head was turned my way. He was whispering something to me that I couldn't hear. He tried to pull me nearer so I put my ear as close to him as I could. His whispered words were hard to hear but I could make them out. He wanted me to forgive him for teaching me to be a homosexual. I couldn't stand his words, forgive him. How could I forgive him when I loved him and what we did was perfectly normal, or so I thought.

"Magnus," he kept on, "forgive me; I can't go to Jesus with sin on my heart." I grabbed him and hugged him and said of course I forgave him. In my heart I didn't know what for but I wasn't about to let him worry. "Jesus loves you, Magnus. You will never be alone if you give your heart to Jesus." I felt his body go limp and he died in my arms, the kindest person I'd known.

I played at his funeral and felt as if part of me had died too. Practicing my horn in the attic helped. The anticipation of college and studying advanced music was now taking up all my thoughts. I left for college, kissed all the girls good-bye, told my Mother I'd write, hugged Prissy, and shook hands with Granny. My Father wasn't there, but what else was new. I drove by Natalie's house and told her I'd write. She grinned and said that wouldn't be necessary because all I'd need to do is wave at her once in awhile. She was going to the same college. We laughed and I said I'd see her around.

I unpacked in the dorm room I was sharing with two other guys, went to the clinic to get my physical exam over with, and then walked to the music department. It had a large stage and several practice rooms. Classes would start in two days and I could hardly wait.

The next day I spent getting things done. I went to the book store, bought my books and supplies, looked around and decided to try out the practice rooms. When I got back to the room to get my horn there was a note on the desk asking me to report to the clinic. I grabbed my horn and stopped by on the way to the music hall. The nurse said the doctor wanted to talk to me. I sat on a chair across from his desk and waited to see what he wanted.

"Magnus, are you a homosexual?" he asked

I couldn't believe he would ask such a personal question. "Why, what difference does it make if I am?" I was pretty irritated at him.

"The reason I am concerned is your blood work needs re-checking. It appears that you have AIDS."

My world fell apart. There would be no future, and there would be no life of music. AIDS, Darrell had begged me to get tested but I wouldn't. Now there was no way out. I hadn't felt bad. I hadn't lost any weight. Maybe the doctor was wrong.

I was determined I wasn't going to give in. I went to every doctor and took a dozen different "cures." I was certain I'd beat it. I went to class and played my horn and tried to forget it when I wasn't in some doctor's office or reading some cure in India or Africa or someplace. Gradually I started to feel it and way deep inside I knew I wasn't going to win. I made it through that year but in the summer I had to tell Mother and Father. Father wouldn't accept that I had lived a gay life, and Mother didn't seem to understand what I was talking about. The girls all knew, but even so just kept on loving me.

We got a telegram from Marianne saying she was passing through and would have about a four hour layover and wanted to see everyone. I went to the train to pick her up. She had been away from home for several years and no one really knew just what she was doing other than going to school. She did write once or twice telling us about the nursing school she was attending. One of her letters said she wanted to do overseas duty when she graduated. When I saw her step out of the train I didn't recognize her until she came up to me and I could see her face.. She was wearing a nun's habit. My sister was a Nun, a Sister of Mercy on her way to China to a mission station near Peking. She only had four hours but in those four hours I heard all about Jesus once more and how Jesus had forgiven her for killing her baby. She was going to China to take care of little sick babies who needed her. I saw such love and kindness on her face I couldn't get over it. I told her about myself and she said she loved me and would pray for me everyday. That made two people praying for me, Darrell's mother, and now my sister. We talked on the drive to the farm and then on the way back to the train.

Gradually my health failed. I couldn't play my horn anymore. I didn't have the strength. I hardly ever saw my Mother. She couldn't stand to see me looking as I did, and she had never really gotten over me being gay. Father stayed away too. Prissy became an angel, I do believe. She cared for me daily, as did most of my sisters.

One day I received a letter from Sister Elizabeth, Marianne had taken a new name.. She asked me if I had given my heart to Jesus and told me there was only one peace on this earth and that was through His forgiveness and love. She begged me to do this before I died. The word was on the page I still hadn't been able to speak. Die, death, I was going to die. Somehow the words on the page of Marianne's letter kept jumping out at me. Give your heart to Jesus. Then I remembered Darrell telling me that the Lord loved me and would never leave me alone. Alone, it seemed as though I had been alone most of my life.

There was a Bible in the bookcase in my Father's study. I sent Prissy to get it for me. I read it from front to back. Then I read the New Testament once more. I tried to pray but didn't really know how. One afternoon Prissy said there was a girl who wanted to see me, named Natalie. Natalie came into the room and sat on the side of my bed and took my hand and was quiet. She never had talked very much and now she just sat there and looked at me with tears in her eyes. I'd never noticed how blue they were. She actually looked pretty sitting there. She told me she'd called and Prissy had explained to her how sick I was. She saw the Bible on the side stand and asked if I was a Christian.

I told her I guessed I was because I'd been baptized as a child, gone to catechism class and was confirmed. She said if I didn't know I really was a Christian then it was time I did. I told her I was gay. It seems she already knew it from college. She told me how she appreciated me taking her to the prom and that my kiss was her first. She hadn't planned to go to the prom because she knew nobody would ask her. Even if she had to sit and wait for me while I played she at least got to go to her senior prom. Then with a small sad smile she told me how she fell in love with me that very night and had been in love with me ever since.

Natalie came back every day. Day after day she talked to me about what I read in the Bible. I started to get into what it said and realized that being gay was not God's plan for me. But it was too late to prove to Him I would never go back into that life style; it was too late for anything. Even though Natalie assured me it was never too late to ask for forgiveness I couldn't. Here I was dying but I couldn't say, "Sure God now I want to live your kind of life." What kind of a God would take that kind of a commitment?

Darrell's mother came for a visit one day and knelt beside my bed and prayed for me. Whenever she did that I was always embarrassed. Being a Godly woman kneeling beside my bed it was hard to take. One day she sat on the side of my bed and held me close to her. She actually held me and told me that I was her son and she had been praying for me ever since I was the boy Darrell had started to teach music.

She didn't know then that he also taught me about homosexuality, but later when she found out about Darrell she realized what I had been to him. She started to pray then for me and had never let a day go by since. She held me and told me she loved me and then very simply said the same words Darrell had used, "Jesus loves you, Magnus. He is your brother if you will just ask him into your heart."

I burst into tears and there in the arms of Darrell's mother gave my heart to Jesus. I guess if the thief on the cross could do it at the last minute I could too.

My name is Sister Elizabeth and I came home because my sister Jane wrote and said that Magnus was dying. I got home in time to tell him good bye. I held his wasted body in my arms as he died. His last words were for me to tell Father that he had forgiven him. You see our Father wasn't home the day Magnus died. He was in Spain buying some horses. He sent a telegram saying he couldn't make it to the funeral. Mother didn't go to the funeral either. She still couldn't believe what had happened. Mrs. Forman was there, a girl named Natalie, Prissy and Granny, and of course all of us girls.

Why have I shared this story with you? I wanted you to know Magnus and his story. I hoped you could share it so others would realize it is never too late to rewrite the end of your story.

This story I took over the phone. Sister Elizabeth was preparing to return to China when someone told her I was taking interviews. I would have loved to have seen her but it was impossible. She insisted I write the story as if Magnus were telling it. She knew he would have shared it if he were alive. We checked with Darrell's mother for some of the details and between Marianne and her sisters we finished the story. We contacted his father, but he told

Marianne that he didn't have time as he was on his way to Paraguay on a horse-buying trip.

As we ended the tape Sister Elizabeth added, "Please know that I shall be praying for the book, in hopes that someone like Magnus can read it and know the truth to change in time, and especially to understand the loving forgiveness of our Lord."

I told Sister Elizabeth good-bye and shared a prayer for the safety of her trip back to China.

2

"Mother, I'm Gay"

THERE WERE THREE TIMES IN MY OLDEST SON'S LIFE, no, four, that twisted my heart turned the corners of my mouth up or down with laughter or with tears. These memories, even now, come to me when I lay down at night. There was a time when the lights were out and the day was finished I would think and pray for seven children, each one with different feelings. Now when the lights are dim and precious memories come to me I think and pray for five. Two of my blessings, a very small daughter and my oldest son, of whom this story is about, are gone. Oh, there are many grandchildren and even some great grandchildren that interrupt my memory and prayer time with their noisy chatter, their constantly sticky hands, and very loving hearts.

I suppose the earliest time that needs to be shared with you was the day they put little Peter into my arms for the first time. His small slit of a puckered mouth was open, emitting a soft little chirp. The sound reminded me of the noise I heard every spring made by baby sparrows nesting in the old oak tree next to my parent's kitchen. Petey opened his eyes, looked into my heart and stayed there for the rest of his life. It had never occurred to me what love really felt like, I mean way down deep where you feel all warm and glowing and safe and excited. Now I knew genuine love. It was all wrapped up in my arms, warm and cuddly and alive.

As I looked into his little face, marked by the instruments which had helped pull him into this world, I knew what was meant by the fierceness of love. He was mine, something I felt was important, a goal in my life, the real reason God had created me. God needed me. I had helped Him create a real live human being.

18

Even as young as I was, without any knowledge of what to really do with a miniature doll, one that moved, needed changing every two minutes, and to be fed regularly, I was excited and thrilled.

I don't remember much else of those ten days spent in the hospital. Ten days you gasp! Yes, in those days you spent ten days or more at the birthing of a child. Today you are lucky to spend three. And now you know why I speak of great grandchildren. Time has silently escaped me. I am old and memories have become extremely important. Isn't it always that way, wanting to go back and have a second chance to make things different and hopefully better.

It was then that World War II was roaring in our ears. Girls were marrying and having their children with absentee fathers in Manila, Leyte, Guam, Germany, Philippines or wherever there were people trying to destroy the American way of life. All over the land boys were marrying girls because that was one way girls could do something for their country. So they married and the boys left for overseas and wrote letters while the girls went back to school. Then there was a day when some received telegrams. Their husbands were either missing in action or had been killed. Somehow the girls mourned but it was hard to mourn a stranger.

I got to know my husband, or the man I dreamed about as my husband, by the pile of letters which came in bunches. There were those long silences between when I would glue my ear to the radio and listen for the five-o'clock news wondering if Peter was in any of the battles they would be talking about in their excited and alarm-trained voices. I will never forget the music which played before the news came on. The music would fade into the background as the sound of the announcer clamored for our attention. In a few seconds, we would know what was happening in the war, for he alone had the latest and the most exclusive information. But then with almost a whisper, as if he were telling a secret, something much more important than any news could ever be, he wanted us to know about Campbells Soup, or Wheaties, or Ivory Soap.

My son was cute. I suppose all mothers think their children are exceptional. But to me Petey was something extra special. He had large brown eyes that twinkled with mischievousness and unruly light brown hair that was always falling down over his forehead even when I put stickum on it. Petey was the "spittin" image of his father, or so I remember. It was hard to place his father in a scene, or even remember his voice. We didn't really know each other very long before we were married and even then we didn't have a chance to understand or become acquainted before he was shipped over seas.

Peter Baker Sr. and I were married in a church wedding with all the trimmings five months after I met him. Two months later Pete and his regiment left for duty somewhere in the Pacific. When Sergeant Baker was called to protect his country neither of us knew I was three weeks pregnant. I planned to finish high school, and then start college. It wasn't until I fainted in chemistry class that I was aware of my coming blessing.

The principal decided being in school was not the correct way of announcing to my class mates that I was pregnant, even though I wore a wedding ring and half the class, including the principal, had attended the church wedding. Pregnancy in those days came with a stork and a trip to the hospital. I learned the hard way there was no stork involved in nine months of carrying a baby. My class mates, the girls I mean, were excited about someone being pregnant. Up until that time our dolls were the closest thing we had to real babies, and peeking in the art books was just about the only idea we had that boys were a little different, down there.

The war changed a lot of things; my best friend's parents got a divorce, which my mother and aunt whispered about in the kitchen. The lady across the street lost her only son in Guam. My husband received a Congressional Medal for bravery, and I had forgotten what he looked like. I had the wedding pictures but the man I had married almost three years before was a dream who rode around on a white horse in 14th century armor. When I went to bed I dreamt of Clark Gable and Tyrone Power, and in the daylight went to school and graduated with my classmates by doing double classes for the time I had taken off to have the baby.

My mother raised Petey along with my younger brother and two sisters. I came home from school, folded diapers, played with a breathing and wriggly doll, and did my home work. After I graduated I went to work at our local grocery store. I worked all day, came home, folded diapers, played with a small doll who was now walking and whom I adored, handed over my weekly paycheck to my mother, and started the routine over with each new week. The girls I graduated with were excited about college, or getting married, or starting their first job. Somehow we didn't seem to have much to talk about anymore and eventually they stopped popping by as they became involved in growing up themselves.

Each week was the same until a telephone call came one evening around eleven o'clock. The voice on the other end was Peter's. He said he would be home the very next day. The man who stepped off the train was a stranger. When he folded me in his arms, I was embarrassed. He took Petey who was holding onto my skirt, pulled his son to himself, took him into his arms, and broke into tears. I was surprised. This man holding little Petey was his father. I had forgotten that Petey wasn't all mine.

Life took on a daily routine: Peter off to work, me doing housework, and trying to make $35.00 a week last until the following payday. Little Peter was beginning to say words that made sense. No longer toddling, he was running wherever he wanted to go. My husband was training to be a telephone man and I was two months pregnant. We lived in a housing unit which during the war had been a barracks and was now made into low-cost housing for kids going to college and in beginning positions. Almost all of our neighbors were veterans and all of us shared a slice of bread, a glass of milk, or an extra dollar when someone needed it. We shared our first babies and several of us were pregnant with the second.

Our daughter was born at 5:33 on a Sunday afternoon and died six hours later, a doctor's mistake. Our neighbor's little girl was born the next day and lived. To lose a child is a terrible loss. To hear a baby crying through paper-thin walls was torture. I went back to school and trained to be a nurse, and left little Petey with a baby sitter. Looking back, I think I know that is where it all started. The feeling inside of me that I needed to accomplish something other than being a mother was a new emotion, but it was strong and approved of by society. Somehow "just" being a wife and mother was not quite as great as being a "somebody" or doing "something".

T.V. was born, the ideal man who played the husband, lover, and father behind the grey and wobbling screen made life inadequate for the average woman, wife, and mother. You had to "be," you had to have a "career," and staying at home was looked down on as if you were a little stupid and lacking in ability. So I became a nurse and left Petey and his brother and sister home with their father while I nursed from eleven at night until seven in the morning. Petey took on the job of being the older brother and a surrogate father. His brother, Orin, four years his junior, and sister, Lucille, thirteen months younger, looked on him to answer their questions, to teach them to tie their shoes, and see to it they got breakfast before they left for school.

I was tired much of the time and their father was having a hard time watching children, carrying on with other women behind my back, and keeping the children from realizing who was on the phone and why Daddy had to go to the store for groceries when Mommy had already been there. We moved out of state to a small town several miles south of Washington D.C. where Peter was put in charge of a lab that was studying better ways of communicating, sort of a think tank. I had to quit work as I was pregnant once again. There was enough money now to pay the bills and to put a little aside for a rainy day. We had another little boy and a short while later one more, a little girl. Peter was still being unfaithful but with all the children and his constantly assuring me of his love and fidelity, I just looked the other way and ignored what I knew to be the truth.

Petey was in Junior High and that is where the second heart twisting thing happened in our lives. Now that I spent my time at home, Petey and I were once again inseparable. I was his best friend and we talked about everything. He was taking Peter's place who spent much of his time in the lab and I suspected with the lab assistant. I had forgotten the man I married, and the man I lived with I didn't like. He walked in and out of the house, changed his clothes, patted the children on the head, handed me money to run the house, and sometimes went to church with us on Sunday. We seldom talked as we once had and I put on a ton of weight, let my hair find its own comb, and became a walking robot.

Peter seldom went with me to anything the children did at school. I was a single Mom who lived with the children's father. Petey adored his Dad and knew that his birthday was coming so he thought if he purchased his Dad a new fishing pole and a license they could spend some time together. For several weeks Petey mowed lawns and did odd jobs around the neighborhood so he would have enough money for a fishing pole and license. The day of Pete's birthday I made a cake, the children all made home made cards, and Petey was ecstatic. He wrapped the pole and put the license in a home made card to give to his dad as soon as dinner was over. I brought in the cake with candles and the gifts. Petey waited until his Dad could open his gift hardly daring to breathe.

Peter opened the smaller children's cards and then Petey's gift with a card taped to the package. He opened the card with the fishing license and with a toss it went onto the table with a "What do I need that for?" The look on Petey's face broke my heart and at that moment I hated his Dad. Then Pete opened the fishing pole just as the phone rang. He went to answer the phone, yelled at all of us he was needed at the lab and left. The fishing pole was stuck in the corner of the closet. The license tossed on the top of the bureau in our bedroom expired without ever being used.

Pete didn't get home that night until after three. I had called the lab and there was no answer. My husband never made it to the lab that night. When he walked in the door I asked him where he had been and he said the lab. I told him he was lying and that I wanted to know. He replied that it wasn't any of my business and started for the bedroom. I grabbed him and told him that he was sleeping on the davenport. I wanted a divorce. Pete moved out and Petey, the other children, and I were glad.

Petey was no longer Petey. He was Pete and graduating from high school with good grades and a girl friend who was the mayor's daughter. A third thing that happened was Lisa, she was a doll, long blond hair, big eyes that were as blue as Pete's were brown, and she adored Pete. He thought she was just about perfect. I remember the afternoon they walked in holding hands, wonderful smiles on their faces and told me they were engaged. Lisa was all fluttery and Pete turned a rather bright shade of red from his collar to the top of hair that was still falling over his forehead and into his eyes when it didn't have stickum on it.

My first question was, "What about college?" They answered together. They were going to State and wouldn't get married until Pete graduated and had a job. Their life was all planned, that is until they told her father. Her mother was in Europe. He ordered Pete out of the house and within the week Lisa was sent to Europe to be with her mother. Pete fell apart. The mayor had informed him he wasn't good enough for his only daughter and asked him who he thought he was aspiring to marry the mayor's daughter when he didn't have a college degree, had a divorced mother, and a dad who slept with anything wearing a skirt.

I tried to help Pete but something had happened to our closeness. It was about a month later he moved out and into a house nearer town with a boy his age, and an older man. I didn't see much of my best friend for over a year until the fourth thing happened that I will never forget.

Pete Jr. called me to have dinner with him. I was happy, perhaps we could go back the way it was before. I thought he was beginning to handle not being engaged to Lisa and maybe even wanted to enroll in college. So I started mentally re-arranging the house so he could move back home. I would have all my kids with me again.

It was raining that afternoon, and when it rains on the east coast it wasn't the pleasant sprinkles I had been used to. It was almost as if someone turned on the tap and forgot to turn it off. When Pete rolled up to the house in his pick-up truck I just knew it was all going to be all right. I remember I was wearing a pink sweater with dark green slacks. I'd put my hair on top of my head. That was when we wore the big barrel curls making us look taller than we were. I was so excited I had my son back and we would be best friends again. Most people thought that Pete and I were brother and sister, we would laugh and he would say, no, she is my mother and we would both enjoy the look on their faces.

I was out the door before Pete could get up the stairs. I grabbed him and hugged him hard to make up for all the times we missed, not really minding the rain that was dousing us both. He put his arms around my waist and half carried me as we ran to the truck. His truck was an eye-sore but he loved it. It could be heard several blocks away. I always knew when he was coming. There was no mistaking the sound of the "buggy" as he had tagged it. I can still remember the smell of that truck, it was musty, smelled like grease, and I can still see the rain running down over the one windshield wiper. The passenger's side wiper didn't work. I memorized the happiness I was feeling at that moment. It was that warm-fuzzy feeling crammed with exhilaration and wonder, the total feeling of loving a child.

Pete was silent all the way to the Mexican restaurant, our favorite. It seemed strange for him to be so quiet. He generally talked a blue streak and seldom let me get a word in between his flow of words. I wondered what was wrong. Instead of asking I decided we could talk over tacos and raspberry ice-tea. By the time we got there the rain had settled down to a trickle.

Peter dropped me off and went to park the truck. I watched him as he walked towards me. He was brooding and some of my happiness began to change places with worry. I recognized the look. When he got into trouble at school and had to tell me before the teacher got me on the phone, or when he had done something I had strictly told him not to, or when he had to show me his report card and it contained grades he wasn't particularly proud of showing. It was that kind of a look.

There was no waiting. The waitress led us to a corner table where we could talk without a lot of people listening. Even after we ordered Pete kept looking away from me, like he was embarrassed. Finally I had to ask him what the matter was. He stuttered and said he would tell me after we ate. I asked him if he was going to register for college. I'd read it would be starting the first of the month. Quietly he said, "I'm not quite sure what I'm going to do." It was strange being silent as we ate our tacos and drank the cold tea. Finally the waitress asked if we wanted desert, Pete said no, just coffee.

The room was humid. I guess it was the warmth of late August and the unrelenting rain. The rumble of voices kept a sing-song sound going on behind us. A child cried at the front of the restaurant and I could hear a mother's scolding words. There was a flash of lightning and then a rumble of thunder, and still Peter fiddled with the straw in his drink. I heard the child cry, "Mommy," and I heard its mother's soft answer. The child was silent. It was then Pete reached over took my hand in his and very quietly said to me, "Mother, I'm gay." I thought I didn't hear him correctly. I gulped. "What did you say?" He held my hand a little tighter and then repeated himself," Mother, I'm gay." I heard the cash register. The child was crying again, and a waitress was asking the next table who wanted soup and who wanted salad. I saw the rain pounding now against the window and I could feel my heart. I could actually feel my heart pounding. Pete was holding my hand very tight and I wanted him to stop.

It had gotten dark. They turned the lights up. Pete sat across the table from me with his hair falling into his eyes, those large brown eyes that held his own certain twinkle which had always made me glad. He was my son. He was older. Where was the little boy? Where had he gone? He looked at me and I could see his dad. Somehow I had never really seen the similarity since he'd grown up. When he was a little guy toddling all over he was a little mirror image of his father, but later he looked like himself. Somehow, at that moment, he looked like Peter sitting across the table so silent and stern, the Peter I hated and hadn't hardly talked to since the divorce.

I remember how angry I was when I asked him, "What do you mean, you're gay?"

I hardly knew what being gay meant. I knew that it had to do with being a homosexual but when I was growing up no one ever talked about such things. I certainly never knew anybody who was a homosexual, well maybe the man who worked at Wayner's Clothing Store on Bartlett Street who wore all the rings. We girls would go and watch him from the hall at the entrance to the rest rooms where he couldn't see us and giggle. When I told my mother she just looked at my dad with that funny grown-up secret society look and said to never mind.

He was so quiet, so unlike Petey; I mean Peter. He kept holding my hand and then with a catch in his voice told me," Mother, I'm in love with Dick Shooster and am going to move in with him Saturday. Dick's going to help me go to college. He can afford it. Dick is a dentist and is a wonderful person. I want you to meet him and love him as I do." It was then he let go of my hand, got up from his chair, and came around the table beside me. Peter pulled me to my feet then took me in his arms and said," Mother, I want him to be your best friend, too."

I remember how I pulled away from this son who was as close as any other human being to me and ran out into the rain. I had to feel clean. I had to do something, I had to understand what was happening. My son, a homosexual? There must be a mistake. He must just be having a reaction over Lisa; that was it, and at last it made sense. I went back into the restaurant and over to the table where Peter was sitting with his head in his hands. I pulled my chair around to where I could be closer and told him I understood and that when Lisa came home from Europe everything would be like it was before.

His face went white, and he pushed me away, "Mother, even if Lisa came back I would still love Dick. I never will love anybody but him. We are in love and intend to live together. Please try and understand. I love him." All I heard was the word, love, over and over and over in my brain. What did this youngster know about love and love with another man. He must be losing his mind. Maybe Lisa leaving like she did hurt him mentally. That must be it. I almost yelled at him, "Are you losing your mind? Has Lisa's leaving upset you so much you aren't thinking straight?" Peter didn't answer me. He quietly took my shoulders and led me to the front of the restaurant and said in the iciest tone I had ever heard him use, "I'll go get the truck, please wait here."

I don't know how I got into the car and what was said as we drove home. All I can remember is the one windshield wiper scratching as it went back and forth and not being able to see where we were going because the rain was so heavy and the wiper on my side didn't work. The baby sitter was playing with the other children and I asked Peter if he would drive her home. I sent the kids to bed without a story. I just couldn't stand even to talk to them. Their brother was a homosexual, a fag, and I was his mother.

For several nights I didn't sleep. I didn't know what to do, how to stop the hurt in my heart, the shame, the wondering what I had done that was so wrong that he would become a gay? I cried, I prayed, I got angry. I yelled at the kids. Finally I went to the pastor and cried out my hurt to him. He told me how it was a sin and an abomination before the Lord and how I had to see if I couldn't get Peter to come in and talk to him. I left his office more hurt and angry than I was before I went in.

When I got home that day the "buggy" was in front of the house. The kids were still at school. I went in and there Peter was with a tall handsome dark-haired man who stood and introduced himself as Dick Shooster. He was older than Peter, dressed in a beautifully tailored suit and very well mannered. Pete came over and hugged me and said that this was Dick and he wanted me to love him too. I couldn't handle it and escaped into the kitchen.

The kitchen was my favorite room in the house. I had painted yellow sun-flowers around the boarder near the ceiling, and the bright yellow curtains had sunflowers appliquéd on them. The neighbors said when they wanted a happy pill all they needed was to come into my kitchen and have a cup of coffee. But on this day it was ugly and horrible and I hated it. I stayed there until I heard the front door close. I knew they had left.

My darling sweet boy was a homosexual. He was in love with another man and I couldn't do anything about it. I couldn't even imagine what it was really all about. I was sick. I threw up in the sink, cleaned it up and went to my bedroom, pulled down the shades and fell on my knees. How could God let this happen? What had I done wrong to be punished like this? Maybe it wasn't what I had done. Maybe it was his father's sins coming out in the son. That must be it. It must be his father's fault. It was then that my anger at my ex-husband was almost to a point of insanity. I stood and screamed and screamed and screamed. I cursed

Peter's dad. I asked God to kill him for what he had done and then, exhausted, I fell onto the bed in a blind stupor and cried myself to sleep.

As all things pass the days went by. Everything became a routine. The children were growing older. I didn't need a baby sitter anymore for them when they got home from school. I had a better shift at the hospital and spent every spare minute with them. I was introduced to Carl, a very nice man, during a potluck at church and eventually married him.

The kids adored him and he loved them. He adopted them all except Peter whom we seldom heard from. He did attend the wedding without the other man and sent a beautiful gift. I can't even remember what it was. I had closed the window and pulled down the blinds on my oldest son. I tried not to even think about him.

Later Carl and I had a small addition to the family, a little girl who almost didn't make it but the Lord gave her to us and let us keep her. I was much too old to bear children. Where was Pete when all this was going on? He left Dick after a year, dropped into the house several times and then took a job in South America with a mining company. Whenever he was in town he would come and see us but he wasn't my Peter. He was a stranger that I didn't know. When he did come to see me and the kids he never spoke about who he was with, but we heard there had been several men in his life.

The very last thing that my memory demands I must share with you. It happened about seven years ago. All the children were grown and out. Some had their own children. Two in college and one who had married early had a daughter who had just married and was going to give us our first great-grandchild.

When the family got together we never spoke of Peter. Somehow they knew it hurt me to talk about him so they seldom brought up his name. He now had a job in Maryland working for a company as their office manager, and had an apartment not far from his office.

Peter called one afternoon, from his office, and asked me to go to dinner with him that night. He said he had some very important news to share. Carl was on the west coast with Lucille and I was alone. In a way I was enjoying a few days of reading and not doing any cooking. I decided to go and when Peter came by to pick me up it wasn't in "buggy" but a shinning new car. I have no idea what make it was. We were silent as we went to the restaurant. It was the new Chinese one on Schaeffer Road everyone was talking about.

The restaurant had little booths in it with rice-paper sliding doors and all the waitresses wore kimonos. As we entered they knelt down and took off our shoes then put silk-embroidered sandals on our feet. The interior of the restaurant was beautifully decorated. In the center of the room a small garden surrounded a pond with large bright-colored goldfish. It must have had burning candles, for a rather sweet smell permeated my nose. I rather liked it.

I remember now how I was taken in by the room's unique beauty and hardly realized Peter was standing quietly beside me. He was a new Peter that I didn't know, not the little boy with the falling hair. This man had on a well-made expensive suit, his hair was combed, and he wore a gold watch and a gold ring with a very large diamond in it. He spoke softly to the waitress and then took my arm as she led us into a small-sized booth, handed Peter the menu, bowed to him then closed the paper doors as she left.

Peter led me to a small table and held the chair until I sat down, pulled out his own chair pushed it closer to me. He reached over and took my hands in his. I shuddered. I remembered the last time he had held my hand and what he had said that day. He said with tears falling from his beautiful brown eyes," Mother, I have missed you so very much. I'm sorry I hurt you so terribly. I'm here to ask you to forgive me for hurting you. Please, Mother, I love you very much."

A flood broke in my heart and I grabbed him to me, my Petey, my darling first son who chirped the day he was born. All at once the hurt was gone and the love I had for this boy came back. No, it had always been there. It somehow now seemed to fall into its proper place. He was my son. I loved him and needed him. He held me for a long time and then said, "Mother I'm still gay but there are things we have to talk about."

I don't remember the exact words but he tried to explain to me that he was trying to break away from his gay life style. He told me stories of how he would break away for a while and then go back, how he had fought it and then a man would come along and give him the love he needed and he would be back into it again. His job in Maryland was only about an hour from us and he wanted me to come and help him decorate his apartment. But I had to remember he said several times, that he was a homosexual. At that moment I knew what Jesus must have felt when he looked out over Jerusalem with such love and caring. I loved Peter but I knew within me the destruction he was facing. How could I help him, and why had I turned my back on him?

I remember the hours we talked as I helped decorate the apartment. I met some of his friends, most of them gay. I tried to remember they were his friends and be nice to them. I tried to be a loving mother and make up for the years when we were hardly speaking. How foolish I had been. How could I have helped him by turning my back on him? I watched him try to get out of the life style. By now the rest of the family knew he was gay and Carl accepted him as his son. He never once said an angry word to him. When Peter would come in, Carl would hug him and welcome him just as he did all the kids. Then at night Carl and I would pray for him and ask the Lord to guide him out of homosexuality.

And now for the last scene, no, the next to the last scene, of Peter's story. It was Christmas and the complete family was, for once, all home. It was snowing, the tree was filled with candy canes, lights, handmade things grandchildren had made to hang on it, and the kitchen was making the house smell like ginger bread, fruit cake, and, oh, just Christmas. Peter had come that morning and there was a look on his face I couldn't read. Carl asked me what was it with Peter. I couldn't answer him.

Peter played with the children and hugged his brothers and sisters. He hugged me every chance he had and even let down and hugged Carl. There was something very different about our Petey. After dinner the grandchildren were all sent up to tumble into beds and sleeping bags spread around in the family room. We

could hear their giggles. Finally there was silence. The excitement and anticipation of Christmas morning, filled stockings and
presents under the tree that Santa had mysteriously left during
the night, had finally closed their small sleepy eyes.

We all gathered around the piano and as Carl played we sang
carols. Peter's baritone filled the room. He had a beautiful voice
like his dad. I was no longer angry with his father because I knew
it wasn't his fault Petey was facing the turbulence in his life. I had
taken it to the Lord and begged his forgiveness and with the years,
and the present happiness from Petey giving me back his love, I
knew that eventually Carl and my prayers would be answered.

We were all tired and needed a cup of hot cocoa, a tradition
that was a warm fuzzy memory in each of our children's hearts.
Everyone gathered around the long kitchen table that had fed all
of us for years. It was then Peter said he had something to tell us.
I will remember his exact words forever. He looked right at me
and then Carl and said, "Mom, Carl, two months ago I gave my
heart to the Lord and I am never going back to homosexuality
again. I have a new love, Jesus Christ, and I want you all to know
that He is my Savior and Lord. I didn't know then that it was
almost too late.

Everyone hugged him and I couldn't speak I was so happy our
prayers had been answered. We were all in tears. Then his
brother Orin said, "What do you mean almost too late? Hey, bud
it's never too late." Petey crossed the room and put his arms
around his brother's shoulders. With happy tears glistening in his
eyes he said, "Orin I found out yesterday I have pancreatic
cancer. The doctors have given me about six months to live, but
that's all right, I know the Lord and I can handle this."

There wasn't a sound. Six months to live. How could that be?
All my children and grand children were healthy, even the new
little great granddaughter was healthy. Pancreatic cancer, why
Peter, why my son? I hardly remembered what he had said about
the Lord. All I could think about was six months, one hundred and
eighty days. No! There must be a mistake. There had to be a
mistake. We would take him to other doctors. I immediately

started to make plans to "make it better" as I had for all the children whenever they had an "ouwee."

Somehow Carl got me to bed, not to sleep but to lay there, my heart aching for my son. That Christmas was a nightmare for me. Peter had quit his job and wanted me to help him move out of the apartment we had decorated. He wanted to move into our spare room, so that when he ——. I couldn't even think it or say the word. I knew I wouldn't have to. I knew God would heal him even after we took Petey to a specialist who did other tests and sadly concurred with the first doctor. Doctor's had been wrong before and they were going to be this time. I had a straight prayer line to God and knew that He would never take my son, especially now that Petey loved Him so.

Peter and I were having a cup of tea at the long kitchen table. The house was empty except for us. He handed me his check book and said he had everything made over to me so that when he died he said the word that I couldn't I wouldn't have any trouble. Then what I remember most happened. I said I was going to give his name to the prayer team and ask the dear Lord for a miracle. He just had to heal my Peter. I leaned over and kissed my precious son and said I was going to fast and pray day and night that the Lord would heal him. It was then that he said, "No, mother dear, I have an appointment with Jesus and I don't want to disappoint him."

We didn't have six months; we only had a little more than six weeks. The day he went to keep his appointment with Jesus he pointed to some clothing that were on a shelf in his room and told me to be certain he was wearing them after he died. I still couldn't say the word. I told him not to talk that way, he just smiled and told me he loved me and then very quietly, turned his head away, his hair fell onto his forehead and he was gone.

When his brother, Orin, took the clothes down to dress him for the undertaker we read what the shirt had printed on it, "Don't be caught dead without the Lord Jesus Christ."

My Peter was gone. My little darling boy was with his real father, one who would never throw a fishing license onto the table and ask what could he ever do with that. I have an idea the very first thing he and Jesus did was to go fishing, and I wouldn't be surprised if Peter and the others weren't there fishing with him.

The lady sitting on the sofa, across from my desk, was dressed in a neat pair of blue slacks and a nicely ironed blouse. She had told me she was 76 years old; she didn't look a day over 50. The man sitting next to her was pleasant; when he looked at her you could tell there was love in his heart for this woman. He looked his 80 years, the lines around his eyes and the wrinkles that surprised different areas on his face gave away his age.

When I started to write this book I let it be known that I wanted to take interviews from family members as well as men and women who were living as homosexuals or had escaped. Carl and his wife immediately e-mailed me they would be happy to tell their story and share Peter with me.

My first question was, "How are you handling Peter's death now, and what would you say to other parents with children who are living in a homosexual life style?"

Before Carl could speak she stood and leaned over the desk as she answered in a voice filled with immense emotion, "I would tell them never to turn away from their children, never, never!" A tear trickled down her cheek as she continued, "Love means to accept other human beings where they are, not where you want them to be. I learned the hard way, oh! how I wish I had it to do over. Maybe Peter would have found an answer long before he did."

Then Carl stood and put his arms around his sobbing wife and told me, "There are days we have a rather difficult time with Peter's death and other day's when we are surrounded by the grandchildren, we are fine."

By now they were both back on the sofa sitting very close together. Carl still had his arm around his wife. I asked, "What are your plans now?"

A wonderful smile came across their faces and each spoke almost in one breath, "We are working in an organization that is helping people living as homosexuals who want to change. And, we are trying to be as close to our grandchildren as possible. Carl takes them fishing and he just finished teaching our oldest grandson, Orin Jr., how to drive so he can get his license."

Carl spoke up "We can't change what happened to Peter but we can make a difference now that we know what love really is!"

3

"O.K. Let's Get Real Here"

"You want an interview; you really want to know all about being a fag. Well, I'll tell you how it really was. You're not going to like it and print in a book; sure, I bet you will?"

MY MOM WAS A REAL PEACH. She went to all my school things, and then there was my Dad, too damn busy. Watching T.V. he couldn't even talk to me when the commercials were on. "Go talk to your Mother," he'd grunt. He was a brain, at the plant, invented some tube that made the gas do better on a rocket. He was a lady chaser; I watched what he did when Mom wasn't looking. Caught him one day at the neighbors with his hands down Thea's blouse. She was Randy's wife. They didn't see me, but I sure as hell saw what they were doing. Boy, did they ever make a good pair, her dotting after my Dad and Randy making out with me.

We lived in a little town about twenty minutes down the main highway from Williamsburg. Dad worked at a plant in Williamsburg and Mom was a stay-at-homer. With us six kids she didn't have time to teach in school and all of us too. Me, I was the second kid, had an older brother and four under me. Bob was two years older, Tommy was about a year and a-half younger, Carlene, Ellie, and Shasta were all younger than him. The girls were Dad's favorite. He'd put them on his knee and bounce them around. Us boys he ignored unless there was garbage to take out, a lawn to mow, or something he could think of to get us out of his way.

We had a big old barn of a house on Fifth Street about eight blocks from town and seven from school. Middleford was a typical eastern town. Had a square in the middle and three churches, we never went. Dad said it was all fairy-tale stuff and

Mom simply didn't say much about anything really. Whenever Dad was in the house she just waited on him hand and foot and nodded her head to the constant flim-flam he dribbled her way. Damn there were times I wanted her to belt him one. But not her, she never even hit us kids, just looked at us and somehow we did as she asked. I guess we all felt sorry for her.

I bunked in with Bob and Tom on the top floor. We had the whole floor, a big room where three singles fit in O.K. We each had our own dresser and enough space that we didn't get into each other's hair too often. There was plenty of space under the eaves for closets so we all had our own. I liked Bob, he was a cool bro. Tommy was a whiner and always getting Mom to kiss an owee or something. He was a damn pest and I guess what I hated worst of all was his using my things.

Finally I put locks on my dresser and also on my closet door. That fixed him. He cried to Mom but she didn't say anything so I just kept everything locked up. Found locking stuff away from people was a great way to get along so they couldn't get nosey. Bob had one of my keys but he never bothered anything. Bob was always reading. He was going to be a scientist and go to the moon or someplace out in space. I thought he was out of it sometimes but when I needed something he was there for me until the day he got killed. Some (drunken) bastard swerved and hit him on his bike. Bob never even made it to the hospital. I'd killed that guy if they hadn't put him in jail. I was ten the year Bob got killed. He had just turned twelve.

I don't know who I hated most, the guy who killed Bob or my Dad. The first time I ever slugged anybody was about two weeks after the funeral. Mom was getting dinner on the table and Dad was reading some kind of plans at his desk in the little room off the big sitting room. Dad said it was his office and us kids were to stay out. The room opened onto the porch and also the dinning room. Mom always had a bad time setting the table having to remember there was one less place. She cried a lot those days. I heard him yell at her to quit her sniveling as I was coming down the stairs for dinner. I made one line for him and slugged him on the side of the head. He was sitting at his desk and it knocked him to the floor. He went out like a light and Mom came in and knelt over him and didn't even look at me.

Dad was only out a minute. I guess I wasn't the Goliath I thought I was 'cause when he got up he grabbed me and beat the shit out of me. I ended up with a missing tooth, a split lip, and an eye that I had a hard time opening for a week. Mom grabbed him and made him stop. She actually hit at him and was screaming for him to stop. I couldn't believe it. She actually fought for me. Nobody would ever hurt her again. She was great. She fought for me, my tiny little under five feet, not a pound over ninety-five Mom plowed into my six-foot Dad and fought like a tiger. Man, my face was nothing compared to what I thought about her.

All during grade school and even up through Junior High I remembered the beatings my old man gave me. There is just so much room inside a guy for hate and my tank was so damn full I fought a kid over just about any reason I could find. I was a great fighter and even the bigger kids stayed out of my way. I only had a couple of friends. Josh was my best friend. I'd fought him in the play yard and he beat the crap out of me. Then there was Ed. He was a little puke and all the kids teased him and some even hit him, so I took him under my protection and anybody getting on his case meant they were on mine. They left the three of us pretty much alone.

I was going to Junior High school that fall if I graduated. I was always in the principal's office for some dumb thing. Mom said she might as well schedule one day a week for a school visit as she was always over there because of me. I hated to hurt her but I was always in some type of trouble. If it wasn't some dumb teacher trying to get me to do something that was stupid, it was some kid calling me names or picking on some other poor slob who needed help, like Ed. I never could stand some rouster beating up on a little kid. One time Crate, as we called him 'cause he was as wide as he was tall, grabbed a kid's candy bar and started to bust him one because the kid hit him. I caught the jab and landed him one in his fat tub of a gut and he threw up all over the lunch room floor. The lunch room teacher said I had to clean it up and I told her where she could go and landed in the principal's office. I didn't give a hang, I'd have done it again.

I got that son of a bitch back. When Crate was walking home that day I got behind the tree just outside of school and when he came by I tripped him. Man did he splatter. I ran like hell so he couldn't see who did it. All the kids knew and the next day was I ever popular, at least for a day or two. Nobody liked him because he was always tattling and whenever you had anything good in your lunch he'd take it. He was so damn big nobody ever fought him back. I put a cork on that. He never took anything again while I was around.

So let's get back to when I started being a gay as they call it now. Hell, there's nothing gay about it. I was about seven. No, I was eight 'cause I'd started third grade when Randy helped fix my bike one day and then fixed me. We were in his garage and Thea was somewhere else. They didn't have any kids. The chain had slipped off my bike and I was in the front yard trying to fix it when he came out and told me to bring it over to his garage and he'd help me. He fixed the bike and then told me to put the tools away in the little room that was in the back of the garage. I was putting the tools on the shelf when he came up behind me held me and reached down inside my pants and started playing with my dick. He was holding me so tight I couldn't move. He had the hairiest arms. I tried to get away. I'd have killed him if I could have.

I yelled at him to stop and he said if I made any noise he'd tell my Dad it was me and who did he think my Dad would believe. When he let me go I slugged him but he was so much bigger it was useless. I told him I'd tell Mom and he said to go right ahead and he'd hurt her if I did. There was nothing I could do, and that wasn't the only time. He always made some excuse to have me come to his house, always when Thea was gone. He'd ask my Maw to have me come over and help him. I'd tell her I didn't want to and she'd tell me that wasn't the way neighbors acted. I'd have given anything if I could have told her the truth, but I doubted she'd have believed me.

It was just a little after Bob was killed that they moved. But by that time I was going of my own free will. Hell, it felt good and Randy started telling me how wonderful I was and what a great guy I was. Somehow in my brain that made it O.K. He made me feel like somebody. I was feeling love from him that I never got

from my Dad and, with Bob gone, I needed something. I knew
Maw loved me but she never touched us boys or the girls either for
that matter. She was quiet and reserved and did all the right
things, kept us clean, made us do our school work, tried to keep
me from swearing, and made us all mind our manners.

Some place in my brain I had switched to having to earn love
and I needed it from a man. Women were shadows, there for
certain things like house work and taking care of kids. The world
was a man's place and woman were additions to do what men did.
You had to make it in the "man's" world and the way you did was
to make it with them by being the best "piece of ass." And that is
how I found myself on the streets of Williamsburg, shooting up
and bedding down. But I'm getting ahead of my story.

Finally I made it to Senior High school and liked it a little
better, maybe because I was older and the teachers didn't treat us
like babies. I usually spent the week-ends away from home. I
couldn't stand the way Dad treated Mom and knew I'd kill the son
of a bitch if I stayed around on the week-ends. I got together with
Eric Sawyer who had his own car and was as gay as they get. We'd
spend our time in Williamsburg. I worked after school at a local
garage so I had some money and Eric had a pretty big allowance
from his Dad. His mother didn't live with them. I never knew
where she was because Eric wouldn't talk about her. One day
when my curiosity got the best of me I asked him where she was
and he told me to mind my own "f———" business. I never asked
again.

I usually told Mom where I was going. I was tagging along
with Eric into Williamsburg, and waiting for him to pick me up in
the kitchen eating a piece of Mom's chocolate cake. Man, could
she bake chocolate cake. I don't remember which I liked best the
cake or the frosting. I asked her if she knew anything about Eric's
Mom. Damn, his Mother had been murdered. Nobody was ever
caught, she said. There were a great many people questioning
Eric's father. They thought he'd done it because she had been
playing around with a guy in Williamsburg. The entire town knew
about it and guessed that when Eric's father found out he'd killed
her, but it was never proven. Eric's father was a salesman and

was supposed to have been in Cleveland that weekend. They found Eric's mother's body in a lake just outside of town. It appeared she'd been hit over the head with, as the paper said, "a blunt instrument."

I never saw Mr. Sawyer much, just once in a while when we'd stop at Eric's to get something. He was generally out of town and I guess he never knew where Eric was. I doubted if he gave a shit. When we didn't go into Williamsburg, I stayed at Eric's house. I can only remember a few times that Mr. Sawyer was there. The couple times he was he stayed in his office and I'd hear him talking on the phone taking orders for some kind of farm machinery. There were brochures lying around and Eric tried to explain his dad sold some kind of machinery used in digging wells. It had an attachment for digging post holes which was different than other types that were on the market. Eric's Dad didn't know Eric was gay. Well neither did my Dad or Mom. I could care less about the old man, but my Mother knowing was a different matter.

Eric was a grade ahead of me and did great in school. He was always at the head of the class and never in the principle's office. In high school I got my act together and stayed out of trouble. Of course in high school it was a different situation. You were on your own more and, if you didn't like a teacher, you could transfer to another class. You walked around to different rooms to go to classes. Everything wasn't with just one teacher and you were not stuck with him or her for the year. It was in high school I met Randy, and he took Eric's place quite easily.

I met Randy during an assembly. I was sitting near the door when he came in late and plunked down beside me. We got to joking over the speaker who was telling us about registering for college exams, what colleges were available, and how to apply for scholarships. Randy didn't need a scholarship. He said his Dad would pick up the tab. I figured I wouldn't either as the only thing Dad ever talked about was when I would be in college and how he wanted me to go to his own alma mater. He was a Harvard man and thought it was the only college that had anything on the ball in the U.S. It was funny. Randy's Dad had graduated from Dartmouth and felt the same way. Later Randy and I figured he'd be going to Dartmouth and I'd be at Harvard. He went to Dartmouth but I never made it to Harvard or any other college.

Randy graduated a year before I did and was off to Dartmouth that fall. I tried to get along without him. I needed someone in my life, but I wasn't a loner. I had my own pick-up truck by then, a little rusty and the paint was chipped but it ran smooth and I kept that motor in perfect shape. I was a good mechanic. Jeff, who owned the garage, told my Dad one day how good I was. Dad just grunted. Being a grease monkey was below Dad's level of understanding.

That night at dinner he brought up the subject of college and told me he intended for me to apply as soon as possible to Harvard. He then actually looked at me and said not to mind he would do it for me. I forgot all about it as it didn't make any difference to me where I went. I loved working with cars but hadn't even let myself think about being a mechanic. If I didn't go to college it would disappoint Mom and I knew Dad would never understand, not that I gave a damn about what he thought.

I still spent my week-ends when I could in Williamsburg and going with any guy I found appealing. I also started shooting up to get a great high. I thought I'd never get hooked. I was too smart for that. I'd just use it once in awhile to have some fun. I got in with a bunch at Crater's, a gay bar on Fir Street. We all tried a little stuff in a rented room at a wayside motel. Some guy from San Francisco got us to try it. He was gay and treated us to a room and a night's fun. I was into group "therapy" ha! It didn't stop there and I couldn't stop looking forward to week-ends and what went with those week-ends. Before long I drove over on Wednesday nights, too, and then it was more nights. I was hooked. I needed a fix. I was a drug addict and I got the money to pay for that from being a male prostitute.

You want to know what it is like being a male prostitute. You want to know the things they do, the beatings, the burning your arms with cigarettes to make it "better." You want to know about chains and whips and how you do anything just to get enough money to shoot-up. Let me show you the burn marks on my arms. Do you want to see the marks on my butt? Want to see the scars from the knife marks and hear about an all-nighter with more than one guy wanting to get his rocks off? It isn't a gay life. It is a life of hell! Oh, heh, I know all gays aren't like that, but try out a bath house or a gay bar and see what happens in the dark corners of the motel and the hotel rooms.

How I graduated I'll never know, but I did. Dad had signed me up for college and I was to leave the last week of August to get settled and use to my new surroundings. I never made it. It's pretty hard to drive to Harvard from prison.

It happened one Friday night. I got off work from the garage where I was working during the summer and drove to Williamsburg to get a fix and give out so I could get some more money. The stuff was getting more expensive and it seemed I needed more all the time. My wages at the garage didn't half cover the cost. I went from my job at the garage to my nightly job at the Crater. There were no "job-benefits."

That night I was feeling pretty high. A new guy came into the club and asked me for a fix, said he was just in from Florida and hadn't made any connections. I was too stupid to know I was being set up. I liked being a big guy and told him about the room at the motel where we all met. He punched me on the arm, patted my butt, and said he'd see me there for more than just a fix. I winked back and was looking forward to it as he was a good looking guy and I needed some fun. He looked well healed. I was going to hit him up for a couple hundred. I was into Chris for a hundred. He knew I was good for it so he loaned me money once in awhile.

Later, after a couple of drinks, I made my way to the motel. The guy wasn't there. It was way past two before he arrived. I introduced him to the guys, some were a little out of it and some others were doing their thing. I took him over to the side of the room and offered him a fix, said he'd have to pay in advance as no one here really knew who he was. He reached for his wallet and when I reached for the money he handcuffed me and read me my rights. The door opened and in walked three policeman who took us all into custody. It was my first arrest. I got six months in the county jail and lost any contact with my Dad. He disowned me and forbid my Mom to even come and see me. Mom snuck out of the house to come and see me anyway. Dad had forbidden any of the kids to say my name and ordered Maw to get rid of everything in the house that was mine. She boxed it all up and hid it in the basement for me so when I got out I could have it.

Jeff from the garage visited me a couple times but that was all. Yeh, a church group came and sang some hymns, and a guy with a collar on backwards preached about forgiveness and sin and how we were all sinners. Hell, what else was new? I didn't do without sex in jail. A great place to have all you want, but it was getting pretty bad. I didn't have any contacts for a fix and no money if I had. Those first two weeks I thought I would die and wanted to but it got a little easier as time went on. One of the guy's gal brought in a bottle and we all got plastered that night. She brought it in under her skirt somehow. When the guards came around and found us all looped they searched everyone the next visiting day and caught her.

Most of the guys in with me were just kids. Most of them because of something to do with drugs. Three had been in the motel with me. One only got three months, and the one who was older, guess he was over thirty, got a year. The other got six months like me. Jail is different. You can't do what you want to. You get up at a certain time, eat at a certain time, bed down when they turn out the lights, and smoke when they say and where they say.

If you are a "f——g queer" the guards treat you like shit and when no one is looking give you trouble. They try and get you mad so you'll hit back and if you do it's the hole. I got solitary once, slugged the damn bastard. Got him good. Spent ten days in the hole for it but I'd do it again. Hell, I did it again and they extended my stay for a year after the judge spent time babbling about me being a bad boy. He said if I'd cooperate I'd get along with the guards. Who the hell wanted to get along with the damn guards? That judge was as thick-witted as most people I knew.

When I had an extended stay at the county hotel free of charge Mom stopped coming to see me. I got a letter, she said Dad had found out she was coming to see me and had forbidden her to ever do it again. I got a note from Tommy that surprised me. He said that Dad had hit Mom pretty bad for sneaking out to see me. When he found out how bad Mom was, he said she had to go to the hospital for a cracked rib— he thought I'd better know. Tommy had graduated but was still living at home. He was going to Harvard that fall. I guess he still was under Dad's rule. From the note I could tell he was getting a little bit of an eye opener. I never heard from the girls. They were all Dad's little door mats so I wasn't surprised. It was a good thing I was locked up 'cause if I'd been out I'd have killed the son-of-a-bitch for hurting Mom.

It gets pretty lonely in jail, especially when no one visits you on visiting day. Most of the guy's parents came and one guy had a sister who came every visiting day. He had her picture pinned up on his locker. Man, was she a beauty. She was in some type of show business and didn't give a shit about him being gay. I often wondered what the girls and Mom would say if they knew I was a homosexual. I could guess the look on my Mother's face, and I hoped I'd never see it.

A counselor came by one day and suggested that some of us younger guys should be thinking about doing some kind of study while we were cooling our heels. I was still determined to have my own garage and work on cars. I laughed to myself when I thought about it and how Dad would go bonkers if I opened a garage in his town under his nose. I'd call it Clark's Garage, and tell everyone that I was Chester Clark's son. I had a goal. It seemed strange to have a plan. I never thought of what or how until that counselor got me to thinking about when I got out.

I wrote Jeff and asked him if I kept my nose clean how about my job back? Everyday I held my breath during mail-call. Then one day they called my name and it was a letter from Jeff. He said he would give me a job, but there couldn't be any dope or it was a no-go. Hell, I knew that, and I wrote him back and told him not to worry. Sure, you can get all the dope you want in prison but something in me got me past those first three weeks when I was stone broke and too sick to even care. I knew I could get along and I made up my mind that dope was not for me. Hadn't considered giving up being gay 'cause that was different. That was who I was and there was no reason to even consider going straight. Hell, who wanted a dumb woman around who did your laundry and waited on you? When I made enough change I'd get a house keeper and keep my lovers. Men were better to be around anyway.

The twelve months were over and I was free. I made myself a promise the day the doors closed behind me. No matter what it cost I'd never be behind those damn "f———" bars again. I'd shovel shit before I'd get into a situation where they could put me back. I never forgot my promise. That was the last time I saw the doors of a prison. I made my first stop Middleford. I had to see my Mom.

The house looked just the same. I made a point of getting there when I knew Dad would be at work, or I thought he would be. I should have called first. I ran up the front stairs and burst into the house wanting to hug Mom. The voice I heard wasn't hers but Dad's. "What's all the ruckus about?" he yelled. I went on through to the kitchen and there she was leaning over the sink.

"Mom, I'm home." I turned her around and hugged her. "I missed you, I love you." I don't remember ever telling her that I loved her.

"Timmy, oh, Timmy," she burst into tears and held me tight.

"Get the hell out of this house and never come back." Dad came into the kitchen and reached his hands out as if to sock me.

"You better make the first one good because if you don't I'll kill you." Somehow the memory of the prison doors escaped me.

I was now nearly six feet tall and shoulders were wide enough and my body strong enough I guess he took a second thought and put down his hands. Then my Mom did a strange thing for her. She walked over to my Dad and said, "My son is welcome in this house or I leave it." My Mom actually stood up to that son-of-a-bitch. The look on Dad's face was one I will remember with happiness for a long time.

"Mary Priscilla Clark, you don't mean that?" Dad yelled at her.

And wonder of wonders she yelled back, "Just try me. Just try me."

He turned on his heels and left, where I could give a damn!

I sat at the kitchen table eating chocolate cake and talking until it turned dark outside.

"Where are the girls?" It seemed strange they weren't around. I knew Tommy was in college but I thought the girls would be popping in. I sort of wanted to see them.

"Carlene is living in a dorm at State. Ellie has a job in Williamsburg, and Shasta is staying overnight with her girl-friend." Mother rattled off the whereabouts of the girls and we went back to talking.

"Tim, you're welcome to stay in your old room until you get a place to stay." I wanted her to say that but wondered at this new set of guts she'd grown since I had been in prison.

"Mom, I can't believe you talked back to Dad. When did you grow a backbone?" I laughed as I chided her.

"The day your Dad hit me so bad I ended up with a cracked rib I decided that was it. I told him if he ever laid a hand on me again I would divorce him and try and get everything I could. With the violence of his actions I was certain I would get a pretty big share of the bank account and no doubt the house. He's never touched me since and I don't take any crap off of him. I hate to say this about your Dad, Tim, but I hate him. I actually hate the father of my children. I know it is wrong but I can't help it." Her face was white and she bit her lower lip as she always did when she was nervous or upset.

I stayed at the house a week or so until I got my first paycheck from the garage. I moved into a small apartment around the corner of the garage. It was cheap rent but I had a goal, to save every penny I could make and get a garage of my own. Clark's Garage was a dream and I planned on making it come true.

I was working one afternoon when a gal came in with a flat tire. She had ridden the rim in. It was a dumb thing to do but by the looks of the car, her clothing and her attitude I guessed money didn't make much difference to her.

She spoke with a southern drawl, "Can you all fix this, Sonny?" She wasn't any older than I was. No one called me Sonny, not a damn bitch of a woman, especially one like her. She had a flimsy top that barely covered her boobs and a pair of white shorts that almost didn't make it around the curve of her butt.

"I'll pay you whatever, sonny, just get at it." She looked up and I saw the most beautiful dame I'd ever laid eyes on. Her eyes were almost purple. Her hair was as black as the wings of the crows that got into the garbage behind the garage, and her eyelashes nearly reached her eyebrows. Her figure, I could see almost all of it, was perfect. My pants got too tight in spots and I thought I'd lost my mind. Me, a gay, and her a girl. What the hell was going on here? I couldn't quit looking at her, especially her hair; it fell over her naked shoulders almost to her waist which I could have reached around with no trouble. I had this damn urge to see what would happen if I kissed those pouting red lips of hers.

"I'll get it changed right away. You can sit in the office while you're waiting." I felt like a damn teenager. My voice sounded as if it were changing and I couldn't take my eyes off her as she walked by me and into the office. As I was changing the tire— had to put a new rim on it— I kept making excuses to go in the office. She sat quietly reading a magazine, never even looked up when I came into the room. Hell, she made me feel like her damn servant. All at once I had the urge to show this little bitch what I was made of.

Why I ever got the nerve to ask her if she'd like to go to dinner with me I don't know. To my utter amazement she agreed. She was staying at the Wayside Motel on her way to Cincinnati. She was driving back to see her folks before the next quarter started at college, and would like to join me.

She ordered me to pick her up at seven o'clock and suggested I wear something appropriate. I felt like belting her but all I did was agree. She paid for my labor with a credit card that had a man's name on it. Her name was Spring Gilbert. It was her Dad's card.

That wasn't the first night she and I went on a date. She stayed over for that whole week and we made out. Me making out with a dame, but with her it was great. I know I was built like a wrestler and not bad to look at. I guess she thought she'd have a sexy interlude. I never dreamed a high-class dame like her would look twice at me seriously. What did I care anyway? Dames weren't for me.

Things were getting all mixed up in my head. I kept thinking about her while I was working, couldn't get her out of my mind. I kept seeing those eyes, as big as eyes can get, and that funny little smile she had, one side sort of crooked. I kept feeling the way her hair felt when I held her, and how she felt naked under my body. How she made me feel important and like a jock. Man she was good and all at once I started thinking about the guys and all and something was changing way down deep inside of me. I thought it would go away as soon as she left.

She didn't leave. She wired her Dad for some more money and stayed another week. I didn't go to my apartment but to get clothes and throw something into the Laundromat. She came to the garage and would sit and talk to me while I fixed a car. She even held the wrench and learned the name of the tools. She was something else again. One night as she lay beside me she reached up and turned my face towards her and told me she loved me. I had a hard time with that one. Loved me? Only my Mom had loved me, and Bob, but he was dead. She loved me. She really loved me and told me she would stay with me until I didn't want her around anymore. Hell, no one in my life time had ever really loved me. I lay there and didn't make a move. This was a moment I didn't want to go away.

We made love and it was sweet, I tell you, sweet. I held her. She was soft and smelled like spring, all clean and crisp and nice. They had named her perfectly, Spring. She was just like her name. Something was very right about all of this. I even lost my head and told her I loved her and told her if she would have me I'd marry her. It was a good thing I was lying down or I'd have fallen down, because she accepted and said the quicker the better.

We went over the state line. Jeff gave me three days off, and were married. When we got back I took her out to see my Mom and she was wonderful. Spring liked my Mom right off and my Dad even shook hands with her and said he was glad to meet her. No one could ever get near her who didn't feel a vibrancy about her. She was like an electric current.

We got a little bungalow on Elm Street and she made it into a doll house. Everything went great. Her Dad came for a visit and left a fat check big enough for me to get a garage of my own. I named it Clark's Garage and wanted to see Dad's face when he saw it. His son a mechanic. I was in for a surprise. Dad came by one day, actually came in the office and asked for a cup of coffee. I showed him around and he said it looked great and would come by again. I wasn't even mad at him. The bitterness was gone and all I could think of was getting home to Spring, seeing that smile of hers welcoming me in the door and holding her in my arms.

Spring was working on my swearing and I was trying to watch what I said. She warned me that when the children came that swearing would have to go. She always scolded with a laugh and then would come up to me and either kiss me on the lips or on the end of my nose. She had to stand on her toes to reach my nose. To top five feet three she had to stretch. I was madly in love and as far as being gay when it hit me between the eyes that I hadn't even thought about it for over two years. No one knew of my past in this town. In fact, I thought there wasn't anyone left anyplace near that would remember me. How wrong I was.

I looked up one day from changing a tire and there standing in front of me was Eric. How did he find me? I told the guys, by now I had two grease monkeys working for me, I'd be right back and took Eric by the arm and walked him into the office. He was passing through and saw the sign and took a chance to see if it was me. We talked for awhile and he asked how things were. I told him I was married and no one here knew anything about my past. He acted as if he were glad I was happy but there was something in his attitude that worried me.

"Eric, no one knows here and I haven't lived that kind of life for awhile and I don't intend to go back to it." I tried to get him to understand.

"Come on, old boy, you mean to tell me you haven't had any for over two years. Man how can you do without a good piece of butt? This dame you're hitched to must be some dame." He sneered as he talked about Spring. I could feel anger boiling inside of me. He sensed it and seemed to gloat over it. I didn't like the way things were going. I felt threatened and I wasn't good at that sort of thing. My temper was still there even though I'd fought giving in to it ever since I'd married.

I reached to shake hands and said, "Thanks for stopping in, Eric, but I have to get back to work." I turned to go back into the garage when he said, "Hey, aren't I welcome here? I think I will stay over at the motel tonight. How about coming over for a fling. You need it after all this time." He grinned and sat down on one of the office chairs. "When do you get off, I'll just wait for you."

I panicked inside but knew better than to let him see it. "Sorry, Eric, I can't Spring and I have other plans for tonight." I walked into the garage and didn't look back. He had to get out of town. When I turned around he was still there. I thought if I just keep working he would eventually leave. He didn't. I took the bull by the horns, wiped the grease off my hands, and went back into the office.

I faced him and said, " Look Eric, I have no intentions of coming to your motel room so you might as well take to the road."

"Hey, you better than me now since you got a garage? Think twice, old man, I can always tell the little lady, you know." He sneered at me and sat back down. "I need a little fun and you were always pretty great, so just plan on it, and bring a couple of bottles when you come. You know the motel, the only flea stop in town. He got up tipped his cap and said, "I'll see you tonight and remember all the fun we had. We'll do it again, you'll see."

"Don't plan on it, Eric, and if you get near my wife you will look like raw hamburger, so plan on that."

"There are ways of letting her know without me telling her, and you can plan on that." He sneered at me and said, "Make it three bottles, I'm thirsty."

He drove off in a beat up old Ford with smoke burping out from under the back.

I went into my office closed the door and sat behind my desk. What the hell, I mean what the heck was I going to do? There was no way I could ever tell Spring. Her Dad, he was a great guy and thought I was just right for her. And my Mom, and even Dad, what would they think? The three girls, how would they take such a story about their "big-brother" who they brought their boy friends to meet?

With Tom away at school I was the big-brother now and I liked it. I liked being who I was. I liked having the money I needed, and I loved my whole family. It was nice loving and being loved. Hell, I mean heck, I'd even let Shasta talk Spring and I into going to church with her one Sunday, and it wasn't all that bad. Several people knew me, had brought their cars in for a tune-up or repair, and it made me feel as though I was part of something. I liked belonging and I wasn't going to lose it. There had to be a way out but I didn't know what it might be. I knew what kind of a man Eric was. I'd been with him long enough to know he was a mean bastard. Good thing Spring couldn't hear me thinking, I'd better watch my tongue.

At dinner, as I sat across from Spring, I kept thinking what she would think of me if she knew my past and my stomach turned. How could I explain the gay bars, the bath houses, the motel and hotel rooms. She had asked me about the scars on my arms and butt and I'd told her I was in a car accident. Spring had been brought up in a southern home which sprouted manners and breeding and above all what was proper. I liked the way she talked, her-a-little-better-than-thou attitude, the way she walked and carried herself. I was crazy over the way she treated me as if I were somebody. I loved the way she had introduced me to her father as if I were King Henry, and the polite and friendly way he had accepted me. What if he knew?

"Dear you aren't eating. Is it unpleasant?" Her drawling question brought me up short.

"Love it dear, best pork chops you've made."

"They are lamb chops. There must be something wrong, can you share it with me?" She laid down her fork and looked at me with those eyes that simply sent me into orbit.

"Spring, it's the shop. I had a bad day dear. I'm sorry as sure as he—."

She interrupted me with a small grin and I knew it was because I swore.

"It was a bad day at the shop honey and I'm sorry to bring it home. What did you do today?"

She shared her day but my mind was not in my body but wondering what Erick would do when I didn't show up at the motel. In front of my eyes I could see the prison doors and hear them opening. I wanted to kill him so that my past would never face me again. I knew that would never be my out. My heart was breaking if a heart can break. I knew the only answer was to tell Spring, knowing Eric he would find some way to get the information to her.

I looked across the table and predicted she wouldn't be sitting there when she knew. She would go back to her father. I would lose the one thing in my life that had ever meant anything to me. I'd better get it over with. I had the feeling the phone would ring at any moment or the door bell and it would be Eric. Hearing it from him would be wrong.

I told Spring I had something to tell her and it wasn't going to be pleasant. Before I told her I had to beg her to understand that I loved her and what I had to say had nothing to do with the present and it would never happen again.

We went into the living room, she sat in her small rocker and I walked the floor like a caged lion. I started at the beginning and didn't leave even the sickening things out, the prison sentence, the bars, the bathhouses, the motel rooms, the dope. I left nothing out. She sat there not moving watching me with those eyes that moved when I did. There was no crooked smile but a tear ran down her cheek and with every new tear I died a little inside. When I was finished I just stood there. My life was over. I knew she could never really understand. How could anybody who hadn't walked in my shoes understand what it was like to be in hell?

It seemed that I had stood in the center of the room my whole life time. I thought to myself, "Oh, God, if you really exist help me." My soul was crying for help. I'd never prayed in my life. I didn't even know how.

Spring got to her feet and stepped in front of me then reached her hand up and touched my face and said, "Tim, I love you and what you did before we were married has nothing to do with us. I have admired you from the day we met and right now I admire you more than any person I have ever known. To be brave enough to tell me these things, not knowing what I would do, is the type of father our baby needs. I love you." Then she pulled me into her arms and stretched up on her toes and kissed me.

What had I ever done to deserve the love of such a woman I will never know? I burst into tears and held her as if she would disappear if I let go. She loved me, me, a dope-head, a gay, a jail-bird, and anything else you could name. Then what she said sunk in, the type of father our baby needed? "Spring, what did you mean, our baby?" I was still holding her to me.

"If you will let me breathe I'll tell you." She broke into that melody laugh of hers and I loosened my hold, but still held her.

"You are going to be a father in about six and a half months." She did her thing and kissed the end of my nose.

A father, I was going to be a Dad. I couldn't handle it. I let her go and sat down on the davenport and sobbed my heart out. I had a woman who loved me enough to carry my baby, enough to ignore my past, enough to even admire me for telling her the hell I'd come from. I couldn't understand. She came over and sat beside me and held my head against her breasts and petted me as if I were a child. No one had ever held me like this, not even my Mom.

I went to the motel the next morning and met with Eric. I explained that I'd told Spring and asked him to leave town and to leave me alone. He didn't believe me and a day later Spring told me some man had called and said he wanted to meet with her because he was certain she would like to know the real man she was married to. Spring told him she knew all about the man she married and his information wasn't necessary. He started telling her anyway but she interrupted him and then told him how much she loved me and that she was sorry he didn't have a woman in his life who loved him and hung up.

Spring asked me to attend church with her every Sunday and I did. She even got me to going to Sunday school. Some of it was rubbing off on me and I liked the way I felt sitting there in church beside her. I didn't really buy all the stuff they talked about but for her sake I went along. The pastor visited and I told him I hadn't ever been to church as a child and that I wasn't ready to be a member just yet but that Spring could if she liked. Spring wanted to wait until I was ready.

One morning I was getting ready to go to the shop, I heard Spring call me from the kitchen. Her water broke and in five minutes we were on our way to the hospital. I did the walking a thousand miles in the waiting room bit I'd heard other fathers talk about. Finally they called me in and put me in a cap and some type of gown and took me into the delivery room. I stood at the head of the bed and held Springs hand and helped her breath like we had been taught to do during classes she took me to. I couldn't stand it when a labor pain hit. It ripped me apart inside but she was being Spring. Not only was she beautiful and a lady but as brave as I'd ever seen a person be.

"Here's the head, now push, little lady." The doctor was giving her directions, then all at once he held a small piece of humanity in his hands who was my son. He laid him on Spring's stomach and asked me if I would like to cut the chord. I passed on that one. I heard a little mew and it was the voice of Robert Foster Clark. Robert for my brother and Foster after Spring's Dad. The doctor took my son and handed him to me. I looked down into the open eyes of a miracle and my heart knew another love of a kind I can't express. At that very moment I understood what God's sacrifice had meant when He allowed Jesus to hang on a cross and somehow I made a second promise to my self: this little boy was never going to know about gay bars and bath houses and motel rooms. He was going to know about the kind of life that included God and happiness and a father who loved him. I was going to be a good father. I was going to see that this little boy knew two fathers, me and God.

I met with Tim in the office of his new garage. The room smelled like tires, and the two chairs beside a stand filled with magazines and papers were straight and rather uncomfortable. Tim sat behind a desk covered with notebooks, papers, and a car part oozing grease onto a pile of newspapers. There were pictures of new and old cars covering the walls and a plastic cup of cold coffee on the top of his adding machine.

At the center of the desk was a picture of a woman and a small baby. I knew instantly it was Spring and little Robert Foster Clark. His wide-set eyes and curly black hair looked at me with the same mischievous look his Daddy had.

We'd finished taping and Tim asked if I would like a cup of coffee. I laughed because when I started taping he'd gone over to the office door and yelled out at the men, in the garage, not to interrupt. At that time had he asked if I'd like a cup? I'd said, yes, but somehow he forgot.

"No, Tim, I'll have my coffee tonight with dinner. What are your plans now, for you and your family?"

"What you really want to ask is will I go back to being gay, didn't you?"

"Not really but as long as you've brought it up, where are you on that issue? "

"When I go home and pick little Bobby up, and hold him to me, and see the look in Spring's eyes as she watches, that is heaven. Why would I ever trade that for hell?" He'd gotten up from behind the desk and was facing me with his two feet apart and all of his bulk staring down from over six feet of muscle.

"Have you heard from Eric?"

"No, and I hope he's got enough sense to stay away."

"Did you ever tell the rest of the family?"

"Spring and I talked it over and she felt there was no need to share the past with the present. I will see there is never a reason for her to want to change her views." I left the office, with my recorder and new tape under my arm, and felt like dancing on my way to the car. Little Robert Foster Clark was a very lucky little baby to have two parents the kind his were.

4

"I'll Think About It Later"

Mom used to say I chewed and Tommy swallowed. My brother, Tom, and I were only twelve months apart and when he breathed in I breathed out. He was the oldest, and I thought he knew everything there was to know, least that is what he told me. I might as well have been his twin because we were inseparable. I wore his jeans because we were the same around the waist; besides I hated it when Mom made me put on a dress. You can't climb to the top of the garage in a stupid dress and our hideout was at the back of the garage on the roof part where we'd built a club house.

The club house was our secret hideout whenever Mom called us to do stuff. We could get behind the cardboard walls that fit so neat between the roof and the first large limb of a maple that leaned over the garage at just the right angle. Mom knew we were up there but played hide and seek with us and always acted surprised when she climbed the tree and found us. Mom was pretty neat; she knew how to climb trees and everything. Every once in awhile she would bring our lunch to the club house and all three of us would eat cuddled together. It was nice to feel loved and warm and wonderful.

Dad never got in the club house. All he ever said was that it wasn't good for the garage roof to have that much weight on it. When we were listening Mom never disagreed with him but I knew she talked to him in their bedroom because he didn't make us take it down. Mom was always on our side. Dad hardly was ever home it seems. He was either at the office or the club. He played golf every week-end and never went to church with us. I saw Mom cry once when he told her not to bother him with that nonsense. He said she could go and take us kids but he wasn't going and that was that. Dad never changed his mind when he said, "that was that."

Mom read to Tommy and me when she tucked us in. She'd read a story from the Bible and before we went to sleep we would say prayers. She'd pushed the covers around our shoulders and kiss us and hug us, and then sit in the rocker beside our beds and sing to us until we were asleep. She had a beautiful voice and loved music. She also loved God and always was thanking Him for something out loud. I saw her one night kneeling beside her side of the bed; she was praying for us kids and that Dad would see fit to come to the Lord.

Tommy and I started school in the first grade together because he was sick one summer and had to stay out. He had scarlet fever and then the chicken pox; somehow I didn't get either of them. I figured girls are stronger than boys. He was six and I was five. I never could catch up with him. He'd turn seven and I'd turn six, it was always that way, but I was taller than him and that made up for it a little. When he was sick I never left him a minute except to eat and sleep. Mom said it wouldn't do any good to keep me away as I'd been with him when he was coming down with them.

I was Tommy's slave that summer. He played King Arthur and I wanted to be Lancelot but he said Lancelot was a boy and girls couldn't be knights so I'd just have to be a slave. I wanted to be Guinevere but he wouldn't let me be her either because I'd have to marry King Arthur and I couldn't because he was my brother and sisters and brothers couldn't get married. So I was a slave, but I made him let me be a slave from Egypt so I could wear a robe and a head piece. Mom made me a head piece that wound around my head and had some make-believe birds on it and even a gold band, one of Mom's old necklaces. I went barefooted like in our picture book of *King Arthur and the Knights of the Roundtable.*

Tommy lost a lot of weight being so sick and I just kept on growing so when we went into first grade we were about the same size. Mom made me wear a dress and I hated it because I had to sit "like a lady" and Tommy could play all the games. I wanted to play ball with him and the boys but they wouldn't let me. The girls played with paper dolls during recess. They had shoe boxes with little pieces of furniture cut out of the Sears catalogue. They made their dolls from the pictures of women in underwear then dressed them with the dresses they cut out in the dress section of the catalogue. I thought it was silly and told that to Marilee the girl that sat next to me in the first row. She called me a Tom-boy and I slugged her.

Mom had to come and be with me in the principal's office, some kind of a school rule. So while parents came anyone waiting to be scolded had to sit on a bench outside his door. I sat there getting madder and madder; nobody could call me a name and get away with it. Tommy came and sat with me on the bench. He didn't want me to be alone. While we waited for Mom he said that when no one was looking he'd hit her again.

Mom was sad I'd gotten into trouble and that Saturday I was grounded to my room. Tommy couldn't even come in and play a game with me. Mom brought my food in on a tray and I couldn't read, just had to stay in the room. It was awful; I couldn't even talk to Tommy. When Dad got home from his golf game he came in and gave me one of his long lectures on how little girls should act. "After all," he said, "you are a girl and it was high time I started acting like one." Then he forbid me to go up in the club house for all of the next week. I really hated that Marilee and she was going to be sorry.

Mom taught Tommy and me piano. Tommy didn't do too well; I loved it and spent a lot of time practicing. Mom played so beautifully and lots of times after dinner she would give sort of a concert. Dad loved to hear her play and I wanted to be able to play the same as she did. I loved the way it sounded when I played a chord. I could make up tunes I heard on the radio real easy. Tommy could hardly play book one by the time I was in the third book. It was amazing to me that I could do something better than him. He just laughed and said, so what, piano was an old girl thing and he wasn't no girl!

It was spring and the ice and snow was melting off the lawns. Along the edges of the street where it was piled into walls all splattered with ugly dirt it was melting and covering the streets with muddy water. The snow was beautiful when if first fell but when the cars went by they got it all dirty. Tommy and I walked the five blocks to school and we had to wear our boots because we would get soaked with all the melting snow.

When it snowed Tommy and I would build a fort in the back yard. We couldn't play in our club house because when it started to rain the cardboard got all wet. Every winter we had to take it down, but that was all right because we could build it again when school was out. We would draw plans during the winter as to what the new club house would look like. It was so much fun because Mom would get down on the floor with us and all three would take turns drawing what they thought it should look like. We'd tape the plans on the door of the fridge and then take them down and re-do them when we got a new idea.

During the winter we had snowball fights. Tommy usually won because he could throw further than I could and straighter. He said he was a better thrower because he was a boy. It seemed to me that God gave boys all the good stuff. Once in a while our Dad would get out and throw too but usually he didn't have the time. Mom was always out with us and she could throw even better than Tommy. She made me believe that when I grew up and was like her I wouldn't need to be a boy to do things well.

One day when we got home from school there were a lot of cars around the house. Tommy and I figured Mom was having one of her lady's meetings. Pastor Jim was in the front room with our Mom's two brothers and sister, and Dad's Mom was there too. Dad was an only child and all the family he had was his Mom. Pastor Jim sat us down on the couch and said he had something to tell us.

"Tommy and Sheila, your mother and father were in a car accident and God has taken them both to be with Him." Neither Tommy nor I really understood those words or what it would mean to the rest of our lives. Our parents had been killed by a drunk driver who had put on his breaks causing him to slide on the melting ice across the middle line hitting their car head on. The driver of the car was a twenty-two year old man who was only scratched a bit. He spent three years in prison but that was all. When we were both older and out of school we tried to hunt him up but couldn't find any trace of him.

For the next year Tommy and I were kept together. Mom's Uncle Pete took us to live with him, his wife, and three older children. He was Mom's oldest brother and felt it his duty to care for us. Tommy was seven and I was six and we weren't allowed to play together as we had at home. Tommy had to play with Harding and Kerry. Harding was nine and Kerry was eleven when we moved in with them. Aunt Meg put bunk beds in the boy's room and a cot for Tommy. I was put in Mary Ann's room. I had to sleep in the same bed with her and I hated it. She was fifteen and kicked me all the time. She didn't want me in her room. She said I was a baby and I was never to touch anything of hers or she'd fix me good.

Almost every night that first year I cried myself to sleep. Aunt Meg came in and scolded me "It's about time you stopped that nonsense and was thankful we are giving you a home." There was never a day she didn't remind me of her and Uncle Pete's generosity. I hated her almost as much as I had Marilee, only I didn't dare slug her. Uncle Pete was sort of O.K. He took the three boys fishing all the time, I had to stay at home. "Now Sheila," he would say, "girls your age should be playing with dolls not going fishing with the boys." There were times I wanted so badly to be a boy so I could be with Tommy and away from Mary Ann and her mother.

It was just after Christmas when I was finally seven and Tommy was eight that Uncle Pete said we had to move. Aunt Meg wasn't doing well and needed a rest. Tommy was to go to Mom's other brother, our Uncle Ken, and I was to go be with her sister, Aunt Martha and her husband Uncle Taylor. Tommy and I hid in the corner of the yard behind a big bush that was all red in the summer and made plans to run away. No one was going to separate us. We didn't have any money and had no idea where to go. We had begged Uncle Pete not to separate us but he just said we weren't old enough to decide things as yet and would just have to go along with the plans that he and Uncle Ken had made.

The day came when Aunt Martha and Uncle Taylor came to get me. They lived in Weinberg about two hours from where we had lived all our lives. One summer Mom and Dad had spent a week in Weinberg when Dad had a vacation. I didn't like their house because you didn't dare touch anything. Everything was like it was still in the store and Aunt Martha was constantly yelling at Tommy and I not to go near her stuff. Mom and she had sort of an argument one day in the kitchen and the next day we went home. I figured it was two days before we were supposed to. Tommy and I were glad.

Tommy wouldn't come into the living room to tell me good by. I knew why because I was feeling just like him, like I wanted to throw up and couldn't. Uncle Pete put me in the back of their car and patted my shoulder and told me that I would be fine and to mind Aunt Martha and Uncle Taylor. I wondered if it were possible to die at that very moment. If I had known how, I would have done it. I'd just die and go to heaven and be with my mother. If there had been a way to take Tommy with me I'd have done that to.

When we got to Weinberg Uncle Taylor pulled into the garage and took my bags and told me to follow him. My room was to be the one at the top of the second flight of stairs. It had a ceiling that came down close on both sides of the bed and had a window at both ends. I think they called it an attic. At one end were a lot of old suitcases and some card board boxes piled to the ceiling. There were some hooks on the wall that I was to hang my clothes on. I was to keep the bed made and see that I didn't eat or bring water to the room as he didn't want the floor damaged. I wondered how you could damage the floor. It was just wide pieces of wood, no rug, and not even painted.

I stayed in the room until I heard Aunt Martha yell at me to come downstairs. It was dinner time and she wasn't going to wait and have to eat cold food. The dining room was on the first floor because when I went down to the second floor all I could find behind the doors were bedrooms all made up as if some king or queen was coming to stay in them. All the rooms were beautiful, I wondered why I couldn't have had one of them.

I ran down the stairs because I was afraid I would be late and Aunt Martha was waiting for me at the bottom. It was my first scolding, "We won't have any running in this house, young lady. You may have gotten away with your nonsense with Margaret but you won't get away with it here. We are civilized and I don't intend you to embarrass me with your actions." That evening was the first of many scoldings from Aunt Martha. Uncle Taylor never spoke when she was in the room. He just made a growling sound in his throat and usually that was from behind his paper.

I wasn't permitted to speak at the table, and was constantly told that I would not be allowed to act as I had at Margaret's house. I wouldn't be allowed to grow up like the animals she was raising for children and how her brother, Peter, could stand living with such a woman was more than she could understand. When dinner was over I was taken into the kitchen and told it would be my job every night to do the dishes. I was to wash and dry them, put them away, sweep the kitchen floor and tidy up the dining room before I went straight up to bed. She wasn't going to have me "cluttering" up her living room.

I started to hate her. She was very fat and always smelled like dead roses. Around her waist was a thick roll of fat which fell out over the top of a girdle that did little to help. When she sat down and her dress was pulled up a little I could see her stockings and at the top of them was another roll of fat, there was a roll over the top of each of her shoes too. Aunt Meg was very thin and had pretty black hair; even as young as I was I thought Aunt Martha was jealous of her brother's wife. In the years I lived there I never heard her say one nice word about Aunt Margaret and very few nice ones about Uncle Pete, her brother. She never had her nieces and nephews in the house; they might damage something she always groaned, so I seldom saw Uncle Peter and Aunt Meg.

I never saw Tommy except at Christmas and once in a while at a birthday party. He was so quiet when I did see him it was strange. He had grown tall and was very thin and never smiled. Uncle Ken and Aunt Kristin lived on a farm. They had three boys of their own, all older than Tommy and all mean to him. Tommy told me he was going to run away as soon as he was old enough to work and get some money and he would come and get me to go with him. I dreamed of that day, the day that never came.

School was about five blocks from where I was living. It was hard keeping up in class because I had to get up early and make Aunt Martha's morning tea and take it to her bedroom before I left for school. She slept at one end of the second floor hall and Uncle Taylor slept at the other end. His bedroom was large and had a room off it that had a desk in it and three walls filled with books. He seldom spoke to his wife, and only grunted at me until one day when Aunt Martha was gone.

I came home from school and went into the kitchen to do the dishes that they had dirtied during the day. I knew if I didn't get them done by the time my aunt got home there would be trouble. I never figured out how, with just the two of them in the house, they could dirty so many dishes. Uncle Taylor worked at home, he did some type of writing and several times a year went on lecture tours. I was standing at the sink washing the cups that belonged to a china set that was really pretty. I was always careful because I knew if I chipped one of Aunt Martha's dishes she would get angry and just add more work for me to do. Uncle Taylor came up behind me and put his arms around me. I didn't know what to do as he had hardly ever spoken to me.

I turned around and he pulled me to him and put his hands down inside my blouse. I screamed. Then he held his other hand over my face and told me that if I told Aunt Martha and if I didn't quit screaming he would kick me out on the street. I began to cry and just then we heard Aunt Martha drive into the garage. He warned me again and left the kitchen. I turned to face the sink and cried my heart out. I didn't know what to do; no one had ever touched me that way. I didn't know that men did such things then.

When Aunt Martha came into the kitchen she saw that I was crying, "So what's wrong with you?" I didn't know what to say. I had picked up one of the cups and had it in my hand it had some soap on it and slipped out of my hand and crashed to the floor. Before I knew what happened Aunt Martha slapped me across the side of the head so hard I saw little flashing lights and fell into the cupboard. She screamed at me for breaking one of her precious cups that belonged to her China set. They had belonged to her grandmother and were worth a lot of money because they were antiques.

I couldn't quit shivering as my head hurt so bad that I felt like I was going to faint. She yelled in my face, "Get the broom you little idiot and sweep up this mess. Then finish those dishes and if you ever break another one I will take a belt to you and you won't sit down for a week." She slapped me again and left the kitchen. I fell into the chair beside the table and wept. What ever could I do? Maybe I could find a way to get to Tommy, but then I knew I'd never make it as I didn't even know how to get to the farm.

The next day at school the teacher asked me how I got the bruise on the side of my face. By then part of my eye was turning sort of purple. I was afraid to tell her so I said I had stumbled and fell. She came over and looked very carefully at the bruise then asked, "Sheila, who slapped you?" I couldn't answer her. Miss Shaw took me by the hand and out into the hall. "Sheila, someone has slapped you very hard. There is even blood inside your ear, and I want to know who did this." As I stood there my teeth felt as though they were glued together because I was terrified of what Aunt Martha would do if I told. The teacher must have sensed it and told me to go back into the class room.

That afternoon someone from the school came to the door and I heard Aunt Martha telling them that Uncle Taylor had slapped me because he caught me stealing money from his dresser. I couldn't see who it was because the sliding doors were closed but I could hear because the window in the kitchen was open and the window in the sitting room must have been opened too. The house was built in an L shape and the sitting room was the length of the house with the dining room and the kitchen the bottom of the L. I kept watching out the window and saw a man in a dark suit leave the front porch.

He hadn't been gone but a minute when Aunt Martha came into the kitchen and took a frying pan off the wall and hit me and hit me across my bottom. "You little beast, don't you ever tell what

goes on in this house again or I will beat you worse than this." I
tried to tell her I never said anything but she called me a liar and
sent me to my room without supper. She kept me home from
school for the rest of the week and made me clean the house from
top to bottom. I worked from early each morning until after ten
o'clock each night. I was so tired and my back hurt so bad I
thought once again that if I could only die it would be better than
living with her.

The following week Miss Shaw asked me why I wasn't in
school and I didn't answer her. I just broke out in tears and ran
into the girl's lavatory. She came right in behind me and demanded to know what happened. I told her how Aunt Martha had
beaten me. She asked to see my bottom and when she saw it she
turned white and told me to stay there that she would be back. She
came back with the school nurse and showed her the bruises. I
was told to go back to class.

I wasn't home but about twenty minutes when a policeman
came to the door and said he wanted to speak to Aunt Martha. She
was in her room and when I knocked she told me to leave her
alone. When she knew that it was a policeman at the door she
came out of her bedroom and glared at me then went downstairs.
I heard her screaming at the man and I knew what was going to
happen when he left. He called me into the room and told me in
front of her that if she touched me again I was to tell him and that
if she did she would be put in jail.

I begged him not to leave. I was afraid for my very life. He said
I was not to worry because Aunt Martha, he was certain, wouldn't
like the food they served in jail. When he left I just stood there
expecting to be hit. She looked at me and said, "I won't hit you but
you had better stay out of my way. This is the thanks I get for
taking you in and feeding you and putting clothes on your back.
Well, young lady you had better see to it that you do your work or
I will dump you out on that street and then who will take care of
you?" With that she grabbed me and shook me until my teeth
rattled then pushed me onto the floor and left the room.

I was turning eleven and I knew Tommy was turning twelve.
How I wanted to see him but there was no way I could. Miss Shaw

married and left school. I had learned to love her and missed her when she was gone. I was promoted to the sixth grade and was beginning to like the new teacher. Her name was Miss Gamelias. She had bright red hair that stuck out on the sides and a little bit on the top. She also had the most beautiful voice when she sang. I loved music and asked if I could be a part of the school glee club. She listened to me sing and said I had a good voice and so I became a member of the school glee club. I'd never belonged to anything before and it felt good inside. I only wished I could tell Tommy. I had no one to tell. No one really cared.

Getting a uniform was a problem; I hardly ever got anything new. Generally Aunt Martha would give me some hand-me-down someone had given her. I never was dressed properly and was always ashamed when I had to stand in front of the class and recite anything. Miss Shaw had gotten me a nice skirt and sweater before she left but it was getting too short and much too tight across my front.

We never went to church so I didn't have any reason to dress except to go to school. Most of the girls left me alone. I could never be in anything because I was so poor and I had to get right home after school to do the house work. Since the police had come to the door there was more work than I could handle. I never got to bed before ten. If I had home work I had to do it after I finished and sometimes it was midnight before I got to sleep. Aunt Martha had gotten so heavy she couldn't do anything. I had to tie her shoes and even wash her back in the tub because she couldn't do it. Since she had to rely on me so much she had gotten kinder. I guess she knew she'd never get anybody else to do what I did. I was the cook, her nurse, and the house cleaner. I did all the laundry and tried to keep up in school.

Miss Gamelias knew I couldn't afford the glee club uniform. One day she called me into the music room and there on a hanger was a new skirt and a sweater with a big G on it. There was also a pair of boots with two large yellow pom-poms attached to the zipper. I was so excited I hugged her and hugged her. She hugged me back and kissed me right on the mouth, then gave me a beautiful pair of silk panties and a matching bra. I needed the bra but Aunt Martha said it was all in my head and I could do without. Some of the other girls were beginning to wear bras and I needed one as I was pretty big in front.

Miss Gamelias bought me other things and each time I would hug her and she me. One day after school she was in her room and I went in to put the music back on the rack before I left for home. She came over while I was sorting it out and put her arms around me and hugged me. It felt so good. She was the only one who had hugged me since Mom died; I missed her so much. I hugged her back and she kissed me and then took me over to the closet where she had her coat and opened the door. We stood behind the door where no one could see and she rubbed my back and then rubbed me between my legs. I was so surprised but I didn't back off because she made it feel good and she hugged me and told me she loved me. I needed to be loved so I just let her touch me and hug me.

When I went home that afternoon I had a million thoughts going round in my head. Was this the way adults loved each other? Did all adults touch each other and treat each other like she was treating me? I had no way of knowing or finding out. I certainly couldn't ask Aunt Martha, and there was no way to talk to Tommy. I had no one. I would just have to figure it out myself.

Aunt Martha was in her room lying on her bed as she usually was when I got home. I heard her yell for me and went in to see what she wanted. She told me to come over to the bed and fix the pillows and rub her back. I rubbed it and rubbed it but it wasn't pleasant as it had been between Miss Shaw and me. I asked Aunt Martha if she liked to have her back rubbed and all she said was that it put the circulation back into it and for me to get to work.

Several days later Miss Gamelias said she would drive me home. I was grateful because it was cold and my coat wasn't very warm. She pulled off the road that went behind the gym and onto a dirt road that circled the water tower. When she stopped she pulled me into her arms and hugged me and told me how much she loved me. Little by little she took off my clothes and rubbed me and kissed me and then asked me to kiss her. I had a feeling this was all really wrong but she was so good to me I went along with what she wanted to do. She had been the only person for the last five years who had cared about me. After that she took me home many times and we stopped and she would love me. Anything I needed she saw that I had. She bought me clothes and shoes, books, and ever so many nice things.

Summer was coming and school would be out in about three weeks. I was wondering how I could get to see Miss Gamelias in the summer. She had become very important to me. Anything I needed she got me and I was young enough to want nice things, pretty clothes and spending money. One night, just before I was to take my final exams, Aunt Martha passed away in her sleep and my whole world changed again.

Uncle Taylor said I could stay there and keep house. He hadn't gotten near me since the time in the kitchen. I had almost forgotten it. I would be in the seventh grade the next year and I didn't have any place to go so I had to stay. Miss Gamelias lived about seven blocks from where I was so we decided we could get together several times as she agreed to teach me piano. There was an old piano in the basement of my Uncle's house and I went down there to practice. I was serious about really learning the piano. I remembered a little of what my Mom had taught me but I wanted so badly to play as she did. It still hurt when I thought of her. I was so angry that God wanted her with Him when I needed her worse than He did.

I cooked and cleaned for Uncle Taylor. He stayed in his room except to go on his tours. I had to see that he had clean clothes and his bags packed. When I was alone I started to feel as though the house were mine and with Aunt Martha gone it really started to be a nice way of living. I took my music lessons and was with Miss Gamelias a couple times a week. I felt loved and cared for and just maybe my life was going to be pleasant.

Uncle Taylor came home one afternoon several days before I planned on him being there. The house was not as clean as he liked but he didn't say anything. He just handed me his suitcase and headed for his room. I fixed dinner and called him. When he came down he was in his robe which was very unusual since I couldn't remember when I'd ever seen him in anything except a shirt and tie and even sometimes his suit coat. He sat down and ate without a word, which wasn't unusual since when Aunt Martha was alive he never spoke either.

I served him a piece of chocolate cake and as I started to place the cake dish back on the backboard he reached for me and pulled me onto his lap. I tried to pull away. He let his robe fall apart and he had nothing on under his robe. He held me so tight I couldn't move and pushed me onto the floor and no matter how hard I tried to get away I couldn't. He tore my blouse off and then ripped a new skirt that Miss Gamelias had given me. I screamed but there was no one in the house that could hear. I hit at him but he just laughed and pushed my hands down so I couldn't move. He raped me over and over and laughed all the time. "Guess the old lady would have liked some of this, eh, girl! No need me having to pay for it when I got it here for free."

I can't remember what happened after that. I know I was bleeding and I hurt so bad I thought it would never quit. I ran up the stairs and grabbed my coat and then ran out the back door as fast as I could to Miss Gamelias's. I pounded on the door and when she opened it I fell into her arms. I cried until I could cry no more. She called the police and they questioned me. They could see that my clothes were torn and I was having hysterics.

The next day I had to go to the police station and sign some papers. Uncle Taylor was sent to prison and, being underage, I had to move in with Uncle Ken and Aunt Kristin. I was back with Tommy and I thought my world was going to be all right. My Aunt and Uncle's older boys were at college and no one was at home except Tommy. Tommy was different and so quiet I had a hard time even talking to him. I helped Aunt Kristin as much as I could and when school started Tommy and I went together on the bus, their farm was about a half hour from the nearest school and quite a ways to Weinberg.

Nothing much happened while Tommy and I finished school. I found a girlfriend named Amy, and Tommy was busy getting straight A's so he could get a scholarship to college. I didn't care about going to college. I just wanted to graduate and be done with school for a while. There was a lot of work on the farm but Uncle

Ken and Aunt Kristin were very fair and let Tommy and me have as much spare time as they could. It was great being in a house where people were fair and even though they were strict they were kind.

Amy and I made close friends and she needed the same kind of love I had gotten used to with Miss Gamelias. One day when we were coming out of the barn Aunt Kristin asked us what was so important in the barn that we were always going there. I couldn't answer her but Amy said she just loved to play in the hay and was it all right? Aunt Kristin laughed and said she had played in the hay when she was a girl and it was O.K.

Uncle Ken and Aunt Kristin went to church every Sunday, something I hadn't done since Mom died. It seemed strange going back into church and the first couple of times it made me miss my mother terribly. How I would have loved to be in our clubhouse with her and Tommy having lunch. I was no longer Tommy's shadow. We were worlds apart. Oh, we loved each other but the closeness we had as children was gone. Tommy was determined to get the best grades he could and I was more interested in Amy than school or him. It was summer again and Aunt Kristin signed me up for High school Christian camp. I didn't want to go because Amy's parents wouldn't let her go, she was Mormon and couldn't visit my church. We were Baptists and I guess there must be different places in heaven for different kinds of churches.

I had never been to a camp before. I'd never been in a group my own age before. I always had to work and Aunt Martha never let me bring anybody home so I had no idea how to really act with all the kids. One of the counselors, a Ted Jay sort of took me under his wing and helped me get into things. Another thing happened that was really different. Several of the boys kept making a point to be on my team, or swim during my swimming time, or sit next to me during lunch and dinner. I guess I was good looking because they sure went for me that summer.

We had chapel every day and devotions before each meal. I felt embarrassed but copied what everybody else did. One evening during devotions around a camp fire a college kid came and talked to us about living a kind of life that Jesus would approve. It never had been a problem with me how I lived. I'd never had a chance to make up my own mind; I always had to do what I was told. I just figured that church was something some people did on Sunday. I had been too young to understand what it was all about when Mom took Tommy and me to church before she died.

One night a girl from Central University spoke to the girls. She talked about sex and what was right and what was wrong. She explained that you should wait until you were married and how being with someone the same sex wasn't accepted and that even though a lot of people said wearing a condom when you were out with a boy was safe that it wasn't and that you could get some stuff called STDs and AIDS. I'd never heard this kind of talk. She said that females who did things with other females were called lesbians and that boys that did things with boys were gay.

I left the camp fire that night realizing that I must be a lesbian because I liked it when Miss Gamelias and Amy and I were doing stuff and I hated it when Uncle Taylor had gotten to me. As I was walking to my cabin, Parker, one of the boys who had always tried to sit with me, walked beside me and told me he would like to walk me to my cabin. It was O.K with me. When we got to the cabin he took me in his arms and kissed me. I ran into the cabin shaking with fear. It brought back memories of Uncle Taylor. I was certain now I was a lesbian and as far as boys went I didn't want them touching me.

The next day the girl who spoke was in the lunch room when it was my time to eat. I knew I had to talk to her because she seemed to know the answers. I sat down beside her and asked if she could answer some questions for me. She was kind grinned at me and said she'd try. I told her everything that had happened to me and asked her why girls being with girls was wrong. Being with a man had been terrible, and I didn't ever want to be with one again.

She suggested we take a walk and led me to the path that circled the camp lake. She found a stump of an old tree to sit on and I sat on a green circle of grass. Then with a smile on her face she told me how beautiful being with a boy was when it was the right boy. She talked for a long time and I asked a thousand questions. No body had ever talked to me before about sex and what it was all about. She said that God was against boys being with boys and girls being with girls. I said I would have to think about it because I never wanted a boy to touch me ever again. It seemed all mixed up in my mind. I remembered how I really hadn't liked girls when Tommy and I were growing up and how I so badly wanted to be a boy like him. As I got older and Mom died and Aunt Martha was so mean I hated her and she was a female and how I had hated Marilee. My mind was confused. The way I found worked best when things got confusing was to simply not think about it. I'd just put the whole problem in the back of my mind and refuse to think about it so it couldn't bother me.

I put that whole summer into my memory bank, went back to school and graduated the following year. Tommy had gotten his scholarship and was going to be a doctor if there was any way possible. He never dated and neither did I. I figured I had better leave the whole thing alone if I wasn't supposed to be with girls and I didn't want to be with boys. Aunt Kristin suggested I take a beauty course and learn how to do hair. It appealed to me so they paid for me to go to Beauty College. It was fun and I loved it. I met some neat girls there and there were some guys in the class too.

I lived at the farm and took the bus in each morning to school. I thought as soon as I went to work and could afford it I'd move into my own apartment and get a car. A couple of the girls were lesbian and two of the guys were gay who were going to the same classes I was. We all sort of hung out together after class and I felt accepted and liked. I didn't pair off with any of them because both the girls were together and didn't bother me and the boys didn't either. We liked each other and that seemed to be all I needed. I was still not going to let the whole thing ruin my life or bother me. My goal was to graduate and work until I could get my own shop. I had dreams of Sheila's shop. I had it all decorated in my mind and knew I had to keep working until it came true.

Our teacher was gay too. He thought I had beautiful hair so was always using me as a model. I went to a conference once and he did my hair there and won first place. At that conference I met Glenn and my world changed again. I'd just stepped down from the stage after being judged and he reached up and took my hand to help me walk down the steps. I'd never seen such a beautiful man before. He was tall and had the deepest blue eyes and his face was tan as if he had been out in the sun all his life. He had wavy blond-red hair and when he said, "Hi, beautiful," I had a hard time catching my breath.

Glenn Whitfield was the owner of one of the beauty shops that were sponsoring the conference. He spoke to me again his voice was as beautiful as he was. When I reached the floor he kept holding my hand and said, "I'll let you go if you will have dinner with me." I gurgled something that sounded like a yes and that was how our relationship started. He took me to dinner, came to Weinberg and took me out several times.

I was wondering why I didn't mind him kissing me and holding me. It was time to try and figure out this whole problem of sex. I was a lesbian and lesbians don't have attractions for men. Or, maybe I wasn't a lesbian at all because I really was beginning to like Glenn. I thought of him and would think about how I felt about Tommy and it was so close. I wanted to be with him all the time just as it had been with Tommy. I liked him and I liked the way he made me feel, accepted and beautiful, and important. Maybe the reason I didn't like men, I thought, was because of Uncle Taylor.

I was getting old enough and talked to enough people that I understood what rape was and how it affected a woman. But I also couldn't understand why I liked the way I felt when I looked at the women in the shop when they came out with their hair beautiful and had that "I'm beautiful" look on their faces. I wanted to hold some of them and have them hold me. I was beginning to get very upset and putting the problem in the back of my mind was not working.

One night when Glenn took me to the theater it all came to a head. After the show he drove out to the farm to take me home and stopped beside a pond that was near the house. He took me in his arms and asked me to marry him. Here I was in the arms of one of the most handsome men that had ever walked the earth asking me to marry him and I didn't know what to say. Should I tell him? But if I did he would never have anything more to do with me. Maybe if I got married I'd forget all about women. So I said, yes, afraid he wouldn't ask me again, I guess.

Glenn and I were married in June. We had a nice wedding, a white dress with lace and all. I cut the wedding cake, threw the bouquet, and we left for Niagara Falls that same afternoon. Glenn had reserved the bridal suite at the hotel. It was a beautiful room with a complimentary bottle of champagne and a large bouquet of red roses on the desk. We had dinner in the dining room and afterwards danced for a while. It was romantic and I loved every moment.

Tired and ready to go upstairs Glenn kissed me as we waited for the elevator. I felt warm and loved. At the door of the room he picked me up and carried me over the threshold. I felt I was in a movie and all the right things were happening. Glenn told me that he would run downstairs for a moment while I prepared for bed. If our whole marriage was going to be like this I thought how glad I was I had said yes. I had purchased a beautiful shimmering blue night gown. I put it on and brushed out my hair letting it fall over my shoulders. Inside I knew I was beautiful. I was a "married lady" and I liked the part I was playing.

Glenn came back and came over to the bed. He sat on the edge of the bed and held me for a minute telling me all the time how beautiful I was and how he loved me. He went into the bathroom to change. I could hear his razor and sort of laughed to myself that he had to shave before he came to bed. Then something happened. All at once I was beginning to shake lying in that big king-sized bed, just as I had after Uncle Taylor had raped me. I couldn't stop my knees from moving. When Glenn came out of the bathroom he had on a pair of shorts and his body was as beautiful as his face. I swallowed the lump in my throat and tried to quit shaking but I couldn't. He got into bed and pulled me into his arms and I started to cry hysterically. I jumped out of bed and ran into the bathroom and locked the door.

Sitting on the edge of the tub I cried uncontrollable until I made myself sick and threw up all over my beautiful new night gown. Glenn was pounding on the door and finally he quit and started talking to me in that grand low voice of his trying to get me to unlock the door. I told him I would but to give me some time. I cleaned up the mess and after awhile I unlocked the door. Instead of being mean to me as I thought he would be he just took me in his arms again and told me he loved me and not to worry things would be all right. I went to sleep that night tight in his arms. He had told me that until I was ready he would wait.

The next morning the sun was out and we went all over, to a wax museum, up in a look-out tower, went to see the falls, rode the boat, wore rain coats to keep the mist off, and then had dinner again at the hotel and danced that night until I was exhausted. In bed I cuddled up to Glenn and he kissed me good night then held me until I was asleep. We enjoyed being together and the next day he rented some horses and we went on a long ride. I had learned to ride on the farm and loved it. He was as natural on the horse as he was doing anything else.

That afternoon we had lunch at a little diner and sat outside under a large umbrella. Glenn asked me, after we were finished and having a cup of coffee, when I was going to talk to him and tell him all about it. I panicked. How could I tell him about being a lesbian and the rape. I begged off but he said it was time I let it all go. He loved me so much that nothing could change his love for me and it was better to tell him than someone who didn't love me. I had to bring it out of my mind and clear it all up, but what if I lost him? I was totally confused.

Glenn just sat there and waited, I thought maybe if I just didn't talk he would change his mind but he didn't.

"Glenn, please, do I have to?" I begged.

"Sheila, the time has come when we have to talk about it. Now is the time to get rid of whatever is hurting you. Someone has hurt you terribly. Tell me, dear, maybe I can kiss it and make it quit hurting." He grinned at me, reached over and squeezed my hand.

Little by little I started to talk, I told him how I had loved Tommy and taken care of him. I told him how I died a little when my Mom died how they eventually separated Tommy and me and then I told him about Miss Gamelias and all the rest, about Uncle Taylor and Aunt Martha. I told him about summer camp and how

I couldn't figure out why I was a lesbian and I even used the word. I told him how when I saw a beautiful woman I had the feeling to hug her and have her hug me. I told him he had married a lesbian and how sorry I was I had cheated him.

Glenn sat there for a long time and then stood up and walked to the edge of the patio where the lunch tables were and looked out over the falls for a long time. I knew I had lost him. I knew that my telling had brought back all the bad and it was never going to be right in my life. At that moment I hated Marilee and Aunt Martha, and despised Uncle Taylor. I even hated Tommy for being different and wanting to be a doctor more than he wanted to be with me. And all at once I was angry at God for doing all these things to me. Why couldn't Glenn and I just keep on being best friends as we had been? Why did I ever say I'd marry him?

Glenn turned around and I expected to see hate on his face but there was no hate. It was a face filled with such sorrow I could hardly stand it. He came to me, pulled me up beside him and said, "Sheila, we're married and together we will work out this problem. I have no intentions of leaving you like your Mom did, and I have no intentions of punishing you as your aunt and uncle and even in a way as your brother did." He kissed me so gently I almost didn't feel it. I couldn't believe what was happening. This man knew all the horror of who I was and still loved me, and even wanted to help me. Of all the people in my life who had ever loved me that much only one came to mind, my Mom. I just stood there still and utterly amazed while Glenn held me. The waitress asked if we wanted anything else and Glenn told her no, but even then he held me tight and firm.

I knew I had to try and be what he wanted me to be. That night I grit my teeth and told him I wanted to be his wife in all ways. He asked me if I really meant what I said and I agreed. Across my mind I could see Uncle Taylor and feel the hurt and the shame, but Glenn didn't grab me or treat me rough. He kissed me and rubbed my back and made me feel wanted. He was gentle and kind and I realized that it wasn't going to be like it had been. Even that night Glenn didn't go all the way. We stayed at the falls for the seven days and the very last night Glenn made me his wife. I was

glad and when we had finished I knew I wanted to be his wife and
that being with a man was all right.

Glenn helped me get my own shop and he kept his. We
decided it was best to have our own space and he financed me and
at last my dream came true. Of course my shop was in Atlantic
City where he had his. I moved and have never gone back to the
farm and Weinberg. Tommy has his own practice in New York
and has since married. We see each other on holidays and once in
a while he flies down and spends some time with Glenn and me.

Kerry, one of my operators was a lesbian and one day she
came in and was broken up so badly that she had to go into the
back room and it was there I found her in tears. Her lover had left
her for another woman. I made the mistake of taking her in my
arms and trying to comfort her, and all at once all the old feelings
came over me and we ended up loving each other. I felt so
ashamed to have betrayed Glenn but she and I spent many hours
together. Each time I wanted to tell Glenn and try and work it out
somehow. Each time I hated myself a little more but I just
couldn't stay away from her.

Why I needed her I didn't know. I thought that I was over such
things because Glenn and I were really happy and our sex life was
wonderful. Something was desperately wrong. It had to be me;
there couldn't be a kinder man or more loving husband in the
whole wide world.

One afternoon a lady came in for a wash and set and was
writing on a tablet on her lap. She said she was working on a
speech. When I moved her to the dryer her paper work fell on the
floor. I helped pick it up and found she was from an organization
established to help people who were homosexuals leave their life
style. When she explained what it was I felt all tight inside and
almost mean. Once a lesbian always one, even if you are married
and your husband is as near perfect as they come. I figured it was
just a way to get money out of people and listened politely but
didn't take much stock in what she was saying. She had a wedding
ring on and I thought little did she know what she was talking
about.

As I was combing her out the things she had been telling me shocked me so much I dropped the comb. She'd been a lesbian and had left that life style and never gone back. She had three children and was happy and glad she could share about her life at the upcoming conference the next day. I had to talk to her and didn't have a clue of how to go about it. As she was paying me she leaned over and very quietly said, "Why don't you come to the conference. I think you will be surprised at what you will hear."

The very first thing I said before I even thought it out was, "How did you know?"

She grinned and said that when I dropped the comb the look on my face gave me away.

"I have walked in your shoes and I know what you are going through. Come to the conference I think it will answer your questions and take that hurt out of your heart."

I never saw her again; I missed her speech. I did go to the conference and then to a counselor. Finally I took Glenn with me. He was hurt when he realized that I had been cheating on him but he knew my story and also knew that I needed help. He forgave me and together we worked out the problem. It is so much easier when you have someone who loves you that understands.

It has now been seven years and I can't say that I don't have a little twinge when I see a certain kind of female, but if the temptation gets a little too heavy I call Glenn and we take a little trip and his love keeps me from straying. Also we have a little boy named Tommy who takes up my time. I'm no longer at the shop every day. Sheila's Shop has grown and has a new manager because in two months there is going to be a little sister for Tommy and they both will need me. I have to learn to climb a tree and help them make a club house and I can't do that washing and setting women's hair.

Sheila met with me at her shop. She came in several afternoons while Tommy took his nap. She said she had an excellent baby sitter but would have to leave around four because she wanted to be home when Tommy woke up.

She was immaculate. Her hair was short and curled close to her head. She was wearing it dark with small highlights that made it glisten.. I looked in the mirror and decided it was time for a re-do.

"How are you and Glenn doing now?" I asked as I turned off the recorder.

"Wonderfully," she quickly answered. "We try and have lunch together at least two or three times a week. I bring Tommy with me. He can use a booster seat now. The three of us love to be together." She kept on bubbling out her happiness.

"Have you been faithful to Glenn? Has it been easy?"

"Yes, I've been faithful to Glenn and have no plans to ever hurt him again. Sometimes it sort of catches me up short when I think what would happen if Tommy ever found out. I don't put myself into situations where something could go wrong. I know I slipped once and even though I would never think of doing it again I just make certain and see I don't have the opportunity." She frowned and pushed a curl off her forehead with a little sigh.

"Has Glenn done well in his shop? It certainly seems this shop is busy."

"Yes, we both have enlarged our shops. We have been talking about joining them together in a building on River Street where the new mall is being built. That way Glenn could manage them both and I could stay home and have a bushel basket of kids." She laughed but I felt she meant what she said even though she made a joke of her statement about children. When I left she gave me a hug and said that a wash and set was her gift anytime. She suggested I also touch up the grey a little when I came in.

I went to the car and sat for a moment enjoying the happiness she had shared with me. I intend on checking up on both her and Glenn to see how many little ones joined their family of love.

5

"Oh, God, Why Me?"

SUNDAYS WERE FOR CHURCH. The rest of the week slid by between prayer meetings on Wednesday night, cleaning the barn, feeding the chickens, milking two cows, and if I was lucky getting to school before noon. My Dad, Chester Carmy, spent his time being sick from one hang-over to the next. My mother worked from early morning until late. Her name was Elizabeth and I loved the sound of it. Dad called her Lizy. I hated that name as much as I hated him. I was scared of my old man and I guess I loved my Mom, sort 'a felt sorry for her.

I don't really remember what it was like before Dad started drinking. There must have been a time because he always blamed Mom. They fought constantly, her saying she'd been faithful and him accusing her of sleeping with some "jerk" called Bonner. He was some guy Dad had hired to help out with the haying one summer. There was a couple times he hit my Mom but that was before I was big enough to stop him. I hated being little and watching her cry. If I were a giant, I thought, I'd really fix my Dad. I'd make him sorry he hit her.

One fall a state worker came to the farm and asked my dad why I was always late for school and missed so much. I heard him cussin' the man out and ordering him off the property. The next day the sheriff came and gave my dad some papers. Dad got drunk that night and hit me pretty hard, made my mouth bleed. My Mom pushed me out of his way and wouldn't let him hit me anymore. It was worth it 'cuz then on I got ta' go to school regularly. I sure liked school and made great grades, better'n the rest of the kids. When I got home I still had to do the chores but

I hurried over them so's I could go to my room, close the door on my parents arguing, and escape into my books. Math was my favorite and I did O.K. in the rest of the classes. I sure liked school and my teacher more'n any man I'd ever known.

Mr. Ford was my sixth grade teacher. I never knew a man like him. Everything I did he was interested in; in fact, many times he drove me home. He was always correcting the way I talked. Gave me a book that was all about talking correct. I read it and sure did try to do what it said. During class he seldom spoke to me but as soon as class was over he always motioned for me to stay. He'd ask me as ta' how school was goin' n' how things were at home? I poured my heart out to him.

Many times Mr. Ford would walk around the desk after all the kids were gone and give me a hug. No man'd ever hugged me before, not even my Dad's brother, Uncle Seth, or any of my Mom's four brothers. Dad whipped me but never hugged me. In fact, sometimes when he was sick from a hangover he would kick me. Mom got in between us to keep him from really hurting me. He kicked her once so bad she had to go to the hospital.

Uncle Kream, whose name was sort of funny, came to the house when she was in the hospital. He was Mom's oldest brother. She said his name was Irish, after their grandfather. Uncle Kream came into the house screaming at my Dad and they had a terrible fight. Dad's eye was all bloody and his front tooth was gone. I heard Uncle Kream yell at Dad that if he ever hurt my Mom again he'd kill him. Uncle Kream was my favorite of all Moms' brothers. He brought me a puppy once but my Dad wrung its neck 'cause it wet the floor. I despised my dad and I was glad Uncle Kream hurt him. I wished he'd killed him. I wanted to be just like Uncle Kream and I'd sure as hell never be like my Dad.

When I turned thirteen I was taller than most of the kids in my class and nearly as tall as my Dad. By then I had learned to talk like most of the other kids and Mr. Ford was very proud of me. My Dad said I was talking like a big shot and laughed at me. My Mom said to do all the learn'in I could so's I'd be able to be somebody.

Dad hadn't kicked me for a while because the last time he did I reached over and pushed him hard and he fell onto the couch. He was as drunk as a skunk but he heard me when I told him if he ever kicked me again I'd beat the shit out of him. I also told him never to hit Mom again or I'd bloody him good. I added that he hadn't hit Mom since he and Uncle Kream fought, but I wanted him to know I was big enough now to keep him from hurting her. Sometimes I dreamt at night that he was dead.

One afternoon when Mr. Ford was driving me home he said he had to stop at his house to get a book and wondered if I minded being a little late. When we got to his house he asked me in. I thought I was something special because he never drove any of the other kids home. His house was on a paved street with sidewalks across the street from the Presbyterian Church.

Our farm was off a dirt road. It had two bedrooms with one large room for living and eating altogether. There was a porch off the back of the kitchen where Mom washed the clothes in an old wringer washing machine. It plugged into an overhanging light that turned on by a string. She hung the clothes on a clothes line strung between our chicken coop and the side of the house. Mr. Ford, had a radio, a piano, and a book case on each side of the fireplace with glass to cover the shelves. The room was real pretty and the furniture was leather and you sank clear down into it.

There were pictures of a lady and man on the mantel over the fireplace and several other things. In the center was a large clock with small figures that came out and made music. I loved music, especially the piano. We never had music at our house. We didn't even have a radio. Edging closer to the piano I carefully pushed one of the keys down. The sound it made was rather peaceful like and made me feel kind inside, something rather new to me. I pressed more of the keys and then made up a little tune. Mr. Ford was standing in the doorway watching me. I thought he would be mad because I touched the piano so I said I was sorry I bothered him. He said it hadn't. Then he came over put his arms around me and hugged me. He laughed and told me to use his piano whenever I wanted to. He kissed me on the cheek and just kept holding me. I sort of laughed at a man kissing me, hell; even my mom never did that. It made me feel sort of funny but important.

When I got home Mom asked why I was so late. I told her that Mr. Ford had stopped by his house to get a book and that I played his piano. She was as mad as a wet hen and slapped me so hard

I fell over the kitchen chair and into the side of the sink. I could hardly believe she had hit me. "Never," she yelled, "are you to go into that man's house."

"Why, Mom? He said I could play his piano whenever I liked."

"You stay away from him or I'll tell your Dad, and then you'll get it. And don't you be taking anymore rides from him either. Hear me boy!"

Mom had never screamed like that at me before. I ran out to the barn to get away from her yelling. She yelled at my Dad and now I was getting yelled at too. Something inside of me turned awful angry and I thought I'd damn well play that piano whether she liked it or not. And I would ride with my teacher even if he had to let me out down at the turn. You couldn't' see the turn from the house and I'd just tell Mr. Ford he didn't have to go up so he wouldn't have to turn around.

Mr. Ford wasn't at school the next day. A sub was teaching who said that Mr. Ford was going to be gone for a while and he was taking his place. That afternoon when I got home Mom was in the kitchen with Mrs. Swanson, the lady who lived on the next farm, and Jenny, her daughter, who looked older than her mother. I didn't like either one of them. They always reminded me of the hens pecking at the grain when I threw the feed to them. They even sounded like it. They were talking real quiet and I heard them say something about Mr. Ford. When I went into the room and asked Mom about Mr. Ford she got sort of red in the face and said, "Never mind, boy, go do your chores."

That night when they thought I was in bed I heard Mom telling my Dad they had fired Mr. Ford because he was a "queer." It wasn't until much later I found out what that meant. My heart really hurt because I liked him and he'd always been nice to me, nicer than anybody else I knew. He cared; he really cared what I was doing and how I felt. I figured that if being a queer was so bad that they fired him and I didn't like any of them, maybe being queer wasn't so bad.

It was nearly summer and time for school to be let out. We had the substitute the rest of the time. He wasn't too bad, pretty strict but that didn't bother me. I went to school and kept my grades up. I'd make Mr. Ford proud of me anyway.

I never saw Mr. Ford again. One day when we got out a little early I went by his house but the blinds were all pulled and there was a For Sale sign on the lawn. His car wasn't in the driveway and the lawn needed mowed. I asked Mom what happened to him and she said, as she always did when she didn't want to answer, "Never mind, boy." It amazed me that she had named me Michael Terrance then never called me anything but boy.

It was during that summer I met Randy Knight. His parents bought the old McGuille farm down the road and were making it over. His Dad worked in town and was some important guy at the mill so they had plenty of money. They were putting in a pool and even fenced the whole place and had a gate you had to open to drive through. Randy was two years older than me. I'd turned fourteen that summer. He was going to get his own car as soon as he passed the driver's test. We sort of hung out together when I had time from chores. Summer on the farm was always pretty busy. He never had to do anything 'cause they had a maid and they didn't farm their land. They planted grass out in front of the house but had a gardener who did all the stuff that needed to be done.

When the pool was finished Randy said I could come over and swim with him. I had never been in a pool before, just in the river at the edge of our property. I could swim pretty good and could dive too. He like to swim and had no one except the maid at the house. His mother was gone all the time to meetings and stuff with her lady friends. She never asked my Mom anywhere and Mom said, "I don't go round in that fancy circle, boy, and 'sides what would I wear anyway." I guessed she didn't have anything proper to wear, we were poor. I made myself a promise that when I got some money I'd buy her the prettiest dress ever. Seemed unfair of Dad that he always had money for drinking but never enough for good clothes for Mom or me.

Randy was sort of a sissy. When I had him over to the farm he just sat around and watched me work, never did a lick himself. One day I was pitching some hay to the cows and slipped on the side of the bin and cracked my arm good. Mom let me get off my chores for the whole afternoon. She put my arm in a sling so that it wouldn't hurt so bad. That afternoon we went over to Randy's and even the maid was somewhere else so we went to his room and decided to watch T.V. We slung ourselves across the bed and pretty soon he was touching me and I was touching him and that was the first time I'd done it.

From that time on we were inseparable. One day we were in the hay loft goin' hot and heavy and my Dad caught us. I thought he was going to kill me. He pushed Randy down the ladder and made him twist his ankle. Mom had to call his parents and they sent a car over for him. He had sprained his ankle and couldn't walk on it for over a week. I guess he told his Mom that he had tripped because they never said anything. Dad said if I ever got near that little fairy again he'd kill me, no son of his was goin' to be a fag.

I was grounded and forbidden to see Randy. I didn't mind being in my bedroom because I could read and in my new found sexual fantasy I continued to dream of Randy. One night I climbed out the window and went over to his house. I threw some sand at his window and when he opened it he saw who it was and came down. We went into the garage and continued to be together, our secret meetings lasting until school started. They sent Randy off to a private school in the east and I went back to public school. I continued masturbating and missing Randy.

Every summer until I graduated Randy and I spent together. I was old enough to go and come as long as I put in my hours doing the chores that Dad demanded. And as long as I went to church on Sunday with Mom she thought everything was all right. Randy and I never let Dad and Mom see us together. His parents didn't care; they never knew where he was. Randy's Dad had gotten him a car and gave him a good allowance, so the two of us mostly did as we pleased. One week we took off and went into Evansville and found a gay bar and spent that week trying out a lot of new things. By then we secretly knew we were both gay.

He was two years ahead of me so when he turned eighteen and graduated that next winter he went to college and I still had a year of school left. I had skipped the second grade because I was ahead of the rest of the kids. There was no chance, I thought, of me ever going to college. There was no money. Dad had said over

and over, "What the hell you want college for just to be a farmer?"
Mom would start crying and I knew they would spend the rest of
the evening fighting. They always fought over me. Mom wanted
me to go to a junior college in town and at least get some higher
schoolin.'

I graduated in June and Randy didn't come home that summer he went to Europe with a buddy. I was alone. I was always
alone it seemed. I hadn't bothered to date any girls because I
didn't have the money to take them out and I really didn't know
what to say to them. They were always giggling and acting silly
and I couldn't be bothered. Calista, a girl in my chem class, asked
me to a dance, girl's choice. I told her I couldn't because I had to
work. She was sort of pretty but I couldn't stand the way she
giggled and put her hand over her mouth.

That summer Dad got pretty sick and I had to take over the
farm. In July he had a heart attack and died. I wasn't the least bit
sorry, in fact I was glad. I kept taking my Mom to church on
Sunday because I drove Dad's car now and was the man of the
family. My Uncles all told me that if I needed help on the farm
they would help. Uncle Seth kept coming over and one day when
we were in the barn cleaning the stalls he came on to me and we
started a relationship.

That Saturday night he took me into town to a gay bar. I felt
needed and accepted. When Randy and I had gone to Evansville
we just hung out together but didn't go with anyone else. This was
different. Seth took off with a guy and two other guys really liked
me. They took me into one of the rooms upstairs and kept telling
me how great I was. There were other men there who wanted me
and made me feel like I was important. I was somebody. Having
very little money wasn't a problem. They didn't make me feel like
some poor clod-hopper farmer. I was right there like the rest of
them, just as good and being pretty good looking was popular,
really popular.

Every Saturday night Seth and I took in the town. I would get
up and take Mom to church on Sunday morning because she had
never learned to drive. Sometimes I'd fall asleep through the
sermon and Mom would push on my shoulder to wake me up. She

scolded me on the way home every Sunday about staying out so late on Saturday night. She thought it was nice that Seth was taking so much interest in me. She adored her brothers. I often wondered what she would have done if she knew what Seth and I did, or if Seth's wife ever found out. Many times Clara, Seth's wife, would get nosey and Seth would tell her that someone had to take an interest in his orphaned nephew.

Dad had an insurance policy that Mom and I found in the bottom of his stocking drawer when we were cleaning out his things. It was a surprise. I called the company and he had gotten it when he was in the navy and for some reason had kept it up and never told us about it. It was a twenty thousand dollar policy and Mom was the beneficiary. I thought we had better sell the farm but it had been in my mother's family and she didn't want to. She said it was for me and my family. My three uncles had adjacent property and all together it was quite a lot.

The three uncles were all married, even Seth, with a bunch of kids. I didn't want to have anything to do with a houseful of crying kids and a wife with hair falling over her face and sticking out in front every year. I wanted to be free of the farm and my Mom, and go to college. There was enough money now with the insurance policy's twenty thousand in the bank, but who would take care of the farm during the time I was gone?

I was torn apart inside. I hated the farm. I wanted to be a lawyer, come back and live on the hill where all the upper class guys lived who I had known in school. I wanted to show them I was as good as they were, the kids that had made fun of my clothes and called me "Old Farmer Brown." I had always gotten better grades than all of them but it didn't seem to make any difference. I was the kid from the "wrong side of the tracks" and they let me know it.

Uncle Kream knew how much I wanted to go to college. One day he pulled up in his old Ford truck and told Mom and I he wanted to talk to us. We sat at the table and he said that his youngest son Mason wanted to move out; he was sixteen and wanted some space of his own. Uncle Kream had seven kids and there were still four younger ones at home. He said that Mason could come and live with my Mom, do the chores and finish school. This way I could go to college for at least two years and we would figure something out after that.

I left for college in September and Mason moved into my room. I was happy. I was away from the farm, on my own, and was going to college. For two years I glued my nose to the books and put in for two scholarships hoping at least to get one. My grades were excellent and the registrar said she thought I had a very good chance. I needed it as I still couldn't take every cent my Dad left. I'd pay Mom back what I had used as soon as I started my practice but if something happened before I became a lawyer she would be without if I took anymore.

I was called into the college office one afternoon and handed the confirmation of a scholarship. It had happened and I was on my way to being the lawyer I had dreamed about. All this time I hadn't dated or had a relationship. I'd even stayed out of the gay bars because I had to get good enough grades to get the scholarship, and I'd done it. I masturbated and even started reading some porno magazines, but I didn't let my problem get in the way of where I had planned to go. That would come later.

That summer I took over and helped Mason with the farm. We had a good crop. Mason loved the farm as much as I hated it. He decided to go to the community college, use my car, and keep up the farm. Things were going my way and I was thoroughly happy for the first time in my life. Randy came home that summer and we took up where we left off. Both of us came to accept the fact that we were gay, but even so we kept our relationship a secret.

Randy never went to church but I couldn't hurt my Mom so I began once again to take her on Sunday morning. Mason was a Catholic and went home to be with his family on Sunday and visit the girl he was thinking of becoming engaged to. She was a silly little blond and I hated her giggling and fawning all over him. He walked around in a daze, sent her little notes, and even picked some of Mom's flowers to make her a bouquet. I was glad I had Randy.

One afternoon that summer I went past Mr. Ford's house and the For Sale sign was down. I wondered how he was so went up to the door and knocked. An older lady came to the door leaning on a cane. I asked if she knew him and she started to cry. She asked me in and told me she was his grandmother and that he had died the summer before. I was hurt. I wanted to see him and tell him what I was accomplishing. I asked what had happened and she dropped her head into her hands and wept loudly. He died of AIDS, she sobbed. He had been a homosexual. I couldn't speak. I didn't even know what to say to her. I just got up and walked out of the house, got into my car and drove for hours.

I didn't see Randy for several days. For some reason I couldn't. I was frightened. I knew there was such a thing as AIDS. I was always careful but Mr. Ford, the man I looked up to and wanted so badly to prove myself to, was gay and had died. At college we had been warned about STDs and to wear condoms whenever we indulged. I'd read the pros and cons of the safety of condoms and really didn't think much about it. It couldn't happen to me. I was young and strong, and had a few relationships at the gay bars, but since then had only been with Randy.

I hadn't really taken it seriously and now I had to think about what I was doing. I finally got the nerve to go over to Randy's and told him we had to talk. We went out beside the pool with our ice-tea and after stuttering around a bit I told him what had happened to Mr. Ford. Randy tipped his glass over and it hit the cement with a crash. He yelled at me," You ever did it with him?" I told him no that all that had ever happened was that Mr. Ford had hugged me and kissed me one time on the cheek. I didn't know he was gay, but why I was disappointed in Mr. Ford I couldn't figure out. Here I was gay and yet I didn't want him to be the same.

Randy took off for New York that summer and stayed with his Mom's sister. He wrote a couple times but was working for a dress designer drawing some designs and had decided to go to college there and work part time in-between. He called one day and said he was going steady with the designer and thought we had better quit writing. I felt lost. It never crossed my mind there wouldn't always be a Randy. That Saturday night when Seth came over to take me to the gay bar I was ready for anything. I'd show Randy that he wasn't the only one.

The next Sunday morning Mom wanted me to meet a girl who had just moved into town and was now a member of the church. Gwen taught the third grade girls in Sunday school and in the fall was going to teach first grade at Evansville Elementary. I couldn't tell Mom why I didn't want to meet the girl so after church she invited her for lunch. Gwen was a beauty. She didn't giggle, and never covered her mouth. Her teeth were white and straight and her hair was the color of hay when it was ready to harvest. She had deep blue eyes, the color of the river when the sky was clear and the water was still.

I hardly said a word during lunch. Gwen and Mom did most of the talking. Gwen didn't mind the hickish way Mom talked. I was so used to it that it didn't bother me. Whenever Mom talked I somehow thought of Mr. Ford and how he had taught me to talk 'more-proper' as Mom called it. I kept watching the way Gwen used her mouth, her lips were wide and graceful and when she spoke she sounded like music. She didn't talk about nonsense but went over the sermon the Pastor had preached that morning. I had slept through it so couldn't enter into the conversation.

I drove her home and she thanked me nicely. There was no foolishness about her. For the very first time in my life I admired a girl. She reminded me of Mr. Ford the way she approached things. I asked Mom if she was going to ask her for lunch the following Sunday and Mom said she would. This became sort of a pattern. The next Sunday morning I stayed awake so I could enter into the conversation.

It was the last of August and about time for me to get ready to go back to college. I had gotten into the habit of having lunch with Mom and Gwen on Sunday after church. I sometimes went with Seth on Saturday night but lately had been going myself because I wanted to get home earlier so I could stay awake on Sunday mornings and besides I was getting tired of Seth always tagging along.

I didn't understand why I was getting bored. It was the same thing every Saturday night, some guy, a room upstairs, and being fawned over as though I was something special. It used to make me feel extraordinary but every guy said the same thing and they didn't even know me. I was still scared of AIDS but I was careful and always used a condom.

That Sunday morning there was a guest speaker, a pastor from Los Angeles. He talked about adultery and homosexuality, and how it was not accepted by God. Our pastor always talked about God's love and never anything that was controversial. This guy was dynamic; there was no sleeping while he talked. I felt like sliding under the seat ahead of me when he started talking about homosexuality. He pounded the pulpit and yelled.

The pastor was yelling at me just like my Dad had yelled. I began to quiver inside and felt sick to my stomach. I was going to hell on the fastest highway there was. All at once I could see my Dad standing up there behind the pulpit, and how he treated me when he found Randy and me in the hay loft. I got up and left the church. I couldn't take anymore. I went out to the car and waited for Mom and Gwen. When they got to the car all they could talk about was how awful homosexuality was and adultery was just as bad. I thought I was going to be sick.

The next Sunday our own pastor was back and things were as usual, but there was something wrong. I had a hard time looking at Gwen, my Mom was O.K., but Gwen was different. When I took her home I told her that I was leaving for college that Friday and wanted her to know how I had enjoyed her company. I asked if she wanted to write and she said that would be fine. I had never kissed her, hadn't wanted to, but that day I wanted to hold her and tell her good by.

When I took Gwen up to her door I reached over and drew her to me and kissed her. I'd never kissed a girl before. I felt strange all over and when she quietly kissed me back there was something there that made me feel like a real man. I kissed her again and told her I loved her. Then I ran to the car and took off like a bat out of hell. What had ever made me do such a stupid thing?

I laughed to myself while I drove home and thought how silly Randy would think I had been. All that week while I was getting ready to leave I kept thinking about Gwen. I'd never thought two minutes about any girl.

The only female in my reference was my Mom and she was a Mom, somehow not related to females. I don't know how that works out but there must be a category for Mom's that precludes her being a female when you are gay. Oh, yes, there were my aunts but they were some where out there in the shadow of not-important-land and I never thought of them except to know I never wanted a wife if wives were like them. I figured someday I'd get a wife to have some kids and be like Seth but that was a long way off. I had to become a lawyer and be a success. Way down deep it had also turned into a desire to become famous and get Randy back. When I got him back I figured I'd brush him off just to pay him back for hurting me.

I was pretty bitter about Randy. I'd called him to let him know I was going back to college and some guy answered and told me Randy didn't want to talk to me. At that very moment I put him in the same category with my Dad and that yelling preacher. It was easy for me to hate. I had been doing it for a long time.

I was finally going to get my degree and had applied at a lawyer's office in Evansville for an internship that summer. My grades opened doors for me and I was ready to show the world how great I was. I decided to get an apartment and not drive back and forth every morning and night. Besides Mason and Mom were satisfied with their relationship and that suited me fine. I was on my own and I liked it that way.

I didn't frequent the Evansville gay bars because I didn't want anyone there to know I was gay. Some of my friends were "coming out" but I didn't want Mom and Gwen to find out. Why Gwen, I didn't know, but I didn't want her to even guess that I wasn't straight.

That summer was exciting. I was a lawyer and was doing great. I was a corporation lawyer and started working on a case for the local mill where my Dad had once worked and where Uncle Seth had worked for several years. Uncle Seth wanted me to go with him on Saturday nights but I said I didn't want to, said I was going straight. He just laughed and said, "Good luck." Why I told him I was going straight was a mystery. Way down deep I was ashamed and I was beginning to feel it. The men I worked with were great and happily married. They seemed to have something I didn't and I wanted it.

Gwen took up a lot of my time. We went to the movies, picnics, and did a lot of ice-skating in the winter. I kissed her when I took her home but that was as far as I ever went. I just couldn't picture myself going any further. One night it was pouring down rain and she suggested I come over for dinner and then we could go to the show. It was Saturday night but I agreed. She had her apartment fixed up quite nice and there were candles on the table and I liked the feeling of being in the apartment with her alone. After dinner we agreed it was to nasty to go out so sat and listened to some great music. She had a wonderful collection of classical music and as we sat in front of her small fireplace which was flickering with its gas lighted logs we cuddled closer and I felt that maybe this was what I had been looking for. That night we went all the way and I felt like I had accomplished something very special. I asked her to marry me and she accepted.

We were married that November. I stopped going to the gay bars, went to church every Sunday with Mom and Gwen, and worked hard during the week. Randy came home that Christmas and looked me up the second day he was home. He walked into my office and I thought I was seeing a ghost. He was so thin and white I hardly recognized him. We went to lunch and even before he told me I knew he had AIDS. He had come home to die. He told his parents and they said he could live with them. His Dad and Mom were on their way to Europe for a month or two and went even though Randy was very ill. They didn't care and had never really cared about anything but themselves. They ended up in the same folder along with my Dad, the preacher—one Randy had also been in.

I had a hard time spending time with Randy. The bitterness over Randy was replaced by a terrible sorrow. The feelings I had for him were gone and so was something else. I was so lonely inside that sometimes it hurt me physically. Something was going on inside me that was making me almost sick. I kept doing great at work but found myself looking out the window many times wondering why I couldn't get things back to where I had been.

Gwen and I were happy, I guessed. She seemed satisfied with married life. She was still employed by the Evansville elementary school but was teaching the third and fourth grades combined. Combining classes was a new idea someone had that was supposed to be a better way for kids to learn. It didn't make sense to me but then I wasn't all that interested in what she did as a person.

We got up every morning and ate breakfast together. She had lunch at school and I was usually with a client. At night she fixed dinner while I was glued to my computer until she called me to come and eat. Every night she would bow her head and say grace and I went along with it. Mom had always done it so I was programmed. I never really listened to her, just said amen when she finished and reached for food. One night she asked me to say it and I groaned out, "You do a fine job go ahead." She never argued with me, always agreeing with what I wanted to do.

There were times I wondered if Gwen really loved me. Our relationship was mutually agreeable. We never fought. I thought we had a perfect marriage. I remembered how Mom and Dad had fought so I compared ours to my folks and figured we had it right. But I was empty inside and felt like I was about to explode.

One Saturday night Gwen was going to a church function and I was home alone. I put on my coat and within minutes was on my way to Sullivan, a town about twenty minutes from Evansville. I went to the gay bar there. I had to find out what was going on. I made it with one of the guys in his van, had a couple more drinks, and left for home. It was the first time since I had been married and I felt like hell. I could see Gwen's small face and those eyes of hers that always made me feel just a little special. I parked the car and threw up at the side of the road. I guessed the drinks had gotten to me.

Our marriage seemed to go into neutral after that. Maybe it was just me. I had no idea. I still was lonely and it was getting worse. Several times I went back to Sullivan, but that didn't help. I started looking at porno on the internet and for a while I really got hooked. Then it became boring and I was back to being lonely and hurt inside. It was beginning to affect my job.

Carl Rasmussen, the senior partner, called me into his office one Friday and asked me what the matter was. I couldn't answer him. I simply didn't know. I will never forget how Bill got up from his desk that day, walked around and sat on the edge facing me, reached over and put his hand on my shoulder and said, "How is your relationship with God, Mike?" I was speechless. No one had ever asked me about such a personal thing in my life. Even Gwen never asked me what I thought or where I was inside. My Mom never said anything to me about God. She just took me to church and figured I was listening.

I remembered how I just sat there and couldn't answer the man. Carl kept his hand on my shoulder and continued, "Mike, I hoped you could put aside your homosexuality being married and doing the kind of work you wanted to do, but I see you haven't been able to handle your problem. Maybe I can help." He knew, "Oh, my God, why me?" How many other people knew.

"How did you know?" I whispered out the question.

"I knew, Mike, because there was a time I had to fight the same battle."

"You were gay?"

"Yes, I grew up thinking I was born that way until I met a real man who really loved me and didn't want me just for sex."

"Who in the hell was that?" I almost screamed. I'd never known a man friend who didn't want sex from me or I didn't want it from him.

Carl took his hand off my shoulder and opened his shirt and there was a crucifix hanging on a gold chain. I was astounded. Then he said, "The man who loved me enough to die on this cross for me. His name is Jesus."

I knew all about Jesus. Good God, I'd heard it every Sunday I could remember. And I heard it every night when Gwen said her prayers kneeling beside our bed. My boss had been a homosexual. I was having a hard time taking it all in.

"Mike, I want you to go to a meeting with me tonight. Will you come with me?" You don't turn down your boss. I went with him to a house where several men were meeting. It was a prayer and

Bible study group. I felt out of place. They all hugged each other but instead of separating off into bedrooms they knelt and prayed. I wasn't about to do that so I just sat and watched. No on said a thing about it. They got up and we all sat around a table. Out came their Bibles and everyone started to talk about Jesus. They acted as if they really knew Him and talked about Him as if He were their friend. I was having a hard time following it.

They read some out of the Bible and then all talked about it. One man started to tell his experience about how he had been struggling in a relationship with a man and had turned it over to Jesus and so far everything was going great. He was gay and all at once I realized they were all homosexuals. But they certainly weren't the kind of gay men I knew. They were happy, their very faces were alive, they had something I didn't have and I wanted it. I didn't know how to get it but I sure as hell was going to find out.

Carl took me with him the next week. I didn't kneel with the guys, but I had found my old Bible and brought it with me. I hadn't opened it since I was in Sunday school and had to memorize something to get a candy bar. I didn't remember what verse it was or where it was in the Bible. That was a long time in my past. A tall colored man who hadn't been there the week before came over to me and hugged me. He introduced himself as Dr. Winifred Washington. I later learned he was head of the pediatric department at the local hospital.

These men hugged each other and there was a feeling between them I had never known. We were reading the Bible about how Jesus was in the garden and asking God to take away what he had to go through when one of the men went to his knees in prayer and asked the Lord to help him. He had met a man at work who was gay and was hitting on him and he was having a hard time with it. All the men got up and knelt down with him with their arms around him and begged the Lord for help.

Something exploded inside of me. That lonely cold place way down deep I could never fill came to the surface and I started to cry. I fell on my knees and wept in agony. The men turned to me and clasped me in their arms and held me as if I were a baby until I stopped sobbing. Carl asked me, "Mike, would you like Jesus to come into your heart? All you have to do is ask Him."

I fell on my face on the floor and poured out my heart to this Jesus whom I knew about but never really knew. I gave Him my homosexuality and He gave me a peace I had never known.

My story doesn't end here. I still had problems with being gay. There came a time I had to tell Gwen. I couldn't keep it to myself any longer. I remember how she said in her quiet way that she had known for quite a while and had been praying for me all that time. I finally told Mom. She was hurt and then angry and then blamed it on Mr. Ford. She just knew it had to be him. I finally persuaded her it wasn't the teacher but me.

I went to Randy's funeral with happiness because I had led him to my new best friend Jesus and knew that I would see him again. I loved Randy but I had to learn to love him as a brother. It took time but when I think of Randy now I think of my brother in Christ. I will always be gay. I know that now, but I will be obedient to my Lord and never disappoint him with wrong actions again.

Whenever I have a moment or two of doubt I have learned to share it with Gwen and the men who brought me to the Lord. I have put aside pornography because it leads me down the wrong path. Being gay I have learned to stay away from temptation. I have learned to love being with Gwen. We have a very good sex life. We now have two little girls and she is pregnant with our son. I am a successful lawyer and a Christian.

When my son arrives I will start right off letting him know he is my son. I will teach him to be a man, to connect with him, to listen to him, and to love him. I will wrestle with him and hug him and kiss his little cheeks. He will know he has a real man for a father, and as soon as he can understand I will introduce him to my best friend. He will know I love him. He will also know I love his mother and his two sisters, but above everyone that I love the Lord, Jesus Christ.

The man sitting in front of me was dressed in a dark-blue business suit and had placed a briefcase on the chair by his side. A very pregnant lady was seated on a couch between two large philodendron plants in front of my office window, facing the bay. When the foliage no longer clings to the trees I can see the water. She was very quiet and seemed quite at ease letting him talk.

We had finished the taping; the room was filled with old memories and many unspoken words. Both Mike and Gwen sat very still, and then Mike stood and looked out the window. I saw him wipe his eyes and knew it had been very hard for him to share his life. He then resumed his seat.

"Gwen, when is the baby due?" I asked.

"Any moment, and I can hardly wait. The girls are counting the days until their little brother can play with them." She smiled a delightful grin and tried to get comfortable.

"Mike, what are your plans, where do you see yourself heading?"

He sat for a few moments, stood again, and walked to the window, cleared his throat and answered, "I haven't the foggiest idea. Work of course. I have the feeling God isn't through with me yet. Whenever I see a kid riding a bike down the street, playing in a park or running through the church on Sunday, I want to take him in my arms and hug him and tell him he is safe with me. I know that would not be a good idea. I've been thinking about trying to talk to all of their fathers. I wish there was someway I could shake sense into fathers who ignore their sons."

Mike started pacing. "Damn, maybe I could convince the pastor to start a program where at least church going men could learn to be good fathers. I'm going to talk to my boss and the pastor Wednesday night and see what we can do."

Mike came around the desk and reached out his hand, "Thank you for pinning me down. I have a responsibility to my son, but it doesn't stop there, does it?"

"No, Mike," I said as I rose to shake his hand. Instead I moved his arm aside and hugged him to me. "You owe it to give little boys the right kind of fathers."

I went to Gwen, helped her out of a couch that never wants to give up its occupant, and hugged her too. I gained two new "kids" that day. I wished they had brought their girls. I have a good idea that soon I will get to know them as well.

6

"There Weren't Enough Pills in the Bottle"

WHEN THE WORLD STARTED ROLLING AGAIN I wanted to cover my eyes to get away from white lights that were blazing above my head somewhere, but somehow my hands wouldn't work. On top of being in this blistering white light my stomach hurt and my throat was so dry it ached too. I couldn't figure out what was happening until I heard my Mother's voice whispering to Robert, my step-dad, "Oh, Bob why did she do it, we could have lost her?" She was weeping so I couldn't hear what Robert said. I heard Caroline sobbing that it was all her fault and that she would never forgive herself. Even with my stomach hurting as though it were on fire I laughed to myself. Here I was, according to my Mother nearly dead, and my sister was playing to the audience as usual.

I figured I was in Community General Hospital in Bayville because it was the only hospital for a couple hundred miles around my apartment. It didn't take me long to figure they had pumped my stomach. I was supposed to be dead. At least that is the way I planned to spend the night, and here I was, wrapped up like a cocoon in a heated blanket, some type of tube running into my arm and hurting like hell. I was having a hard time talking because my throat hurt too much. Why did they have to interfere? Why couldn't they just have left me alone. I didn't want to be here, but as usual my Mother ruled the day, time, place, and everyone involved? When hadn't she called all the shots? That one I couldn't answer?

Alex hadn't come to my apartment for several days. His mother found out where he was spending his nights and put a stop to his visits. I challenged him, his age, and his manhood over the question, but his mother won. I'd tried, but nothing I could say or do changed Alex's mind. He said that if they were going to pay for his college and as he said "tote the bill," he'd have to skip a few pleasures.

"And all I am is a few pleasures, is that all our love has meant to you?" My words still rang in my ears and his answer that broke my heart, "Come on, Pat, don't make a federal case out of this. We can get together when the old lady isn't around; after all I'm not dead, old girl." We had been going together since the tenth grade and had planned to get married. I'd been a virgin and he was the only person I'd ever been that close too. I dreamed constantly of our marriage. I had my wedding dress wrapped in tissue in a gold covered box on the shelf in the closet waiting for the day.

There hadn't been much of an excuse to live so I chucked down a bottle filled with sleeping pills. I was having a problem trying to figure out how I'd ended up in a hospital. More than likely Mom had come by to check up on what I was doing and see who was in the apartment with me. I'd moved out, paid all my own bills for nearly a year now, but she still treated me like a kid who needed a constant reminder that Mother knows best. She wanted me to move back but as long as my stepfather, Robby boy was in the house that was out. Someday I'd tell Mom why I thought he was a dolt, but she thought he walked on water. I didn't think she needed to know that he was quite aware of where the rocks were.

My twentieth birthday was just a little over two weeks away. I thought for certain Alex was going to give me a ring as a surprise. He had asked me what size I wore at Christmas but the subject hadn't come up since. It was wiser not to say anything because Alex wasn't the kind you could push. I had moved out of the house the day after graduating from high-school. That one I had planned. I'd saved enough money from working at the florist shop in Greenville, a small town just eleven miles south of Bayville, during summer vacations.

I wanted to get away from my Mom and her sicko husband, Robert, and from my sister Caroline. What I hadn't wanted was to get away from Alex. Alex and I'd been going together now for almost four years. We had planned on getting married when we graduated then go to college together. Alex decided we had better put off being married for awhile and save up some money because we would need it for college. I was going to be a horticulturist and he was planning on animal husbandry. We thought it would be a good combination. Well, that was before Ransom and his mother got into the act.

Ransom went to school with Alex and me and was a little on the sissy side. He never played sports and always had his nose pasted in a book. Alex and I were in every sport we could get into and as far as books went they were a necessary evil to get where we wanted to go. Both of us had above average grades; we knew we had to keep a good average if we were to be accepted in the college we'd chosen. Ransom shadowed Alex wherever he went. It got to the point that Alex even brought him to the house when he visited me. Ransom had tagged along even before Alex and I graduated and I got my own apartment. I guess Ransom spent some time at Alex's house when his parents went to Florida the summer before our senior year.

Alex's father was a druggist and his mother a surgical nurse at Community. All I needed was for Althea to join the crying crew that surrounded my bed and my day would be a complete disaster. Althea was about as domineering as my own mother. She'd never wanted Alex and me to get together and made it uncomfortable whenever we were in the same place at the same time. One more reason I wanted an apartment was so Alex and I would have a place to escape when we wanted to be together. Alex was her only child and she never let him forget it. She always put on this "how lonely she was act" whenever he was gone more than a couple of hours. Then she'd give him a guilt trip saying how unfair it was for Alex to spend so much time away from her. After all she wasn't going to live forever. There were times I wished her predictions would come true.

Alex had to call in when we went on a date and was never allowed to be out after eleven. She worked from seven in the morning until three and was always around when he got home from school. George, Alex's Dad, worked a swing shift at the hospital in the pharmacy. When she got home he went to work and so she clung to Alex as if he were her real husband and George was just something thrown in for good measure.

George was sort of funny. He made Alex and me laugh and yet when Althea came into the room he would be quiet and leave to do something in his garden. He had a beautiful rose garden; in fact he was president of the Bayville Rose Society. Every year he would win some type of prize for the best roses. He was thrilled about Alex and I planning to go to college together. He thought it was the thing to do but would never speak up and say so to Althea. I can't remember him ever disagreeing with his wife. As I lay there thinking about the whole mess I couldn't seem to remember George hardly ever talking to her. I liked George but I sure couldn't say the same for Alex's mother and that was where the whole thing started. Well, it was part of the problem.

Alex never disagreed with his mother either. In fact he was a carbon copy of his Dad. If Althea said jump both George and Alex would ask, "How high?" I was created an independent being and just couldn't understand giving in. I tried to be respectful of my mother but I wasn't about letting someone else rule me. I got in trouble in school because I didn't want any teacher making a puppet out of me. Alex and I got along great. I didn't order him around as his mother did and he let me have a free reign. It was always a little surprising though how he let Ransom tell him what to do.

Whenever we wanted to be together we had a telephone code so his mother wouldn't give him a lecture about being too young to be dating. Good grief he was nineteen years old and still tied to his mother as if his umbilical chord were still attached. That is the only argument we had and it always centered on his mother. He was a Mamma's boy; I tried to cut the chord and landed in the hospital having my stomach pumped. Alex chose his mothers side and I chose a bottle of pills which evidently didn't have enough in the bottle to do the job correctly.

Caroline was still bubbling tears, Mother was crying on Robert's shoulder, and Robert was, as usual, doing nothing. Caroline came over and kissed me and begged me to forgive her.

"What in the name of God do I need to forgive you for?" I felt like bopping her but that was normal and I couldn't get my hands out of the covers.

"Oh, Patty dear, you know you aren't supposed to talk like that." She pulled this better-than- thou attitude on me which she had perfected by a lot of practice.

"Cut the theatrics and tell me why you think you had anything to do with me popping some pills?"

"Mother asked me to stop by and see how you were and I forgot. Clayton was driving me home from work and we got to talking. You remember Clayton, the manager of the sports-wear department, the tall blond one. Well he asked me..."

I interrupted her manuscript reading, "Caroline, for crying out loud, so you forgot. You aren't my keeper you know."

"But Patty, dear, if I had stopped by you wouldn't have taken the pills."

"The hell I wouldn't. I'd taken them sooner." I'd had it with her blubbering.

"Patty, sick or not I'll not have you swear," my Mother said always correcting me.

"So how did I end up here?" Maybe I'd get some answers.

"I came by after Caroline came home and said she hadn't stopped to see if you were all right. And what a blessing, if I hadn't you might be dead. Oh, Patty, Patty why did you do such a thing?" Mom started to cry again. Thank heavens the nurse took that moment to tell them visiting hours were over.

Richard Foster, my father, wasn't in the room; he'd never come any place near where his former wife might be. Dad was cool and I knew the minute they all left he would pop in if someone had called him. More than likely Caroline had. She took any opportunity to play the "good" sister act. My dad was about as handsome as a man could get. He always had women hanging on him but never seemed to pay any attention to them. He told me he'd been burned and he had learned his lesson. He'd had all the women he wanted and marriage was a once in a life time commitment so he didn't plan on trying it again. My father was a lawyer and a mighty good one people told me. Boy, would he be mad about what I'd done. I didn't give a hang about Mom, Sicko, or Caroline but I was beginning to feel squeamish about Pops. He had been for Alex from the beginning but now I wondered if he would think he was so great.

Alex was missing and I knew Caroline must have called him. She took every opportunity afforded her to talk to men, and especially unattached ones. And though Alex was definitely mine, or had been, it made little or no difference to her. If it breathed and wore pants it was fair game. I'd never liked Caroline from the day I was born, or I figured it went back that far. She was three years older and was Mother's favorite. From the time I could remember I had always been compared to Caroline. Caroline the little lady, Caroline the good student, Caroline who always treated her Mother with love and caring, Caroline this, Caroline that! There was no way that anyone in this world could come up to Caroline in my Mother's world.

I didn't look a thing like Caroline and she didn't look like anybody in the family. Caroline was tall, nearly six feet, and her hair, almost white, was absolutely straight. She had a strong rather large nose, and her cheek bones were high and firm. I was of average height about five feet five, had thick auburn hair that curled so tight at times I had to brush it with curl-out to get a comb through the strands. I had the same coloring as my Dad including his green, brown speckled eyes. My square jaw went along with the stubbornness that Mother said was "just like my Dad," My oversized front caused me some whistles even in Junior High school. Now that I was older they were sort of nice and I didn't resent or try to hide them anymore.

"Hey Squirt, you awake?" It was Daddy. I knew he'd come.

He came over and put his arm behind my shoulders and lifted me off the pillow then hugged me as if he were going to break me into separate pieces. There were tears on his cheeks and he didn't even bother to wipe them away. This was my big strong Dad who never cried, always laughed, and never saw the bad in anyone I knew of. He looked at the world through rose-colored glasses and always seemed to understand how it was to walk in the other guy's shoes. Maybe that was what it took to be a good prosecuting lawyer.

"Oh, Pops, I'm sorry. I didn't think about you. I was hurting so bad I guess I just didn't think." If I'd known how I would have hurt my Dad I'd never done such a stupid thing over a dumb s— t like Alex. I was beginning to hate him and for some reason Ransom as well

"Come on, tell your old man what made you pull such a dim-witted stunt." Pops laid me back down onto the pillows with those big hands that could be so gentle, pulled up a chair and leaned onto the bed.

I didn't know where to start because I didn't think he knew that Alex and I had been living together, well together and apart, since I had moved into the apartment. I took myself in hand and told him everything. After all I'm the one who had been stupid, and not to face it now was being a coward, and that we Fosters weren't. I'd kept my own name when Mother married Robert Harding. I didn't want his name or anything to do with him. Caroline took his name, the twerp. I decided to even tell Dad about Sicko. I guess it was show and tell time so I just let it all hang out!

When I got to the part where Mom's new husband caught me in my bedroom when everyone else was out and tried to make out with me I saw his face turn red, even his ears.

"What do you mean, make out with you, Patricia?" It was always Patricia when he was going to be stern and Squirt any other time.

I told Dad how Mom and Caroline were out shopping. They were always shopping. Robert had goobles of money and Mom and Caroline knew plenty of ways of spending it. He had offered me an allowance once and I, not too politely, told him where he could put it. I'd just gotten home from school and was getting out of my school clothes and into some shorts to go play tennis with Alex. Robert came into my room without knocking and when he saw me in a bra and panties he whistled and told me I was a good looking gal and he was going to show me how to feel good. He pushed me down on the bed and started to take off my bra. I grabbed his hand and bit down as hard as I could, then kneed him where he didn't appreciate it. He left the room swearing he would get me for this. I yelled that if he ever came into my room again I'd kill him. He never did.

"I never told Mom. I didn't want her hurt," I said.

"I'll get that creep; see if I don't, I'll get him. I should have plastered him before." Dad was angry, I'd never seen him that angry, and in fact I couldn't remember ever seeing him angry.

"Why would you have gotten him before?" I asked.

"Caroline! Caroline isn't your sister. She's his kid. I married your Mom when she was three months pregnant, thought it was mine. When Caroline was born and when I saw who she began to look like I made Phyllis tell me the truth. You are my only child and from now on young lady you are going to come and live with me and I'll have no sass."

Then I knew what it was about Robert that I always thought I'd seen him before. He was over six feet tall and had that white thin hair, just like Caroline. Mother was short like me and had light brown hair that was rather pretty. She had to have permanents all the time to keep it looking nice. Caroline, the goody-goody daughter wasn't even my real sister. Well, she was my half-sister and as far as I was concerned that wasn't enough claims on me to count. I was feeling great inside. She didn't have any of my Dad in her and that made my world a little brighter, even in a white hospital room.

I was thrilled; I was going to live with Pops. He had a very nice house in Greenville, it had four bedrooms, a pool, and it would be away from where Alex lived. I was going to "kick the dust off my feet" of the whole mess of them. I felt free and ready to live.

"Oh, Pops, really, you really want me?"

"Twirp, if it hadn't been for Phyliss I would have kidnapped you many moons ago. The courts gave her custody and I didn't even try to fight it. Being girls they would have awarded you to her if she'd had three heads. If I'd known about that creep making a pass at you I could have gone back to court. But that's all over and as soon as they let you out of this place you are on your way to your own bedroom, bath, and home with me! Mazee will love it. Incidentally, she is a pretty old lady but I think you will love her too."

"Mazee, who is she?" I was curious. Dad living with a woman?

"Mazee, my dear, is a nine year old white poodle who thinks she owns the place."

It was a week later I moved into my Dad's house and thought everything was going to be great. He let me take my pick of the three remaining bedrooms and I chose the one that had a little balcony over the backyard garden and the pool. Not having to pay for my expenses I thought I could save enough to start college that fall. Even that wasn't necessary because Pops registered me, paid the tuition, then bought me a little red T-Bird so I could come home some week-ends and holidays. Pops said it was wonderful having someone in the house and he would be lonely with me gone. I thought I really had a handle on life.

College was great, I signed up for the classes I needed as a freshman, put up some of my own pictures in my room, and waited to see who my roommate would be. She was a girl from India and could hardly speak English. She was beautiful with olive colored skin and hair as black and shiny as I'd ever seen. She was shy and her name was hard for me to pronounce. It was spelled Sinchong and pronounced Sinch-shong, or pretty much that way. She spoke with such a quiet and low voice that it was sometimes hard to hear. When she talked she wouldn't look at me but kept her face turned downward. It was exciting to know someone who had been overseas and was foreign.

The first week went well. I attended classes and was bound to get good grades so started out disciplining myself to study every night. It was on Tuesday afternoon when I ran to the store to get some more paper I ran into him. There at the counter was Alex with his buddy, Ransom. I was standing by the book rack on the other side of the store and was certain he hadn't seen me.

My heart came clear up into my throat and I was finding it very hard to breath. I had made up my mind I wouldn't even say his name and never to think about him again if I could help it. I stood very still hoping he wouldn't turn around. The clerk gave him some change and I heard Ransom ask him to grab a package of gum. The gum was on the rack behind him and as he turned to get it he saw me.

"Patty, what you doing here?" He came straight to me, grabbed me and hugged me.

"Heard you were in the hospital. I was gone and didn't know until I got back in town. Ransom and I took a boat trip down the Columbia River and when I tried to look you up your apartment had an old lady in it. She didn't know you or where you'd gone. Called your house and Caroline said you were living with your Dad. She didn't know the address but said it was somewhere in Greenville, and that she hadn't heard from you for some time."

I was tongue-tied, me the one who had a remark for everything. I grumbled that I was glad to see him, which I wasn't, and asked if he were a student or just visiting.

"Visiting, no way, old girl. Ransom and I are students. What hall you in?" He was so good looking, with broad shoulders and sandy hair that looked as if it were constantly combed. Several freckles covered his nose but that just made him look sexy. I remembered what it was like to be held tight in those muscular arms of his and began to bubble with anger way down deep inside. It was going to explode, I knew, and I'd better get out of there before it happened.

Picking up the paper and walking to the check-out stand with my face turned sideways, I mumbled, "See you later." He shouldn't have followed me but he did.

"How about a coke, Patty, let's catch up. How come you're living with your Dad? Caroline started to cry when she said she hadn't heard from you. You girls have a fight?" He stood as close as he could and I could almost feel him. I had to get away or put my fist through his freckles, my anger was going to be uncontrollable.

"Yeh, but can't have a coke today, have to study." With that I grabbed my purchase signed the charge slip and almost ran out the door and right into the arms of Cam, a student in my English class.

"Heh, the store on fire?" he laughed as he leaned over and picked up the sack with my paper in it.

"Hi, Cam, just wanted to get away from someone." I thought he would let me go but held onto my arm until I stopped jiggling.

"The sheriff or an old boy friend?" He took his hand away still laughing. He had bright red hair and, talk about freckles, there wasn't a spot on his face that didn't sport, not one but two or three, all piled on top of each other.

He looked behind me and saw Alex and Ransom walking out of the store. "Don't like queers I see, no wonder you're running."

I thought he must be talking about someone else but Alex and Ransom were the only ones in our view. "Cam, what are you talking about? That's Alex Crisp and his friend Ransom. They're from my home town. I've known Alex for years."

"You may have known them for years lady, but they're as queer as a three dollar bill. You keep your head in the sand?" He laughed again and waved as he ran after a girl he seemed to know quite well.

Homosexuals, I couldn't seem to get the picture but then little by little things began to fall into place. The excuses Alex used, blaming his mother for not being able to stay at the apartment some nights. Then there was Ransom always at his shoulder, soft-voiced Ransom who never played sports or was ever in anything in school. It hadn't been his mother at all who broke us up. It was Ransom. Alex had to choose and it wasn't me who won. I'd nearly killed myself over a gay guy. I ran back to the dorm, threw open the door to my room, fell onto the bed, and cried my heart out.

It took me days to get a grip on where I was coming from; I had made love to a gay man. Then I started wondering what was wrong with me that a gay man would even get near me, get near me enough to make love to me and plan on marrying me. Why, was I gay bait? I couldn't talk to Sinchong. She would never understand. Talk to my Dad; let him know I had been making love to someone gay? There was no place to turn. The college counselor was a drip; she was at least three-hundred pounds and talked in a high canary chirp. We all called her names and whenever she called us into her office we'd laugh about it together for days.

My grades were suffering. I just couldn't get hold of the whole picture. I saw Alex every once in a while going from class to class with his shadow tagging along. I felt like going up to Ransom and punching out his lights. It was only that I'd get kicked out of college that kept me from doing it. It was spring break and I drove home to see my Dad and see if there was any sense in this whole bit of nonsense.

As always Pop was glad to see me and put aside a conference so he could be with me. We went to a couple of shows, had dinner together and on Sunday he suggested I go with him to church. I almost laughed. None of us had ever gone to church. No, that isn't quite right, the neighbor girl had taken me to Daily Vacation Bible School one summer and I'd loved it. Oh, yes, when Aunt Ruby came to visit she made all the family go to church with her, well except Bob. Even my Mother couldn't order him to go.

"When did you start singing in the choir, Pops?" I was giggling when I asked him. He didn't laugh which surprised me because I could always make him laugh.

"Oh, I go quite often, Squirt." He looked serious and I felt I'd honor him by agreeing to go.

"OK, I'll go," I answered in a flippant manner which seemed to sadden him.

Sunday morning we went, not only to the church service but to a Sunday school class. The teacher was an older man who seemed to know my Dad very well. In fact all the people knew him. He introduced me to a whole bunch of people, and when church time came and they took up the collection my Dad helped. He was an elder; my Dad was an elder in the church. I was amazed. I asked him when all this happened and at lunch after church he told me the story.

It was a little restaurant that had small tables and only two chairs per table. They served soup and sandwiches and different kinds of tea. The tables had red and white checkered table clothes and cloth napkins. In the center of the table was an old wine bottle with a candle and melted wax drippings down the sides. I sometimes wonder how I can remember all the details but in a way I know because that was the day I grew up.

It is hard for me to tell this story now because I have a hard time keeping from breaking out in tears. This man I thought I knew so well had a story I could hardly believe. He started his story back before he and Mom were married. As he was telling me he would stop at intervals and let me absorb what he had said. The silences were awful but later on I realized it was kindness on his part. This caring and laughing and loving man really did love me. It felt good to be loved that much.

Dad had lived in Greenville all his life. My grandparents were immigrants from Ireland and worked a farm. Both of them died from a flu epidemic while Pops was in college. They'd worked their life away, had put my Dad through college, and hadn't lived to see him get his degree. Dad adored his Mother and had little to say about his Father.

Pops worked on the farm every summer while he was in school and helped in the evenings after school as well. It was a hard life. Dad said one of the reasons he wanted to be a lawyer was because he felt there was a great deal of injustice, especially for immigrants, and he wanted to be part of the cure. He met my Mom his first year in college and married her the day he graduated. He had a job in a local attorney's office and here was where the story took a turn I would never have expected in all my twenty-two years.

"Patty, there is something I have to share with you. I'm not too proud of it but it has to be said. I know you think I'm a pretty wonderful Dad. I have tried to be these last couple of years, but it wasn't always so." He reached across with those great big hands and held both of mine in just one of his, the other he let lay on the table as if it were useless.

"Patty, do you know there are people in this world who are called homosexuals. They are attracted to their same sex not to the opposite sex." I thought for certain he was talking about Alex and my mind raced as to how he had found out.

I blurted out, "How did you find out about Alex and Ransom? How long have you known Dad?"

"What are you talking about Patty? Alex is gay? My God, not Alex. Oh, my darling little daughter, not you too?" He stood up and walked over to the window and just stood there. I saw him take his hanky out of his pocket and wipe his eyes then blow his nose. Finally he came back to the table and asked me to tell him all about it.

It felt good to share my hurt and how I was still in love with Alex no matter what he was. I'd realized the day I saw him in the school store, and knew it was why I was so hurt and confused. How could I be in love with a gay man? I knew there must be something wrong with me.

"Oh, Daddy, there has to be something wrong with me. It isn't natural to be in love with a homosexual is it?"

My Father came over to me and pulled me into his arms, then sobbed out the words that nearly killed me, "There isn't anything wrong with loving a homosexual dear. Your Mother did."

"I thought there was something wrong with Robert, how could she live with him?" At last I knew what was wrong with Mr. Sicko.

"Patricia, it isn't Robert that is gay, dear. It's me."

"Daddy, don't be silly. You are a man's man for goodness sake!"

"Sit down, Patty, and listen." I had seldom heard that tone from my father.

I sat down and picked up my tea cup. The tea was cold. I really didn't want it so I sat the cup down and watched as my father put his large body onto the little tea-chair that had a white-wire heart on its back.

"Patty, I want you to listen carefully and not interrupt. I am, or was, a homosexual. I guess I still am but I don't follow that pattern of life anymore. When you came to live with me I decided to try and break away. I didn't want you to find out, but I couldn't do it by myself. One of my gay friends told me about an organization called Exodus. I visited and they suggested a counselor. I made an appointment and went for counseling. The man was a Christian and showed me how he had turned from homosexuality, had gotten married, and wouldn't go back to the way he had lived again for anything.

He and his wife asked me for dinner one night. They had a little boy and when I walked into their house I knew there was love there. His wife had helped him; she loved him dearly and stood by him. He fell back several times but one night when his little boy was sleeping in his crib he realized there was no way he wanted that little boy ever to know the hell of being a homosexual. He said he knelt down beside his son's crib, took his little hand in his and promised the Lord he would never again act out his desires for another man. He said it was hard at first when he met someone he had had a relationship with but little by little, with God's help, and his wife's love made it possible."

There were large beautiful tears running down my Dad's face. It reminded me of the spring rain that cleansed the air of winter. There was a look on Pop's face I will remember the rest of my life; it was a look of peace. I'd never experienced that kind of peace. He looked radiant. Then all I could see was Alex's face and something inside of me pushed aside the bitterness and hate and all the love I'd had all my life for Alex seemed to wash away all those feelings. Something was happening to my streak of hardness. The tears running down my Dad's face washed away a meanness and bitterness I'd carried in my heart and in it's place there was a new budding feeling of really caring about him and my Mom and even Caroline.

My father went on to tell me that when he met my mother they had dated a couple times when he was having spats with his lover. She called him and told him she was pregnant. It was at a bad time as he had just broken up with a lover he'd lived with for several months. He was in a black mood of depression and Phyliss was panicking because the guy she had been going with dumped her for another woman. Out of anger against his lover and because my Mom wanted to show the guy she'd been going with she didn't need him, they agreed to get married. Daddy assured her he would raise the child as his own. So Caroline came into their life. Daddy was settling into his law practice and money was no problem.

They lived together for nearly four years and my Mother grew to love Pops and he respected and tried to be a good husband to her. Mother got pregnant with me and they thought they were going to have a good life. Dad said he hadn't had a relationship with a man for nearly three years and when I was born he felt he had put his past away forever. Then Robert came back into the picture and Mother started seeing him on the side without Daddy knowing it. One night Daddy came home early and there was Robert in the front room playing with Caroline. Daddy walked out and never came back into the house again.

He said he hadn't been able to forgive my Mother until he became a Christian and had written her a letter asking her to forgive him. She had called him and asked him to forgive her. By then Daddy said he was a Christian and forgave her willingly. However he said he was having a hard time with the fact that Robert bothered me and came into his own house without him knowing it, but that forgiveness meant to forget and he was trying to.

Daddy told me about the life he had lived. After he moved out he seldom made time to see me. He was busy being the new Greenville prosecuting attorney and then was elected as a judge. I didn't know he had been a judge but during the time I was growing up he'd sat on the bench for seven years. Daddy said he had had several live-in lovers and it was simply a blessing he had never contacted AIDS.

"How did you ever get to be an elder in the church?" Somehow the story he had told me and reality didn't seem to match.

He didn't smile when he said, "I kept my private life separate from my public life, dear. It is easy to hide in this world those things you want kept a secret, especially if you work at it."

He told me how it was important to his social life to be the right kind of man and so he joined a church and did all the right things: gave to the building fund, attended church regularly, went to their membership class and eventually was asked to be an elder. After all a judge was above suspicion.

He'd rented out the guest room to his lovers and no one thought too much about it as he was such a macho-man and a respected member of the community. He made it a point to never be seen in public with a lover and would immediately kick them out if they gave him any trouble. Daddy said he really didn't love any of them, and that he never found a woman he really loved. He said that he was so determined to make something of himself that he never took the time or effort to get involved with his heart, only his body. Once his sexual needs were cared for he went on to what was important.

It was when I came to live with him that he realized how very much he loved me. It was then that his homosexuality became something he couldn't handle. As he was working with a sex counselor who was a Christian he found the emptiness in his heart that was there because he had never filled it with the Lord. His parents had been very firm Catholics and had never missed a Sunday's Mass, confession, or a feast day. They had insisted he go with them and do all the things they did. It never made much sense. The Mass was always in Latin and not eating meat on Friday didn't seem very logical. Fasting was a hardship as he was growing up and always hungry.

Even attending church as an adult, being an elder, and going through the motions were exercises he'd jotted down on his calendar and kept as he did the rest of his appointments. The night he went to dinner with his friend change his whole life. After they had finished dinner their son climbed up in his lap and asked him for a "round-room-ride."

"He hugged those little chubby arms around my neck and slid around to my back, as I imagined he had to his Daddy many times. He called out "Giddee-up." I stood up and pranced around the room. He hadn't had enough, but his Dad came over and took him off my back and asked if I would like to help him tuck his son into bed."

Dad told me how he couldn't say no because the little boy told him he'd say a special prayer for him if my Dad would come upstairs and help "tuck him in."

Pops continued, "His Dad took him potty and helped him brush his teeth as I stood in the room besides the crib waiting. As I stood there I thought about all the time I had missed with you and Caroline and how I'd filled those years with business that at that point seemed pretty futile. My friend came back and put little Timmy in the crib. Timmy sat up on his knees and held two little chubby hands together and for the first time in my life, Patty, a child prayed for me. He said, "Dear Jesus, take care of Mommy and Daddy and my new friend who knows how to give bestess round–room-rides. Thank you Jesus, Good night."

There was silence as Pops tried to get hold of his emotions, and it gave me time to wipe my dripping eyes as well. Dad got up one more time and went to the window. He stood there for a long time then came back to the table.

"I don't know how to explain how I felt, Patty. All the pretense, and sham, and sin, and helplessness, and anger left me at that very moment. I had to rush out of the room because the moment I was in the hall I began to sob as I had never cried in my life. Grown men don't cry Patty, but I did. Jim came out into the hall and took my hand and we both knelt there outside of Timmy's room and for the first time I really gave my heart to the Lord, and Patty I'll never take it back."

Pops was quiet and the love on his face was beautiful. If a man can be beautiful he was. Then he said, "Patty, please forgive me for the hurt I have done to you. I intend to ask Caroline as well. After all I took her as my daughter and even though Bob is her blood father I did not treat her fairly. I have cheated you of a father's love as you were growing up. Even though I will try with all my heart to make it up to you, I can't go back and teach you the things I should have. I should have taken you to Sunday school and church and taught you how to trust and love the Lord. I have been a very poor father and I beg you to forgive me."

I just sat there. I didn't have any idea what to do. This large wonderful man was asking me to forgive him and somehow it didn't make sense. How could I forgive him when I adored him and even now, knowing what he had been and done, I loved him with all my heart? There had to be an answer.

"Daddy I love you. I could never find fault with you."

"Please Patty; I need you to forgive me."

He needed me to forgive him, great, what about all the nonsense I had done during my life. If I forgave him, Caroline's and Mom's, Alex's, even Bob's faces passed in front of me. How could I forgive the nicest man I had ever known?

"Daddy I don't understand. I have no right to forgive you. I'm not lily white you know and I thought only God forgave people."

"Patty, I sinned against you. When we have sinned against somebody, Jesus asks us to go to that person and ask forgiveness so He can forgive us. Dear, please find it in your heart to forgive me." Pops reached over and took both my hands in his and the love I felt for him at that moment almost burst me apart.

"Oh, Daddy, of course I forgive you, don't you know how much I love you?"

Patty told me how she went back to college and made a promise to herself to talk to Alex. She got together with him and told him about what her father had shared with her and that she loved him and wanted him to meet with her father. He wouldn't even talk to her about his and Ransom's relationship, said it was none of her business and that he was just fine.

The next weekend when Patty went home to spend with her Dad she shared what had happened. He told her to give it time. There would be a day, he said when Alex would find that the hollowness of a homosexual relationship would catch up with him and he would need a friend.

"Just be there, dear, when he hits a rut in the road. He will. But, little daughter, it is time you put aside the feeling you had for him and find happiness yourself."

I followed Pop's advice. Cam asked me out one afternoon to a ball game and I went. We are going to be married in June. I won't be a virgin my wedding night but I will be a happy bride as I have learned to love Cam. He is a wonderful man. My Dad is giving me away and Mom, Caroline, and even Robert will be at the wedding.

Oh, yes, we are going to be married in Pop's church. Cam and I attend there regularly now. I've got a lot to learn about being a Christian but Cam and Dad are working on me. You see Cam is going to be a pastor and I'd better get used to church and church people.

I had asked Patty to send me a wedding invitation, and she did, but it was across the country and impossible for me to attend. She assured me she would send me wedding pictures as soon as they returned from their honeymoon. They were going to a cabin his folks owned on a small island at the tip of Florida.

Their wedding pictures arrived one afternoon and I was thrilled to see her beautiful dark face surrounded by a frothy cloud of white lace. She was beautiful. Tiny and not quite five feet tall, she stood next to her new husband, a man who was not at all handsome but pleasant.

I called them and Patty answered the phone.

"How are things going, Patty?"

"I love Cam more than I thought possible. It is a different love than I had for Alex, but a better one." Her voice bubbled with happiness.

"Have you seen Alex?" I asked.

It was silent for a moment. When she answered there was concern in her voice. "No, and I have decided I'm not going to look for him. I shared with him and he turned it down. He will have to find the truth on his own. I'm sad over his choices and know he will suffer but I can't help him. My responsibility is with my marriage and my new walk."

"Patty, when you get settled, send me your address and keep me informed. You and Cam are important to me."

"Oh, I will, and just as soon as Cam is in his church will you come and hear him preach?" The pride in her voice forced a positive answer, and I hoped that when that day came I would have the time and be able to travel.

7

"Fatty, Fatty, Two by Four"

WHEN I TRY TO REMEMBER THINGS FROM MY CHILDHOOD I can't keep this rhyme from ringing in my head, "Fatty, fatty, two by four, can't get through the kitchen door." It started the day I entered the first grade at Jackson Elementary, a small school in a very small town in Minnesota.

I didn't know I was fat until that morning. I had this idea that I was beautiful, that I was a princess, and that everybody loved me. Mother had told me how pretty my eyes were, that they were so like my father's. When she brushed my hair each night before she sang me to sleep she would say how beautiful my hair was and that it was the same color as my father's mother.

I'd never seen my grandparents or my father. There were two pictures of a tall, very handsome man with dark eyes and a crop of dark curly hair. One picture of my father was in a clock-locket which had a small diamond on the cover. I never knew my mother to take it off. The other picture of my father was in a gold frame on our fireplace mantel. He was smiling in the picture and I always thought it was just for me, because he loved me.

So many times Mother told me that when Daddy came home he would think I must be a princess because I was so beautiful, and how he would hug me and love me. She was kind and gentle and always told me wonderful stories of what my father was doing and why he couldn't be there with us. It wasn't until I was much older when I heard Mother and her sister, my Aunt Katy Ann, arguing in the kitchen that I knew my father had been a married man living in Florida, and that I was a bastard. I was old enough by then to know what the word meant.

121

I hated grade school. I never made any friends except Carol who was almost as heavy as I was. She and I would eat lunch together in the basement of the school, sitting at the end of the third table near the lunch-room monitor's desk. If we sat there the other kids wouldn't dare throw spit-wads at us. But the kids would whisper so only we could hear, "Hog feeding time, suee, suee."

I cried and cried to my mother but she would put her warm arms around me and always say in that sweet, tinkling voice of hers, "Now, now, Katherine, they're just naughty children and can't understand what a beautiful woman you're going to be." Then she would take a piece of chocolate out of her apron pocket and give it to me. "Here dear this will make you feel better." Whenever I was sad or angry, or hurt, she always gave me sweets to make me smile.

As I grew older I wondered why she never watched my diet or tried to help me lose weight. Even when I became a teen-ager and put myself on a diet she would always worry I wasn't eating enough and would put another helping on my plate. If I didn't eat it she'd tip her eyes down and say very quietly how sorry she was I didn't like what she had cooked. She made me feel a little guilty so I'd eat it and then hug her and tell her how good it was. I would get that beautiful smile of hers whenever I complimented anything she did. It never failed to make me feel good all over, warm and loved. At least she loved me, but as I grew older I found it wasn't enough.

The summer before Carol and I entered high school we promised each other we were going to lose weight. We exercised and practically starved ourselves; in fact when we did eat we'd stick our fingers down our throats so we'd throw it up. Carol's Mom caught us and really got mad, but when she wasn't looking we did it anyway. Carol and I took turns sleeping over at each other's houses and trying to eat together to be sure we stayed on our diet. We were determined to go into high school in the fall the same size the other girls were.

One night when Carol's Mom and Dad were at the movies and I was there a boy called and made some pretty smutty remarks to

Carol. She burst into tears. I felt so sorry for her I hugged her to get her to stop crying. That was when it happened. She hugged me back and then kissed me. Something seemed to take away all the hurt and we just kept kissing and kissing. Then somehow we stopped and were terribly embarrassed. She started to cry again and I picked up my books and went home. We only lived two blocks from each other. I didn't sleep much that night and for the first time in my life I didn't share what had happened during the day with my Mom.

Carol and I sort of kept out of each other's way the next day but by evening I ended up telephoning her with the excuse of seeing if she had stayed on her diet. We both had lost almost ten pounds by then and were pretty excited about it. We got to talking about what new clothes we were going to wear and pop everyone's eyes out when school started. Somehow we just didn't talk about the night before.

We exercised every day so hard that by night we were completely worn out. Carol's parents had to take a trip to visit Carol's mother's sister who was going to have an operation and so Carol automatically came to stay with me. We had stayed with each other ever since grade school, slept in the same bed, giggled under the covers at books we peeked at with a flash light while we nibbled on crackers and cheese. We both started our periods within a week and commiserated on being females and how lucky boys were they didn't go through this once a month. We bragged on our first bras, went to church-camp together, and practically lived like twins.

Even though Carol was a Catholic her parents sent her to camp with me, a Presbyterian. I liked the inside of her church better than mine. It had candles and tall statues and was beautiful. My mother let me go to church with Carol when she went off to visit her sister. Mother said that God was in all the churches and it didn't make any difference which one we went to just so we went on Sunday morning. I asked her why we didn't go to the Catholic Church, but she said my father preferred the Presbyterian and as the whole family was Presbyterians she wanted me to be one.

The first night Carol and I spent together after the kissing episode was sort of odd. I dressed in the bathroom with the door closed and so did she. Before we'd thrown our clothes every which way, pranced around the room without anything on and laughed at the new ways our bodies were changing. I had black hair and Carol's was almost white her hair was so blond. We slipped into bed with a very large space between us and started to read. There was no giggling and we were sort of embarrassed. It was a feeling new to us and we weren't quite certain what to do or say.

Carol broke the silence. "Cathy, do you suppose we're O.K?" I knew then she was as concerned as I was. She threw her book on the end of the bed, sat up, and there were tears in her eyes. All at once we both started crying and before we knew it were locked in each others arms sobbing our hearts out. Before long things were happening that I didn't know how to handle and neither did Carol. But we kept on and feelings we had never felt before were overwhelming us and we answered them in the only way we knew how. Out first experience was over and we declared our love forever.

The next morning with the sun coming into the room it was different. There was no darkness to hide our faces. We both felt stupid and wrong and somehow didn't know how to handle that either. Neither of our mothers ever talked about the feelings we had experienced or about what went on between Carol's mother and father in their bedroom behind closed doors. My mother told me it took two to make a baby but it was in such vague terms I really didn't understand her red-face and her stuttering over eggs and sperm. When Carol and I talked about kissing boys and all that stuff we sort of made up stories as to how it would be in bed with a naked boy. Neither one of us thought we'd ever do that. It had been mostly the boys who'd hurt us so badly growing up.

I guess when you don't know what to say, you sort of ignore it and try to pretend it didn't happen. That is what we did for several days but it was always there like a cloud that just followed us around wherever we went. We also didn't see much of each other for awhile. We both made excuses not to pop into each other's house. My mother even asked me if Carol and I had had a fight. I told her we were just busy and hadn't the time to visit.

It was only three weeks until school started and I'd lost over twenty pounds and could get into several sizes smaller than when school was out in the spring. Mother took me shopping and I had a brand new wardrobe. I was so anxious for the kids to see me. When I looked in the mirror it was exciting. My hair was beautiful and my eyes were large. When I touched them with mascara I had to admit I wasn't bad looking. I had olive colored skin. I knew it must have come from the man in the picture as he was rather dark too. My mother was very pale and when we were out in the sun she always burned and I just got darker.

Carol and I had been so close for so long I just had to run over and show her my new clothes. She was as excited as I was, she had lost a couple pounds more than I but she was shorter and we came out both wearing the same size. We changed our dresses several times and thought nothing of being our old selves. The excitement was all we needed to go back to where we were before. Inside I felt good again and I knew she did too. I guess it was just some silly thing; maybe all girls went through it.

School started and the first day was a success for both of us. Carol was so blond and rather pretty with her hair nearly to her waist. We both got whistles and Tom asked me for a date to the show Saturday night. I said I would go if he got a date for Carol. Our first date we were both so keyed up we couldn't even eat that day. Tom was pretty good looking and he was going to bring Jensen along too. Both were popular and Carol and I thought we were finally "in." It took Carol and me hours to fix our hair that Saturday, and I do think we changed our dresses a million times. Finally when the door bell rang—we were at my house—my mother let the boys in and we gave each other a sister-hug and went downstairs.

Tom had borrowed his dad's car and we left for the theater. All of us bragged about because Elmersville, eleven miles down the road, didn't have one and they all drove over to use ours. I don't remember what was playing but I remember Tom reaching over and holding my hand, and I saw Jensen holding Carol's hand. We had arrived.

After the show we had banana splits and then home. Both of us had been told that eleven o'clock was the deadline and it was up to us to see that the boys understood there would be no second time if we overstayed our curfew.

When Tom pulled up to the curb in front of my house he grabbed me and kissed me on the lips. I was so surprised I slapped him. I heard Jensen laughing in the back seat and Carol telling him that he had better not try it. Tom said that I had a pretty selfish way of paying for the show and treats, got out of the car, opened the car door, and walked me to the porch. Jensen and Carol were behind us.

We heard the boys laughing as they got into the car and saying something about guess they had better take a trip to somebody's house. I couldn't understand the name. We did hear Jensen telling Tom, "Boy what a couple of duds." We were shocked. What had we done wrong? That night we went over and over what we had said and done and came to the conclusion it was just their way of talking. The next day at school I went up to Tom and thanked him for a great night. He laughed and said he guessed it was O.K.

Carol and I waited for them to take us out again but nothing happened. We watched our diets and lost a few more pounds. Carol was in the Glee Club, I was in Latin Club and the band. High School was different than grade school. We moved from class to class and Carol and I were seldom in the same one. I started making other girl friends and so did she. Our lives were beginning to change. I seldom stayed over night as I was so busy with the band and trying to get excellent grades so I could get a scholarship for college. My mother got a monthly check from somewhere but I supposed it wouldn't be enough for college.

One of the things that troubled me was where my father was and if he were married as my Aunt had said in the kitchen maybe I had brothers and sisters. I asked mother about him and all she said was that someday she would tell me. Every time I asked it was the same answer. Finally I just gave up asking because she wasn't about to tell me. She would just give me that sweet smile and say, "Darlin,' he'll come home some day, you'll see." By then I knew it was just a fantasy. My mother was living in a dream world when it came to my father. I was almost seventeen and so far in all those years I had never heard a word from him, no phone call, and as far as I knew no letters.

One day mother was visiting her sister, my Aunt Katy Ann whom I was named after. She lived in Atlantic City with her husband, my Uncle Bob Highland. I was old enough to stay by myself and hadn't done the wash. I needed a pair of socks and went into mother's room to borrow them. I had never gotten into any of her things. She was a very private person and raised me to be the same.

I opened the top drawer and realized that the bureau's top lifted up. Curiosity made me lift up the lid and there were several letters all tied up in a ribbon. I just had to see who they were from. Inside of me I was hoping they were from my father. One of them was post-marked only a few days ago. I opened it and started to read. It was from my father. Then I realized from the post mark that he was in the Florida State Penitentiary. I read every letter there. He had been married to a lady in Oregon, had killed her and another man, and was in prison for life.

I heard my mother come in but I just sat there on the bed sobbing. Mother found me there crying my eyes out over the letters. She gently took them from off my lap and the bed where I had been sitting, wrapped them up with the ribbon and tenderly placed them back into the bureau and closed the lid. Her face was white and there were tears in her eyes as she told me the story of the man she had fallen in love with one summer when she and her parents were in Florida on a vacation. He had been working in the hotel they stayed in, and it wasn't until after they had made love that he told her about his wife.

Her parents were only in Florida for two weeks and when she had to leave my father told her he was getting a divorce and would come for her as soon as he was free. Mother said he wrote her every day and they loved each other dearly. Two months later she realized she was pregnant with me and wrote him about it. He was frantic and demanded a divorce but his wife wouldn't give him one. One day he went home early from work and found her with another man and he was glad for he thought that she would now grant a divorce but she refused.

I asked my mother where the check came from each month. I had always dreamed it was from my father who secretly loved my mother and would until his wife died and then they could be together. How romantic you can be when you are sixteen going on seventeen. The monthly check was from my father's parents who I always thought were my Uncle Bob and Aunt Katy Ann. These two people who loved me dearly and always treated me so special were my very own grandparents and I never knew it. It seems they were quite wealthy and my father had been doing some extra things around one of the hotels they owned. He was working his way through all the positions so that when he took over he would know the hotel business well.

So my Aunt Katy Ann wasn't my aunt at all and when she and my mother were in the kitchen they were talking about my father. His name was actually Robert Jennifer Highland, the Jennifer was for my great grandmother from where all the Highland money came from. Even my name wasn't real. I wasn't Catherine Mary Holmes. I was Catherine Mary Highland. I hadn't been born in Minnesota, I had been born in Atlantic City and stayed with my grandparents until I was nearly three. It was then they thought for my sake that I should be out from under the stigma of my father, and so they helped mother move. Holmes was my mother's name and the one she always used when referring to my father. Mother decided to move to Minnesota because she grew up here and knew several people.

My mother then told me there was plenty of money for college and that I would eventually inherit a great deal from my grandparents who were owners of several large hotels in Atlantic City. Now that I knew the story mother said she was going to call them. She said they would be so happy to be my real grandparents and that I finally knew the truth. My aunt, I mean grandmother had wanted to tell me before but mother thought I should be older before I knew the truth.

I had to get to Carol's and tell her. As I was walking around the corner to see Carol it all hit me, all at once my world fell apart. My father was a murderer and I was the illegitimate daughter of a prisoner, not the wonderful and elegant man I had always dreamed about. How could my mother have ever lowered herself to such an extreme as to get pregnant by a prisoner? My gentle loving mother, the beautiful quiet lady who had been my life, who had always been there and who had told me such exciting stories about the man who was my father and how he had done so many wonderful things, had lied to me. She had lied to me all of my life. She had lied about his name, about mine, about my grandparents. It was all lies, lies, lies!

By the time I got to Carol's it was nearly dark and I was almost in hysterics. Carol's parents were across the street playing cards with the Walkers and Carol was putting up her hair for school the next day. I fell across her bed and screamed the news that I was a child of a prisoner. Then I told her the whole story, crying my heart out at the deceptions and the lies. She sat on the bed beside me and took me in her arms to comfort me. I clung to her as if I was dying and she was all I had. I don't know how long I cried or was held but I know the lights went out. We climbed into bed and Carol held me tight and kissed away my tears and told me how sorry she was. Once again we found ourselves in each others arms doing what we had done before.

In the morning we didn't shy away from each other. Carol pulled me to her and hugged me and said that we needed each other and that it was O.K. what we had done. She said she read in a book about being a lesbian and guessed that was what we were. Somehow because it was in a book it sort of made it all right, why I don't know. I liked the way I felt and I certainly hadn't felt that way when Tom kissed me in the car that night. So, I guess we were lesbians. I wasn't quite certain what a lesbian was but Carol seemed to know and that made it so.

Carol and I went to the library and looked up everything we could find about it. How the Greeks and Romans accepted it and how it had been around since day one. At church I'd read in the Bible somewhere that it wasn't right and once the preacher hinted at such things and said that God hated those kinds of actions. But Carol and I thought that we were made that way so there must be a mistake somewhere.

We didn't tell anyone and kept our secret life even from our parents. Being hush-hush made it sort of mysterious and exciting. We tried to find everything out we could but there really wasn't much anywhere written about it. So we made up things about how we got that way and how we were special. We lived in our own little dream world way out there where no one else could enter and it was our very own where no one could touch us or hurt us.

Before long we didn't watch our diets and little by little we both started to gain weight. My Mother never said a word, just said I was growing up. Mrs. Carter, Carol's mom, became quite upset. She took a strong hand with Carol to see that she lost weight. After all Carol was becoming a young lady and no boy would look at a girl who was obese. Carol's mother put a stop to our overnighters. She made Carol eat every meal at home where she could count the calories and see to it that Carol lost the weight she'd put back on.

We were finally going to graduate. Carol had lost weight and was quite pretty. I had kept the weight on but as long as Carol loved me, I thought, nothing else mattered. I could be a jailbird's bastard daughter but that was not as important as knowing I was loved. And then my world fell apart again.

Jensen asked Carol to the senior prom and she accepted. Lately they had sort of spent time together. Carol told me it was because they were both in chemistry class and he was helping her because she was such a dolt. I got angry and asked why she would even care to go to the prom with him. She said her mother had heard Jensen's mother remark about him asking her to the prom and so she had to go.

I didn't go to the prom. No one asked me and I wouldn't have gone if they did. I didn't have anything to wear that covered the fat. The next day was Sunday and after church I changed my clothes and ran as fast as I could to Carol's. She was a Catholic and I went to the Presbyterian so I hadn't seen her at church. When I got there Jensen was on the front porch talking to her. I saw them from the side-walk and stopped and watched. She was actually smiling at him and then he reached over and kissed her on the mouth and left. She waved at him all the way down the street, then twirled around and hugged herself.

I screamed at her from the yard and she went in the house and shut the door. We never knocked and so I ran in and upstairs to her bedroom and there she was grinning from ear to ear. I asked her what she was doing letting Jensen kiss her like that. She grinned and told me that he had asked her to go steady and she had said yes.

"What about us?" I cried. She answered with words that were like knives cutting way down deep inside of me. "Catherine, for goodness sake, what we had was just nonsense, sort of a fad. I guess some girls go through that sort of thing at times. Besides I wouldn't want people to know what we did, heavens, my parents would have a cow!" Then she showed me his school pin he had made into a necklace for her. I turned, left the room and went home.

We graduated. I was glad we wore robes because I couldn't find a dress that hid "me." I didn't talk to Carol for several weeks. I couldn't. I was so hurt I didn't know what to do. My mother thought I was sick, and finally she took me to the doctor. He gave me a clean bill of health. Mother said that I should go and stay a couple weeks with my new-found grandparents. I had visited them many times as my aunt and uncle but never as their granddaughter. They were thrilled I was coming and I looked forward to getting away from our town.

Atlantic City was a big city compared to Emeryville, and it was exciting to belong to people who had a maid, a butler, and a chauffeur. They gave me a checking account with my own checks and told me that they would register me at whatever college I wanted to go to. I asked them if it were possible to see my father. My Grandmother broke into tears and said she would try and get permission.

The day I saw my father was terrifying. We went through some large gates with barbed-wire rolled up at the top of the wall. We had to be searched and finally went into a waiting room. They called my name and I went through a door that clicked because a man in uniform behind the glass was watching. I went into a small room that had another door and he clicked it again and I went down a hall to a large room filled with table and chairs. I had to go through another door that clicked to open and was in a large room. There were several people in the room sitting at tables. A man at each table had a badge clipped to his shirt.

A tall grey-haired man came up to me and said in a very deep voice, "Catherine, you must be Catherine; you look like your mother." It was my father. He wasn't the man in the picture. He was as tall but there were lines in his face, his eyes were not as dark as in the portrait, and he wasn't smiling as he had smiled at me for nearly eighteen years. He was sad and there were tears in his eyes.

He stood straight and stiff and waited for me to speak. I mumbled something about being Catherine and then he stepped towards me and took me in his arms and held me close. He held me close like I had dreamed of all my life and he cried and his tears fell onto my shoulder. I let him hold me. I didn't pull back because something very wonderful was happening. This was my father and he loved me for he was telling me he did. Something burst inside of me, something that had been tight and dark way deep where I could feel my heart pound once in a while. There was that something way inside where I couldn't touch. I felt as though I couldn't stand it another minute and then all at once I started hugging back and crying as if I would never stop.

This was my father and he loved me. He took me to one of the tables in the corner and started talking. He told me how he had wanted to be there when I was born, how he had loved my mother with all his heart, and how he had lost his senses when his wife wouldn't give him a divorce. He told me that when he found her with another man and that she still wouldn't give him a divorce because she wanted his money. He simply lost it and killed them both. He told me how sorry he had been but then it was too late.

My father took a plastic picture holder out of his pocket and showed me several pictures. They were pictures of me growing up. My mother had kept him constantly in touch with me by pictures and letters. How one-sided. I felt cheated and then I was angry. He reached over and touched my arm and told me it was both my mother's and his decision not to let me know until I was old enough to understand. Every time my mother had visited her sister, actually my grandmother, she had visited him and once when she was here they had married.

Married, I couldn't believe it; I was actually legal after all. "Catherine, he said, you may call me daddy or father. I would be so proud."

"Daddy," the word sounded strange but very wonderful, then I repeated it, "Daddy." He laughed and my heart burst with love. There was the smile I had known all my life. This really was the man in the picture on the mantel.

I can't remember everything we said. I do remember I had to go before we were through with all the years we were trying to cover. I visited my father every time I was allowed that summer. I learned to dearly love my grandparents and they loved me. I lost over thirty pounds and had a beautiful new wardrobe. They registered me in Brown University for the fall term, bought me a car and took me to everything they went to. I was happy and things were going well for me.

When I entered college that fall I lived in the dorm with other girls my age, most of them from rich families, and well-known ones. My grandparents were in the upper-crust as it were and I was traveling in a new atmosphere. I liked it and played up to it like a pro. We had drinking parties and co-ed parties and one night I was a little tipsy and a boy form Harvard and I "made-out." I was shocked at how brief and unloving the whole thing was. It was almost over before it started and I was left out on a limb as he rolled over and went to sleep. I cried myself to sleep that night missing Carol and wondering if she missed me as much as I missed her.

My first year in school was in and out of class rooms, dances, games, beds, and I never stopped long enough to even really think about the consequences of, as they say, burning the candle at both ends. It was new and exciting having anything I wanted. Money was no problem. I had lost enough weight that I never was without a date and carried condoms in my make-up kit so I wouldn't end up pregnant as my mother had. I never told anyone about my mother or father. In fact I hinted they were both dead and I lived with my grandparents after a car accident had killed them both.

Then it was summer again and I went home for a couple weeks to visit my mother. She said she had been talked into moving to Atlantic City with my father's parents. She was excited about living near me, and being closer to my father. I stayed and helped her pack and get ready for the moving van. One afternoon I was bored and walked over to see what had happened to Carol. She had married Jensen and was home getting a divorce. We got back into the habit of spending a great deal of time together. We were too old to have night overs and never mentioned our actions of two years ago.

One night we had popped some corn, opened a couple of Cokes and were watching T.V. We ended up sitting close to each other on the couch and before much time had lapsed were in each other's arms and finally in her bedroom. We resumed our way of living. I told her she had to move to the city with me and get a job there so that when I came home from college during the breaks we could be together. She said she would think about it.

We wrote almost daily and called each other as much as possible. Carol started working for her dad and I went back to school. The whirl-wind didn't blow quite as hard as it had my first year. I was getting serious about being a pediatrician and started to keep my nose to the books. I didn't date as I had all the letters and phone calls from Carol I needed to satisfy that side of me. At Christmas I had her come to the City to spend the holidays with all of us. Working for her dad she got the time off and came. No one thought much about it as we had grown up like sisters and in fact some people even thought we were.

I visited my dad whenever I could. I wrote him and he wrote me quite often. I called him all the time. One time I started to tell him about Carol and me but I lost the courage. He and mother had what they called trailer-visits. She could go into the prison in a certain section and stay for two nights and a part of three days with him about twice a year. She looked forward to those times as if every waking minute had to be counted off until the next visit. I wondered what it would be like to love a man that deeply. I guessed that was the way I felt about Carol, but there always seemed to be something missing. I never shared our feelings with anyone because I was a little ashamed way down deep, but Carol needed me and I needed her, and that made it all right.

A routine was established and my life could be fitted into a pattern: school, Christmas vacations, spring-breaks, summers, living with my grandparents and mother, visiting my dad, and spending time with Carol. We went to church on Sunday when I was home. I never did at college. I was usually pounding the pillow at 11:00 on Sundays trying to make up for Saturday night.

I was in psyche class one afternoon when a substitute teacher taught. He was tall and strikingly good looking and talked with the voice very like my dad's, that low rumble which sounded like a man should sound. He was tall and had dark-auburn hair and the greenest eyes I had ever seen on a human being. Eyes like his should be limited to cats, I thought. During class I was tongue-tied for some reason. He stood and talked about child-discipline and how parents should treat their children with firmness and yet with love. He went on and on and all at once I wasn't really listening. I was watching every movement he made and drinking in every word he spoke. I was mesmerized. I couldn't take my eyes off him. He noticed me staring and grinned, I quickly bent over as if to pick something up to hide my red face.

When class was over I couldn't get out of the room fast enough. I ran down the hall, out the door, and to my car. When I turned around he was standing one the side-walk watching me. I couldn't find the key. Finally I realized I had already put it in the lock. I drove away with not even a peek back to see if he was still standing there. I couldn't' figure out what was wrong. I suppose it was because his voice reminded me of my father. That was it, how silly, I thought, that I had been so flustered.

Two weeks went by and I hadn't heard from Carol. I phoned her at work one day and she wasn't there. They said she had been ill. I called her house and she answered. She had been sick with the flu, she thought, but the doctor had told her that morning she was pregnant, nearly three months along. Carol had never been regular so when she missed she hadn't thought much about it. We had always laughed about my every month clock and her whenever time. She was devastated. What would she ever do with a baby?

She was angry. Jensen it seems had been dating a girl at the college where he attended and was going to marry her as soon as the divorce went through. It was then Carol asked me what I thought about abortions. She said her parents had forbidden it. As Catholics, it was against their religion. I had no idea what Presbyterians believed. I told her that I would catch a plane and spend the week-end with her and that we could work it out together.

Her parents met me at the airport and drove me back to their house. When I got to the house I ran up to Carol's room and found her looking out the window with her back towards me. I went over and took her in my arms but she pulled away and told me never to touch her again. I stood there, not having any idea what was the matter. Then in anger she told me that Jensen was coming that afternoon. Her mother had called him and told him about the baby and he was coming to get Carol and take her back with him where she belonged.

I had no idea what to say. I sat down on her bed and just stared at her. Why did Carol even need Jensen. We could handle the baby between us. I had enough money and her parents were not hurting for money either. After all she had been married and the baby was legal. My mother had been able to take care of me and I wasn't even legitimate at the time. I talked and talked to Carol that morning. All she said was that Jensen was coming and she had to get ready to leave. Again I was saying to her, "What about me?" And again she was saying that what we had was just one of those things people do when they don't have anybody else.

I left before Jensen got there. I didn't even tell her good-bye. I just called a taxi and had the driver take me to the airport. I sat in the waiting room all afternoon until I could get a flight out for

Atlantic City and home. I needed my father. I was praying I could get in to see him. I was going to tell him about Carol. I had to tell someone.

When I got to my grandparents I tried to get in to see my father, but visiting days were Tuesday and Friday and it was Saturday. You had to make an appointment several weeks ahead for special visits. I wasn't able to visit with him. I stayed that night and visited with my mother who was living with my grandparents and tried to get over the dead feeling that was inside of me. Everything in my world was all figured out and now there was a hole in the plan. I just figured that when I got out of college and started practice in Emeryville Carol and I would move in together. Now all I had left was college.

That next quarter I studied. All I did was study, I didn't even go out with any of the girls and when a boy asked me for a date I snapped a quick, no. No one else was going to hurt me or lie to me and the only way I could keep from being hurt was to keep to myself. I was getting outstanding grades and doing some great work in child psychology, in fact I was chosen to represent the class at a psychology conference in New York that October. I was going to be a good pediatrician, I could tell.

I hadn't heard from Carol, but my mother had heard from her mother. Carol had a baby boy and was living at Dartmouth with Jensen who was still in college. They had named the baby after Jensen's father and according to Carol's mother were doing great. I covered up the place in my heart that had been Carol's and tried to forget how lonely I was. I never told my father. Somehow I didn't want to see the hurt in his eyes. He had been hurt enough in his lifetime.

My grandfather and grandmother had started a new case with a rather famous lawyer to see if they couldn't get my father released from prison. They had done this once before but the court ruled against them. Now their son was married and had excellent behavior records, and as it was a "crime of passion," there was a little hope but not too much. I couldn't imagine how wonderful it would be to have him with us, so I didn't even hope.

All the family was praying for his release. I hadn't prayed since, well, I couldn't remember when. I was angry at God, so why be a hypocrite and talk to Him.

The conference was exciting and on the second day the speaker was the teacher with the green eyes. I was sitting at the table with the other school representative and he came over to shake hands with us before he spoke. I was writing in my journal and didn't notice until he said in that rumbling voice, "Aren't you going to shake hands with me, young lady?" I looked up and into those green eyes and could hardly breathe. I stuttered some dumb thing and shook hands, then he laughed and said, "Aren't you the girl that was in my psyche class?" I stuttered something else, agreed that I was and I think I said how nice it was to see him again.

While he spoke I was a zombie. Once again I couldn't keep my eyes off him and all I heard was his voice. I have no idea what he said. As soon as he was finished he came back to the table and stood in front of me and asked me to go to lunch with him. I have no idea what I said but I ended up sitting at a table trying to act as if I had a brain and to talk intelligently with him. His name was Dr. Quinton Hallsely, a teacher at one of the leading colleges on the West Coast, and had been brought to the conference as a guest speaker. When he had taught at my college he was finishing his degree and had already been hired to teach in California.

The conference was finished the next afternoon and he asked me for dinner that night as he wasn't taking a flight out until early the next morning. Again I was sitting across the table from him. Each time before we ate he asked if I minded if he blessed the food. I thought it was a little funny but I said, of course I didn't mind, and bowed my head as if it were an every day thing with me. We talked until after midnight just sitting there having cups of coffee one after the other. He didn't drink and didn't even ask me if I wanted one, which I certainly could have used.

When he finally took me back to my hotel I knew all about his childhood, his parents, about his two sisters and three brothers, and that his father was a general practitioner in a place called Spokane, Washington. He told how all of them had been brought up in the Methodist Church and that two of his brothers were ministers and one of his sisters was a missionary, married and had two little boys. The other sister was just entering college. He didn't say anything about his other brother.

I learned how he had worked in the summer to help pay for his college and that he was going to be a doctor until he started working with his father in an orphanage and got to understand where some of these kids were coming from. It was then and there he decided to be a Psychiatrist so that he could help heal their minds as well as their bodies. He was teaching for a couple of years, he said, while he did some more research and then he intended to open his practice.

He asked me if I had a steady. I laughed and said I didn't need that sort of thing to muddle up my life. He had a very funny look on his face, then laughed and said he guessed that was why he didn't have a steady either. When he took me back to the hotel, he went up in the elevator with me. He took my key, opened the door, went in first, then laughed and told me he had chased all the boogie men out and I could come in. It was rather strange having someone take care of me. When he reached the door to leave he pulled me to him and very slowly and carefully kissed me. I didn't push him away and I didn't mind it at all. He was so gentle and kind I felt safe and sort of funny all over.

I went back to school and he left the next morning early. He called me before he left and said that he would like to write me and asked if I would answer his letters. I agreed and even though it was early in the morning and I was standing in my nightie I felt sort of warm and safe when I heard his voice.

School was a tight schedule. I was taking eighteen units and they were all pretty stiff. I liked challenges and spent my time in the library or in my room studying. I talked once in a while to the other girls but begged off when it got to be party time. I seldom went to the cafeteria but ate a lot of junk food. One morning when the jeans were too tight to zip up I realized I was putting the weight back on. It was a fight I supposed I would have all my life, but this time I was the boss and made it a point to choose the apple in the automat instead of the candy bar. It wasn't long before the jeans zipped and I felt pretty proud that I had been able to discipline myself without Carol. I often thought of her and wondered how she was but gradually it got so I could handle her absence.

Summer rolled around once more and I decided to stay in school and take a couple summer classes. My grandparents were still going to court about my father but so far nothing had happened. I wrote Quint several times and each time he wrote back long and interesting letters. His school was almost out and he asked, if he came east, if I would spend time with him. He planned to rent a cabin on the beach for a month. I wrote back that I would be glad to see him and way down deep I meant it.

When I got home from summer school, I drove up to my grandparents' house and, Mason, who had been with the family for years, came out to get my bags with a happy welcoming grin. I felt I belonged and I did. I ran in expecting my mother or grandparents to be in the living room but it was empty so I ran back to the solarium where they loved to sit and have tea. They were there, and sitting next to my mother holding her hand was my father. I was so excited I couldn't keep from crying and laughing and hugging. It was a wonderful surprise and that with Quint's visit made the summer a very happy one.

Quint kissed me good night many times and I started to look forward to it. He would come over in the afternoon and we would go swimming or to the lake or even take long walks on the beach. I teased him about being a sleepy head and never getting there until afternoon. One night after we had taken in a show he asked me if I would go with him the next morning and let him prove he wasn't a late sleeper. I agreed thinking he'd hit the floor early and take me somewhere just to prove me wrong.

At exactly eight o'clock the next morning he was at the front door. He was wearing shorts and a T-shirt that had some writing on it. I grabbed my purse and was in the car ready for the day. We drove quite a ways then turned into the bad section of the city. He pulled up in front of a rather beat up park, let me out, locked the car, and I followed him amazed at the poverty. I'd never been in this part of the city.

A small building was at the end of the path surrounded by at least fifty or more kids, all colors and all sizes. I was speechless.

What in the world was he bringing me here for? As soon as the kids saw him they surrounded him chatting, each one pushing to get closer. I spent the morning watching and helping Quint be with the kids. He sat them all down on the lawn and told them story after story, as he said, his best friend a man named Jesus. He taught them songs, and games, and health hints, and ways to take care of themselves. He told them how important it was to stay in school and get an education. At twelve he hugged them good-bye, put his arm around me and led me to the car.

I never said a word driving back to my house. There wasn't anything I could say. He stopped at a small lunch stand, ordered hot dogs and a coke apiece, put the top down and we sat there eating. Finally I couldn't hold it in any longer. I had to ask him what he was doing with those kids. Quint was helping with a church program that worked every summer with inner-city kids. Then he popped the one-hundred dollar question, "Want to help me the rest of the month, Cathy?" I had planned on being a nice-white-coated pediatrician not a summer baby-sitter, but there was something in Quint's face that wouldn't allow me to say no.

For the next three weeks I worked every morning with the kids. It got to the point they were as happy to see me as Quint. I didn't tell the stories. I just helped with the games and teaching good hygiene to the girls, for many of them were budding into young ladies. Every night when Quint kissed me good night I was thrilled. I was doing something with my life and I felt good. It was time for Quint to return to the west coast and I wasn't looking forward to being alone.

It was Friday night and Quint asked me to go to dinner, a rather expensive place on the boardwalk. He said he was going to get gussied up and wanted me to wear a formal as there was dancing and he had made reservations for the evening. It was exciting getting to really dress up. I had my hair fixed up on top of my head, got a new pair of gold shoes and a matching clutch. My dress was trimmed in gold sequins that glittered when I moved.

We were finished eating when Quint reached into his pocket and took out a small blue-velvet box. He laid it on the table then reached across the table, took my hand and with his heart in his eyes asked me to marry him. I was startled, marry him? I hadn't even thought of such a thing. How could I marry him with the past I had of being a lesbian. How could I be a wife to him when I preferred to be with Carol? I hadn't been with another woman, but I also had never really liked being with any guy that first year in college.

I didn't know what to say. I liked Quint but had never put love and marriage into the picture. With Carol gone I had planned on being a pediatrician and that was that. This was a new thought and I didn't know how to handle it. I just sat there and looked at him. He repeated the question, then came around the table and took me into his arms and kissed me quite differently than he had ever kissed me before. It was a kiss that made me feel like I wanted more. He kissed me again and all at once I was kissing him back. Somehow I said yes, he put the ring on my finger and when he took me home that night he went in and told my family, they were all excited and thrilled. They like Quint very much.

That night I lay in bed in a panic. Why had I said yes? Had I lost my mind? I went down to the kitchen and poured a glass of milk and sat at the table with tears streaming down my face. How could I do such a cruel thing to such a nice guy?

"What's the matter, Cathy?" It was my father. He took me into his arms and held me tight. He was the father I had dreamed of, he was real, and he loved me. That night I poured my soul out to my father, all the hurt, all the lies, all about Carol, and then my worries about being a lesbian and marrying Quint. My father just sat very still and let me rant on. He never said a word until I literally ran down and was out of breath. "Have you finished dear?" he asked. He took a napkin that was lying on the table and wiped my eyes.

I also told him how I had gotten angry at God and even though I went to church I thought that is was a waste of time. He said, "Yes ,dear I know. I could tell by your attitude. I have been worried but didn't want to say anything because I felt you would talk to me when you were ready."

We talked until nearly dawn. He told me how in prison he had met the Lord and how he would never have been able to handle prison life without Jesus. He told me how the Lord freed him from the guilt of killing two people and then he said, "Dear, if God can forgive me for killing two people I think He can handle your lesbian actions." Before I went to bed that night I was on my knees next to my father begging the Lord to forgive what Carol and I had done and how I had flipped around my first year at school.

The next day I took Quint into the park at the bottom of our street and told him everything. When I was finished I knew he would ask for his ring back so I took it off and handed it to him and said, "I know you will want this back, I am sorry I ever took it, please forgive me."

Quint never said a word, he reached over took my hand in his and put the ring back on my finger. Then in his rumbling man voice he told me we would be married at Christmas time when all of his family could be together and my family could plan on visiting the west coast.

We were married that Christmas and he has never mentioned my past. I saw Carol a year ago and she had two children, not by Jensen but by a man named Ralph. She had finally divorced Jensen and was now remarried and said she was very happy.

Quint and I have a set of identical twin girls and two little rough-neck boys. I don't have time to practice and one doctor in the family is enough. Quint has his own practice and I help out once in awhile.

My mother, father and grandmother come to visit often. My grandfather passed away last summer.

We all traipse into church together, the twins off to their Sunday school class, the boys to theirs and Quint and I to ours, which he teaches. I have learned to love the Lord and will teach my girls especially that they must wait for the right kind of love. Of course they will have their big tall rumbling-voiced daddy to keep them hugged, and I have their daddy to keep me hugged as well!

Katherine sat across from me at the restaurant. She'd left the children with a baby-sitter: there would be no safety for us at her house with all four of the rug-rats awake. She did bring pictures of them and Quint. The girls were mirror images of each other and, as the two small replicas of their Dad, looked like mischief personified.

"Cathy, do you and Carol ever communicate?" I asked.

"No, that part of my life is a closed book. I have four precious little gifts of God I must care for. I can't let them stumble as I did. I will know what to watch for. The girls will never have an eating problem because I have started them off learning to like good food, as I did the boys. And all four of them know that Quint and I adore them. Oh, we discipline their dear little back-sides once in a while. Whenever that is necessary we always give a double portion of love afterwards."

I picked up the recorder and the check. Cathy took it and said she wanted to pay for lunch. She said it was like paying for a re-run, and had made her remember to be more cautious and never forget.

She stood and even though she was a little heavy she was quite attractive and certainly not fat.

"You look very nice, Cathy."

She laughed and touched her hips. "You would think with the amount of running around I do chasing kids I'd be skinny. Guess I'm just not the type. Quint says I'm just right for hugging, and that's what counts!"

I walked her to a large van filled with toys and a dog that took up one row of seats.

"That's Pest. He came to our front door one day and we've had him ever since. We didn't quite expect a very small half-starved puppy to turn into a horse. The kids adore him, ride him, and sleep with him. Quint loves him, and guess who takes care of him?"

She received several dog-kisses as she got into the van, laughed pushed the dog back, then turned to me and said, "Thank you, it helps to share memories. Gives me a chance to take them out, dust them off, and remember where I am now. I hope the book helps someone keep from tumbling around like I did." She pushed the dog back again, waved, smiled and drove off into traffic.

8

"In the Grip of Hell"

I DON'T KNOW WHAT HELL WILL BE LIKE but my youth must have been a preview, or maybe you could call it a training ground for unhappiness and hurt, physically and mentally. My Dad was a fag; anyway, that's what the kids at school called him and in their eyes that made me one too. I can't remember my Mother, all I ever knew about her was that she died in prison; some gal knifed her because she wouldn't give out.

My Grandma brought me up and she never talked much about her daughter. All she ever said was that if Barbara hadn't married my Dad she'd be alive today, and no doubt she was right. My Grandpa died in the Second World War, so did his brother, so Grandma took me over and put every bit of love she had left over into me. If it hadn't been for her arms and her love I'd never have made it.

The courts made me go to my Dad's every other week-end, a month during the summer, and one major holiday a year. I hated to go there, and that's why I want to share my life. I'm thirty-seven, just got married three years ago and have a little eleven months old boy named Mason Jr. Our son will never go through the hell I went through. Crystal, my wife, and I have learned that children are a very special gift and should be treated as a blessing, disciplined correctly, and loved every minute.

Grandma passed away when I was fourteen, just going into high school, and I ended up with my Dad. I thank God I had Grandma as long as I did or I would probably be either in prison or dead. I'll tell you why, but I'll have to start back as far as I can remember so you will understand what it was like growing up in a house where my Dad was a homosexual. The very early years I don't remember. Must be when I was five or so that things began to fall into place, or I should say fall out of place.

Grandma had me in Sunday school; it was a Lutheran Church in Meadville, a pretty small farm town. We went over to Union City sometimes and when we really wanted to go to the city we took the bus into Pittsburgh. Grandma had a cousin there, Nettie, where we would go for a week-end. She lived in what they called a flat, second floor up. You walked up a flight of stairs and there was a living room, dining room, bath, kitchen and three bedrooms all in a line down the side. Her husband was a mailman and funny. They called him Skitch and I loved being there. No one laughed at me or called me names there. Miss Nettie and Mr. Skitch, as I called them, loved me and treated me as Grandma did.

Grace, a girl my own age, lived in the flat under Miss Nettie's and we played together in a large back yard, all fenced in with high wooden slats. She didn't know about Troy. I never called him Dad to anybody and only to him because he made me. I had to call the guys that lived with him uncle; he'd tell people they were his brothers whenever we went anywhere together. Dad owned a hair stylist salon in Union City. He had pictures of Cary Grant and Randolph Scott on the walls, and a special addition built on the side where he kept several parrots. He called them his babies. I hated them as much as I hated him. They were dirty and bit me whenever I had to give them water.

There were two sides of my growing-up coin, the times I was with Grandma and the times I had to be with my Dad. Oh, by the way my name is Mason Lester Ashton, Mason after Grandma's father and Lester after my Dad's uncle. I certainly thanked whoever named me for not tagging me Troy after my Dad. Even knowing him was bad enough and having to live with him as much as I did was hell.

When I was around five, as I started to say, I remember him picking me up at Grandma's. She packed a little fuzzy-bear suitcase with my pjs, and an extra pair of jeans, socks and shorts.

There was no need to pack my church clothes as Troy never went to church. He laughed at me for going with Grandma, called it nonsense and said only little girls went to church not boys. He asked me if I wore a dress on Sunday's, said I would have to let my hair grow so I could braid it. Grandma hated letting me go to Troy's but she said the government said I had to. Every time Troy came to get me she would cry when I left.

Grandma had little or no use for the government, and proudly told everyone that she had never voted and never would because of what they made her do to her grandson, forced her to send him into the den of Satan. She would scream at Troy and say terrible things when he came to pick me up and told him if he didn't have me back exactly on time she'd call the police and have him put in jail. How I wished he would have been late getting me back, just once, so he'd be put into jail. He was never late and never missed picking me up. Grandma would watch the time and not let him take me out the door until her big grandfather clock over the fireplace rang the correct hour.

One day when I was older and knew how to change the time I sat the clock back an hour, but Dad had a watch and accused Grandma. He was being so mean to her I admitted doing it and he slapped me right there. Grandma picked up the fire tongs and was going to hit him but he grabbed her arm and stopped her. I guess it was best he did. If she'd hurt him he might have put her in prison and then he'd get me full time. I begged him not to take me with him but all he did was pick me up when I was little and carry me to the car. When I got older I knew there was no chance he'd let me stay so I'd get into the car in the back seat so I didn't have to sit next to him.

I don't remember much about the first time I went to be with him but there was a time, before I went into first grade, I can remember. From that week-end on, I guess, is when I started to hate him with every fiber in my body. He came to pick me up and one of his boys was in the car. I forget what that one's name was. Doesn't make any difference anyway. He was sitting in the back seat and Troy put me in beside him. He hugged me and hugged me, said I looked just like "his" Troy. I had no idea at that time what a homosexual was or wasn't, at five you don't have a good handle on such things.

When we got to Troy's house—it was a big one with lots of rooms and a pool in the backyard he had his friend take me to my room while he put the car away. The man carried me into the house and up the stairs to the one I always stayed in and put me down on the bed. Then we said how cute I was and came over and hugged me several times. Troy came into the room and pushed the man out into the hall and I heard them fighting. The man kept yelling, "I wasn't going to f— him." It wasn't until I knew the facts of life I understood why they were fighting.

That night when we had dinner the guy served us like he was a servant or something. Troy had lots of money and I never had to do without because he paid Grandma what the State said he had too and then more. He always handed me a twenty or more when he took me home, even as a little guy, but I always gave the money to Grandma. When she passed away I found she'd put every cent he'd ever had his hands on in the bank that was a pretty hefty sum helped put me through college. She was an angel and if you were to ask me where she is right now she is probably giving God what for because of Troy. Grandma was pretty outspoken but as fair and as honest as they make them.

Dad spoke to me as though I were one of his pet bulldogs. He had three of them and at first I was scared to death but later they were the only thing I liked in the house. He always ordered me around, never talked to me as he did to his boys. I never could understand why he even wanted me there. When I was little he would order me to do something and if I didn't do it fast enough he'd slap me in the face and tell me he'd take no lip and I was damn well going to obey him. I'd not get by with things like that old lady let me.

Troy hated Grandma and would never have left me there if she hadn't gone to court. The state made him let me stay with her most of the time when I was a baby, then when I was in the second grade Troy went back to court to get me full time but lost the case and then he really hated Grandma. I can't remember a sentence he ever spoke to me that he didn't run her down or call her a bitch or something worse. When the court made me go and live with him after Grandma died he came at me one day about her and I hit him in the mouth so hard it knocked him into the wall. I told him if he ever mentioned her name again I'd kill him. By the time I was fourteen I had an inch or two on him, took after my Grandma's side. All her men folk were over six feet. She often said, there's no runt in my family generally meaning Troy who was short and heavy.

That night I went to bed glad to get out of the room and away from the man who talked as if he owned Troy. I'd taken a few books with me and got them out crawled into bed and read. The best thing I ever did was to read. I loved any book I could get my hands on. Grandma took me to the library once a week and let me check out the five books they allowed on my card. I took good care of them and never bent the corners back or let them be thrown on the floor.

I guess I must have fallen asleep because when I woke up the books had fallen off the covers onto the floor and I'd never have let that happen. I heard some strange sounds in the hall. I thought maybe the dogs had gotten out of their pens. My Dad's bedroom was next to the room I used so I jumped out of bed to see if it was the dogs and to tell Troy. I went into the hall and then into Dad's bedroom. I will never forget what I saw. That man and Dad were naked on the bed and doing things I didn't believe. They heard me and screamed at me to get out. I ran out of the room and into my room and closed and locked the door.

I heard my Dad demanding I open the door but I wouldn't. Finally he stopped pounding and I eventually fell asleep. The next morning that guy was gone and Dad was in the breakfast room eating breakfast that a lady fixed every morning. She came to work early and stayed there all day, fixed dinner and then left. She rode a bicycle to work, as far as I know even when it rained. At the table I couldn't look at Troy and he didn't say a word. That afternoon another man came and moved into the same bedroom that Dad was in. And that was how it was, there was always a new man, and always nothing said between Troy and I when I was little and didn't know what I'd seen.

It was horrible when I went to school. There was a bully in the third grade that picked on us first grade boys. One day while we were on the playground and I had the swing he came up and tried to tip me out, when he couldn't he yelled at me, "Fag, fag, Mason is a fag and all his dogs are fags too." I had no idea what he was talking about and neither did most of the other kids. No one liked him and they started throwing the little pieces of gravel at him that covered our play yard.

When I got home I asked Grandma what a fag was and she said, "Never mind, Mason, it isn't a nice word and if I hear you using it I'll wash your mouth out with soap." Then she ran into the living room, covered her face with her apron, and cried. I knew I'd hurt her but I didn't know why. I learned quickly enough because the kids at school must have asked their parents and the next day two or three of them wouldn't play with me. The bully kept yelling it at me and I ended up running into Mr. Appleby in tears. He was my first grade teacher and helped me get through his class and onto the second grade even then I had to get used to being the son of a fag.

Children are cruel little beings and when they get onto a way to discriminate they take it and explore ways of being kings of their own mountains. I had to go to that school for six years and there never was a time that I wasn't known as the fag's son. I was bigger than the rest of the kids and one day when I was in the fourth grade the bully, now a sixth grader, decided to really get to me. I fought him, got a terrible black eye out of the scrape but I also broke his nose. Grandma was called into the principle's office and I was suspended for three days. She never scolded me one second, just took me by the hand and out to the car and home. In fact she never said a word about it. She helped me make up the three days I'd missed so that I wasn't behind the class, and took me back to school on the fourth day.

By that time I knew what a fag was and I knew what Dad did in the room with the different guys he had stay there. Once in awhile he had a party and the rooms would be filled with men and some women who came together, music, dancing, and booze. I would stay in my room with the door locked because they would roam around the house. One day, that was before I learned to lock my door, two men came in, pushed me out of the bed onto the floor and did what I'd seen Dad and that guy do. It was disgusting and I slid over into the corner and hid my face but I couldn't keep from hearing the sounds they made. I told Grandma and she went to the police to see if they could keep me from having to go to my Dad's but they said it was a court order and he had his rights as a parent. She really had it in for the government after that.

When I got into high school it was in Union City and no one there knew that Troy was gay. He kept it pretty much under the table owning a local business and belonging to the Chamber of Commerce and several other organizations. By the time I moved into his house he was as wide as he was tall and had high blood pressure, took a handful of pills every day and didn't go to the shop very often. He was not well and I could have cared less. I often thought why hadn't it been him instead of my Grandmother.

I stayed away from Troy as much as possible, though I had to have dinner with him every night. It was an order and even though I was too old for him to slap me, he demanded I sit at the table with him and usually one of his boys. I never spoke to any of his gay friends if I could help it and if they started to carry on a conversation I left the table. I wasn't going to have anything to do with them and I let them know it. Troy would fight with me over it and one night slugged me pretty hard because I wouldn't talk to the new one who had moved in with him.

When Grandma was dying in the hospital she made me promise I would never miss a Sunday at church if I were able to attend and I promised her. I liked church and went to camp every summer. As I got older I became a swimming instructor, had a Red Cross life-saving badge and worked during the summer for church camp. I loved being out of doors and was leaning towards being a Youth Pastor and then Grandma passed and I had to go to Troy's because I was a minor.

Troy laughed at me every Sunday morning. I told him to mind his own business and that even though I had to live with him the minute I was of age I was out. He would laugh and tell me I'd be back when I had to support myself or when I wanted enough money to go to college. By then I knew I had enough money in the bank to take me through college. I never to this day have understood why he wanted me around. He didn't love me; he treated me like s—, and made cutting remarks to his boys about me being a sissy.

The day I turned sixteen he handed me the keys to a new car, with the insurance paid, and with the new car a checking account. It seemed he was trying to buy me. I thanked him for my car and checking account and knew better than to throw it back in his face; I'd done that once when he bought me a new T.V. for my room. I said I didn't need anything from him and found myself flat on the ground. I had a broken rib.

At the hospital they asked me how it happened and I told them. Troy laughed and said why would he ever hurt his only son. He told them I'd gotten mad at him because he wouldn't allow me to go out with a group of my friends and had tripped on the stairs. He put on his I'm-a-good-citizen look and said he didn't think the boys I was going with were the kind he wanted his son to be associated with and they bought his story.

I took the car and was secretly glad because it was an escape for me and I could care less what it cost him. I could go and come as I pleased without relying on the bus. It was freedom for me; I started attending Thursday night youth meeting at the church and never missed a Sunday morning. I was doing great in school and had decided seriously to be a Youth Pastor.

One Thursday night a kid from Meadville attended and let it be known I lived with a Dad who was gay and had other gay men in the house all the time, and what were they doing letting me have anything to do with the younger kids. I was a senior then and helping with CYU. I was graduating in June and was going to work at camp through the summer and then go to Seminary in the fall.

The pastor called me into his office the next day and told me he thought it was better if I didn't have anything to do with the younger kids. I told him the whole story and what I thought about Troy's life style but he said that appearances were important to the parents of the kids and it would be better if I didn't. My world fell apart. My future had been set in cement and now there was no future because the college asked for a statement from two elders and the pastor to qualify for entrance.

I went home that afternoon and if I hadn't had such strict training from my Grandmother I would have killed Troy and the creep that was living with us at the time, some young kid who needed the extra money Troy threw at him for bed-favors. I knew why these kids took to this nearly two-hundred and fifty pound tub of lard who had lost most of his hair and was red in the face from the booze and I figured pot as well. I felt sorry for them at times but stayed out of their way. Troy was there that afternoon and asked me to come into the office he had built at the side of the living room as sort of a parlor. He had all his office equipment in there and it had an outside door so that the men who worked in his salon didn't have to go through the house.

I sat down, hating even to look at him, crossed my legs and picked up a magazine hoping to ignore him. I was seething inside from my meeting with the pastor and was in no mood to put up with this man who had not only probably in a way killed my mother but had made life miserable for me.

"Damn you, look at me," was the way he started, "I have some things that you have to listen to and you're going to, hear me?" He was shaking. I figured his blood pressure was getting out of hand. Maybe if I made him mad enough he'd pop a blood vessel and that would be it

"You know I'm not a well man. Somebody is going to have to take over the business and it might as well be you, after all you are my son and whether you like it or not my heir. I had the lawyers draw up my will last summer and everything I have will go to you. Hell, it's about time you started earning it. I've never said much about money but the business, house, bonds, and bank account are worth over two million. The day you graduate you're going to come into the business with me sending you to Business College so you can do it right." He leaned onto his desk and held his head up as if it were too heavy for his neck.

Me go into his business, with all the men who worked for him being as gay as he was? There was no way I'd ever do that. Then it struck me like a bolt of lightning. I wasn't going to be a Youth Pastor, then just what was I going to do? I hadn't had time to digest what the pastor had said and now with this added to the problem my brain registered tilt.

"By the way I've never told you about your mother. Upstairs in the attic are all her things. There is a photograph album you may want to have. All that stuff is yours. I met her at a dance my first year in college and was blown over. Oh, yes, I was gay and even had a live-in lover at the time but there was something about her I couldn't get on top of. She went for me in a big way and we eloped to New York on spring break and tied the knot. She was living in the girl's dorm at Brown University and I was at my fraternity house. You know your grandparents were well-healed, lived in Boston with the rest of the hoity-toities and sent me to Yale. We kept our marriage a secret and I kept my lover. Obviously she got pregnant and was sent home. I sent her money but wasn't about to leave college."

I could tell he was tired but I didn't care, "How did she get into prison if she had money?"

"She started going with a guy from Pittsburgh after you were born. He turned out to be a gangster and she was in the car the day he held up a bank. They gave her four years because it was her first offense. I sent her enough money for a good attorney but she sent it back, damn her hide. I could have gotten her off. All it would have taken is money and a good lawyer and I had plenty of that and knew a good lawyer, but she wouldn't even use him." Then he did something that surprised me nearly as much as what the pastor had told me. He put his head down on the desk, into his arms, and blubbered like a baby.

I didn't know what to do. I'd never seen any emotion in this man as long as I'd known him, well not this kind of emotion. I'd seen him mad plenty of times and suffered the consequences. "What happened to her in prison?" I had to know.

"Some gal slit her throat because she wouldn't give out, but that was like her, that was like her." He repeated the statement shaking his head in sorrow it seemed, pushed himself out of his over-stuffed desk-chair and left the room. I could hear him laboring up the stairs and into his room. That was the first time in my life I had any feeling for Troy other than hate and being ashamed of him.

I went to the attic and found two chests and a cardboard box with her name on them. It was late that night when I had finally gone through everything. Most of the things were her clothes, she must have been very tiny because they looked like a little girl's clothes. The photograph album I took down to my room and looked through it carefully. I had never seen a picture of my mother. Grandma had put them all away and in her sorrow would not talk about her only daughter.

My mother was beautiful. She was tiny and had long black hair that fell to her waist. There was a professional colored picture showing that her eyes were very dark brown and had a look of kindness in them I couldn't get over. She had tan skin like Grandma's from the Italian in her background and a little Indian from what Grandma had told me of my heritage. There were many pictures of her and Troy, some showing very loving gestures, kissing, holding hands, and as I pored over every picture I could hear Grandma's words, "If she hadn't married your Dad she would be alive now."

Had she found out about Troy? How badly was she hurt when he left her to have me without him being there? Why had she been taken in by a crook? Was it in desperation, revenge? I felt such sorrow for her. How could he have treated her as he did? Why had he married her when he knew he was gay? There were a million questions in my mind. I was so totally exhausted from the emotions I'd had to handle all in one day I fell across the bed, fully clothed and went to sleep.

The next morning Troy wasn't in the breakfast room with his plate piled with eggs, bacon or sausage and rolls, and cups of coffee. I asked the housekeeper where he was and she said he had left early and he'd asked me to come to the salon as soon as I woke up. It was only a week from my graduation. I'd taken all my finals and I only had to check out at the library, clear my locker, go to the office to sign some papers all seniors were expected to sign, and that would be it.

Friday night was the senior prom. I had a date with Meg for that night. I'd ordered a corsage to be delivered to her house. Meg and I had dated a couple times. I never dated much because I didn't want to have to bring girls home with one of Troy's flakes around the house. No one at school knew about Troy and I didn't want them to know. I seldom went around with many kids because I didn't want them popping in. I was pretty much a lone, except at church and helping with the kids at camp. That was one reason I loved camp, a whole summer away from Troy.

Sunday afternoon was graduation, my cap and gown were in my closet, my shoes polished like glass and my suit brought back from the cleaners and hanging beside the gown, all ready for me to wear to a day I had looked forward to for a long time. It was the day I planned on escaping from this house. I'd even looked into a small storage unit to put my things in while I was at camp and through the next few years while I was in college. I wanted to break the chord and never come back.

I went to the salon and into Troy's office. I hardly ever went there. I didn't like the guys who worked there and I didn't like their clientele. Troy was sitting behind the desk and he looked terrible. He was a shade of yellow. I'd noticed his coloring for the last few months but figured it was his blood pressure.

"Sit down, Mason; I need to tell you something." He was so serious I decided not to argue with him but listen. He handed over a raft of papers and asked me to look at them. It was his power of attorney, and a copy of his will. Everything was in my name. I had no say about it. Everything he owned was mine. I couldn't take it all in. What was I to do with all these new responsibilities? It was overpowering.

"Where are you going, Troy, and why are you leaving me with all this?"

"Mason, I'm not going anywhere. I'm dying and from what the doctor told me last Monday I will be lucky if I have a month. It's time you took over your inheritance, so there it is. Do with it what you want. There is enough money to last you the best part of your life. Sell the salon if you want to. I could care less."

"What do you mean you're dying, why?" This was too much, all these papers there on the desk in front of me, and the man I had wished dead many times sitting there behind the desk telling me he was dying. "What am I going to do with all this? I don't know how to run a salon and I certainly don't know much about the rest of your investments?" I stood up and walked back and forth across the office like a caged lion, thinking there must be an escape some way out of this mess.

"Sit down, Mason, you're making me nervous. There is more I have to tell you." He pointed to the chair I had vacated. "You are also heir to my parents' estates in Boston. I've never shared it with you but they owned a great deal of property. It's being managed by a corporation but needs constant supervision. When I took the trips to Boston that is what I was doing, attending a board of directors meeting and visiting your Grandmother who was in a hospital. She passed away a year ago and left me her estate as well."

"Why didn't you ever take me with you to see my Grandmother?" Was this nightmare ever going to stop?

"The reason I didn't, Mason, is that she would not have known you. She was in a mental hospital completely insane, and had been ever since I was about eighteen. Your Grandfather took care of her all those years never missing a week, hoping daily she would come out of the fog and be herself once more. She never did, and until the day he died he loved her dearly." He sounded like a machine repeating memorized portions of some speech he had heard a million times.

"Mason, there is one other thing I've wanted to talk to you about. I know I've been a damn poor father, and I know you hate me and have for a long time. You're ashamed of my life style and hate the "boys" I've had living in the house. I've never been able to break away. You can't understand that. It's a hell of a life, Mason; for God's sake leave it alone. Don't even start. Don't try it out, get the hell away from it. You want to know what is killing me, well it's AIDS. Me, I thought I was smart, always used protection. Protection, hell, look at me, nothing's safe, Mason, not a damn things safe in this life." He was angry and pounded his fist on the desk.

Here was a man I didn't know. This side of Troy I'd never seen. I didn't know what to say. I just sat there watching and listening to the angry words of a dying man who happened to be my father.

"You won't believe me but I love you. You're the only thing I've ever given a shit about except your mother, and why, don't ask me. Me, who has spent his life going from one guy to another, who has told them I loved them, and then told the next one the same thing. Love, that wasn't love, Mason, that was just damn lust of some kind. Maybe it was a sense of power, I don't know. With your mother I felt a relationship that got into my guts. Maybe if I'd had the right training, or the right background, or even your church, maybe I would have left it alone and stayed true to Barbara, who knows? But I didn't and that's that."

"You love me. How can that be? I don't understand?" I was beginning to feel that nothing that was happening here was real.

"I guess its love. It sure beats what I felt for those, boys, as you call them. Sometimes I'd be so angry at you I'd strike out in anger because I knew what you were thinking and knew you hated being with me, but I wouldn't let go, I couldn't let you go, Mason. You are the only sanity I have to hold onto, you are real. I'm some kind of a flake. Maybe I'm even insane like my Mom? I just know that if what I feel for you is love then son I love you." He sat there and stared behind me. On the wall was a picture he had taken of me when I was around eight. He'd hired a pony and had a professional photographer take it and frame it. The picture had been on that wall ever since I could remember.

This man loved me. No wonder he'd never let Grandma have me. How could he have loved me and treated me the way he had? I didn't know that kind of love. I knew the kind Grandma and Nettie and Skitch gave but this kind was strange. How could he even call it love? Could it possibly be the only way he knew how to love? Can a man love a son and not do the very best for him possible?

"I know you can't understand that I love you, so forget it. I should have kept that to myself. It's my problem, not yours." He reached over answered the phone and turned back into a business man and the Troy I recognized.

Troy died about two week after the scene in his office. In fact it was only two or three days afterwards that he was in the hospital and never left it. His funeral was private and the casket was closed. I was the only speaker. When we read his instructions we were directed to follow a simple and singular plan. I was to speak and there was to be no flowers or any other show of farewell. I wondered if he didn't have it that way because there may not have been anyone else there.

I sold the salon, the house, and moved to Boston and my Grandparent's house. It was a big old family home near downtown Boston surrounded by a square block of gardens and was gated with a security guard. It had been kept in good repair by my Grandfather's directions in his will for Troy and for his children. I often wondered if his father knew the type of life his son lived.

There were family portraits on the walls of a long hall that had eight bedroom doors interrupting their procession. In the library a photo album listed enough names to introduce me to some of the faces hanging on the wall. Most of the portraits were very old and I had no idea who they were. The album also told of some who had come from England in 1870 and bought up a great deal of Boston. One of my great uncles was the minister of the Presbyterian Church in Boston and another uncle was a judge. The rest had nothing written about them, only their names, wives and children.

Caring for everything that Troy left me to manage took up nearly every waking moment. I was on several boards and had little time to actually think where I was going or even why. I was just reaching my twenty-first birthday, had a full-time job, and hated every moment of it. I was empty, making money, but empty. I hadn't been to church for nearly a year when one day I opened the Boston paper and saw a picture of a new church being built in the downtown area. It would be about four blocks from my house and I thought that would be handy. I was feeling guilty having broken my promise to my Grandmother. But I had been so bitter over what happened the year I graduated that I was angry at the church and anyone connected with it.

Every day I walked by the site of that church on my way to the office. I walked because I had remembered how fat Troy had gotten and I didn't want to follow his pattern. Even though I was so much taller I still felt I could put on a few inches in the wrong places if I weren't careful. I would stop and watch the men building every morning, counting the floors and silently supervising the men in their hats and hammers and drills.

Eventually the building was finished and I attended the opening. My curiosity had to be satisfied. It was beautiful inside and the choir was absolutely perfect. The pastor that spoke told us about Christ's love and how He came for every sinner walking the streets of Boston and if any of us thought that didn't mean us we were out on a limb and Satan was carefully chopping it off. He was funny and clever and filled with ways of getting us to look carefully into a mirror. I walked home and ate a cold lunch. I always let the servants off on Sunday, and at least Grandma would have praised me for that.

I got into the habit of attending every Sunday morning. I was beginning to get over the bitterness. Every week Pastor Newhouse shook hands and asked how I was, and one Sunday morning asked if he could visit me. I invited him to my house for dinner the following Wednesday night and found myself looking forward to company, something I hadn't had since I'd moved into my grandparents' house.

The Pastor was prompt and we had an enjoyable dinner. We adjourned to the library for coffee and shared a few bits of political information. I told him what I did and then he commented on my age and the house. Then he quietly asked me if I would like to share why I was so bitter. I was utterly shocked at his remark and made some dumb comment about why he think thought I was bitter. Without blinking an eye he said he had watched me and was sad I was so lonely. He told me my expressions had no joy or happiness in them.

Like an adolescent kid I blurted out practically all that I have shared with you. The pastor did not move or speak until I'd finished. I came to several closes and then repeated or added more, each time remembering something else. It seemed I had to get every little feeling and happening out until I knew he understood, so the more I repeated the more I added. He sat there with his head lowered, acting as if he had seen his hands for the first time in his life. He never changed his position. I must have talked for over an hour, repeating over and over those parts that had hurt me the worst or when I had been the angriest.

I went over and over my feelings for Troy. Strangely, the more I repeated the more I needed to repeat and I found myself calling Troy my Dad. I had no idea why that was. Sadness began to replace anger in me after telling it so often and my feelings began to soften towards Troy. Somehow I began to understand the pastor and his concern for the children I was teaching at summer camp, and his hurt in having to tell me I couldn't work with the kids.

When I was finally totally emotionally wrung out I sat very quietly. Pastor Newhouse still didn't move or talk. We sat in silence. It was getting dark in the room; I didn't even get up and turn on the light. It was summer and the days were long. The wide library doors opened onto a patio and a large rose garden someone had started a long time before I moved in. The smell of roses and the summer warmth surrounded us both and it was pleasant and I liked the way I felt.

"Mason, I'm glad you have shared this with me. Now we can become friends and you can start making plans for your future." He raised his head and smiled at me that same sweet smile I'd seen on my Grandmother's face so many times when she had finished scolding me for something I had done that had hurt her.

"My future? I have no future but taking care of all these things that have been left for me to do."

"No, Mason, you have school to attend so you can become a youth pastor and eventually the senior pastor you have dreamed of all your life, and you have a promise to fulfill that you made to your Grandmother." He stood and walked through the open doors out onto the patio that allowed us a small breeze. I followed him and we both sat on wicker chairs.

That was nearly fifteen years ago while I was in school. I managed to hire a corporation to handle the business until it was all sold. I kept the house and there was plenty of money to keep it up. My plan was someday to marry and bring up my family with their ancestors looking down on them. That may come in time for Mason Jr. and any brothers and sisters who come along. My location is across the country from Boston.

My first call was to a small town in the Midwest where I met Crystal and where she became Mrs. Ashton and the mother of my son. I have been a pastor now for several years and when I stand in the pulpit I remember my Grandmother and would have liked to have looked down and seen her face looking at me with pride. And way down deep my one sadness is that my Dad never knew what it meant to have the peace that passes understanding.

This interview was taken over the phone, so I didn't have an opportunity to see Mason. After I turned off the tape, I still needed some questions answered.

"Mason, what are your plans concerning homosexuality or is that a subject you seldom talk about to your parishioners?" I wondered if his background had influenced his pulpit.

"Presently, I direct a program for gay and lesbian people needing help. We are connected with an international organization and attend their conferences and use a great deal of their material. I have just started a program for young people this year and am excited at how it is answering their questions and helping them. We are thinking of adding other sections which will include programs for any kind of sexual brokenness out there, and also one for people who have AIDS."

He sounded excited and a little bit like he was preaching. I had a feeling things were going down the right path after he had control of his life.

I thanked him for his time and he thanked me for asking him to share his life. I'm planning on traveling this summer and will stop by, hopefully, on a Sunday and get to know him face to face.

9

"I Didn't Understand"

TOMORROW I WAS GOING TO BE MARRIED to the nicest and kindest man I'd ever known except my Dad, whom I'd adored ever since I could remember. Tomorrow, at exactly eleven o'clock in the Middlewest Presbyterian Church, my Dad was giving me away. My name would be changed from Elizabeth Maria Armstrong to Mrs. Gerald Arthur Pence. Everybody called me Tazz. How they got that out of Elizabeth is a mystery but somehow, for as long as I could remember, I have been Tazz to my Dad and three older brothers.

When I was born the Lord left me and took my mother in exchange. I thought it was unfair but Daddy told me God knew what He was doing and it wasn't nice to tell Him differently. I had a hard time because I know how much Daddy loved my mother, but then Daddy was God's right hand man and knew things other people didn't. Whenever I had a problem Daddy always knew the answer. I was in love with Gerry but I loved my Dad—it is funny how you can love differently—and then there were the three musketeers, each brother about two years apart.

I was eighteen, then Nelson, twenty, Meyer, twenty three, Vincent, twenty five, and my Dad, Brogan, going on fifty. He had been going on fifty for a couple of years and reminded us that he would be going on fifty until he got smart enough to tell people he was half a century old. I never quite understood all of that, but as four of us laughed each time we gave him a surprise birthday party he repeated his plan of advancement as he called it.

I loved my Dad's name. It made him sound like an Irish chief or something. I saw a Celtic picture once where the main character was named Brogan McKenna. The story was how he saved the town of Brenner from the English. If I ever had a son I was going to name him Brogan after my Dad and his middle name would be McKenna. It sounded so noble and brave.

Married! In about fifteen hours I'd be married and on my way to Niagara Falls. Several of my girl friends had gotten married. Some went to Hawaii, but Cathleen and Robert went to Vancouver B.C. and then up to Banff. I'd always wanted to see the falls and Gerry told me I could pick so I did. Dad and my Mother had gone there and I wanted to see it. At least I could see where she went even if I would never see her until I went to heaven. I always wondered how I would know, her but Daddy had shown me lots of pictures and he assured me she would know me immediately because I looked a great deal like her Mother who was there with her. I guess when I went to heaven I'd see a lot of relatives.

The three boys were going to be in the wedding. I laughed at them because they were older and I was the first to leave the house. I knew that Daddy was sad because being the only girl he would miss me terribly but Gerry and I were going to live in the same town and I'd see my brothers and Dad everyday I wanted to. Gerry was the high school principle at Lincoln High School on Alder Street. He'd been there for a year before we met at a church camp helping with the kids. I'd been teaching some girls to swim and he was teaching the boys. Everyday at the same time we used the pool, I was at one end and he and his boys at the other. We started dating that summer and by fall were going steady. Now it was June and not even a whole day until the minister would pronounce us man and wife.

I was a virgin and proud of it. The four boys, I always called them my four boys, even though one was my Dad, were sort of responsible. Whenever I dated I always knew that behind the scenes one of the boys had instructed my date about the facts of dating their sister. It was a wonder any boy ever asked me for a date, but plenty did. Eleven o'clock was my deadline and Daddy would always be in the front room with all the lights on including the porch light waiting for me. I felt special and loved.

Sometimes all four of them would be sitting playing cards, or Daddy and Vincent would be playing chess and Nels and Meyer would be watching T.V. or have the backgammon board between them arguing over a play. Nelson and Meyer were always arguing. They were the youngest until I came along and I didn't count because I was a girl and was under the protection of them all. Poor Gerry had to pass inspection from them all. How he made it is a mystery because no one was good enough for their Tazz. Now I would have five men of my own and it felt pretty wonderful.

The girls at school always wanted to come to my house because of the three boys who were all at least six feet. After all Daddy was six feet two. And they all had black curly hair like my mother. I had blondish red hair, pretty straight, like my Dad's. I had pale blue eyes and almost black eyelashes and eyebrows. The boys had brown eyes and tan skin like Mother. Next to my very white skin it made them look like Indians when they got tanned in the summer. I burned, pealed and burned again.

One summer I went swimming without my sun screen and got such a bad burn I landed in the hospital overnight. Daddy was furious. He'd told me over and over to take my sun screen. I was with a bunch of Girl Scouts and having so much fun I forgot to use it. I never forgot again. The boys were such darlings when I came home from the hospital. They were right beside my bed and got me anything I wanted. I know I was pretty spoiled but Daddy kept such a tight reign I don't think I was obnoxious. He wouldn't let the boys go overboard and there were even times the boys took sides with me against him, but he would win and I always ended up doing what he had told me to do.

Gerry was on the phone but the boys wouldn't let me talk to him. There was some type of a mystic about the groom seeing the bride or talking to her the day before the wedding. I tried to get the phone away from Nelson but he was taller and kept it from me. Nels was my favorite. I guess, being closer to my age we had a little more in common. He was the one who teased me the most but when the other boys would start to tease he would take my side. Nels was in his sophomore year in college. Meyer was graduating this coming year and Vincent, already working with

Daddy, was planning on going back to get a doctorate this fall. Vincent was the smartest one of us all and was planning to be a psychiatrist like Daddy. He didn't want to work with prisoners as Daddy did but for the state at different mental facilities.

Daddy was on staff at the Federal prison between our town and highway seven. We lived in Williamsburg. The prison was exactly seven miles from our front door and seven miles south to Jacksonville. Daddy was the government's psychiatrist and pretty important. He was called by different organizations all over the state for conferring with psychologists and counselors on different cases. Meyer was going to be an engineer and Nels didn't know what he was going to be. Me, no college for me. I was going to be a housewife and a mother.

Daddy had tried to tell me what marriage was all about but Aunt Maggie sat me down and told me all the gory details and seemed to have fun doing it. Aunt Maggie wasn't Daddy or my Mother's sister. She was a neighbor and had, in a way, helped raise us with some kind of cleanliness and good manners. She was about Daddy's age and married to Williamsburg's chief of police, another reason the boys got through their teens without any public display of male passage problems.

Uncle Ben and Aunt Maggie lived across the street and didn't have any children except us. We were in her house as much as our own; in fact there were times all of us would be plunked around her table for dinner and many nights in one of their five bedrooms curled up and dreaming. She loved me best of all because when she and Uncle Ben were first married they lost a little girl, and since she could never have any more children I sort of became hers by proxy. Daddy didn't mind. He said many a time that girls needed a woman around and Aunt Maggie was all girl. He would tease her and he and Uncle Ben were best friends.

Uncle Ben would tease Daddy about sharing Aunt Maggie with him but only up to a point. Daddy would pick Aunt Maggie up and twirl her around and set her right down on Uncle Ben's lap and all three would laugh. Aunt Maggie and my Mother were the best of friends before God exchanged us. She was only about five feet tall, the shortest of all of us, and wouldn't tip a hundred pounds with apples in her pocket as Ben would say. She wore a size smaller than I did. I was about five seven and had a neat figure. I wasn't fat, but firm and curved in just the right places. Gerry had told me I was just right. He was as tall as my Dad and had deep auburn hair that sort of curled around in the back where it met his collar. He had blue eyes like mine and when he was upset they almost turned a deep green.

His parents were coming for the wedding and would be in around six o'clock. They were going to stay with Aunt Maggie. She'd invited them and was doing so much for the wedding you would think she was my Mother. In a way she was, she'd taken me home from the hospital only three days old and had taken care of me until I was old enough to stay with Daddy and the boys. I was four when the big day came and I moved across the street into my own room. She missed me terribly and I her but I was in her house so much and she popping in to see that everything was all right in mine that I guess we never really moved away from each other.

Mr. and Mrs. Pence lived in Jacksonville where Gerry grew up. His younger sister Carla was in college and arriving on the eight-fifty-five plane. Vincent was going to pick her up. She was staying across the street too. Gerry was living in our new house on Baker Drive that overlooked Lake Cushman. Our lawn went right down to the lake and Gerry had built a dock. We were going to buy a motor boat and some skies. We were both sports minded and loved to ski, play golf, hike and camp out. Of course every time we had camped out at least two of the boys had been with us or Daddy. I wondered what it was going to like to be with Gerry alone.

Every minute brought the marriage closer. I was going to be Gerry's wife and be alone with him and in bed with him. I was getting a little worried about the alone in bed bit. All we had ever done was some heavy petting. Aunt Maggie had told me everything that would happen and I supposed it would be O.K., since all married people did it and there were a lot of married people. I couldn't imagine Daddy doing such a thing but then he was older and single so he didn't count.

I hadn't seen the Mr. and Mrs. Pence. They'd gone straight to Aunt Maggie's. She'd fixed dinner for them. They knew each other even before Gerry and I started going together. The ladies at church had dinner for us and Gerry was out with a batch of bachelors who were treating him to his last night of freedom, as they called it. Daddy suggested I pop into bed early so I would be wide awake in the morning. He said it would be a long day with the wedding, reception, and the drive to the Falls. Gerry had reserved a room at one of the hotels there. He'd even gotten the wedding suite.

There was no way I could go to sleep. My mind wouldn't shut down. I heard the Grandfather clock strike one and then two. I must have dosed because the next thing I knew Aunt Maggie was shaking my shoulders and telling me to get up, that this was the day, and I needed to get into the shower, fix my hair get on my wedding dress and get ready to go to church. Mrs. Pence and Carla came in just as Aunt Maggie was putting the wedding dress down over my head. When they saw it they oohed and awed quite appropriately. It was a beautiful dress. White satin with little bead pearls woven into the cuffs, around the neck, and down the back of a train that went out quite a ways. I felt like a princess at her first ball.

Holding onto Daddy's arm I was walking down the aisle towards Gerry who waited for me at the alter. Daddy handed me to Gerry. We stood before the minister as he read the marriage ceremony, and then we said our wedding vows, promising to be faithful to each other forever. Our wedding day must have been made in heaven as everything was perfect.

The reception was held in the church basement. I cut a beautiful cake, fed the first piece to Gerry, danced the first dance with him, the second with my Dad, then all three boys, and finally Uncle Ben who hugged me with tears in his eyes. I knew how much they all loved me and felt as if God had sent me a special blessing. I prayed my Mother was watching and knew how happy this day would have made her. I always felt her near, in my imagination I suppose, but I really didn't believe it was just that for her presence was too strong.

Soon I was upstairs in one of the Sunday School rooms changing into traveling clothes. We ran out of the church. I threw my bouquet and Lynn, the church secretary, caught it. She was over fifty and a widower. Oh, well, maybe she would be next. The church janitor was known to clean her office more carefully than all the other rooms.

The drive to the falls was wonderful. Gerry put the top down on his convertible and we sang and laughed and acted as I supposed all newly weds acted. It was after ten when we reached the hotel and as I signed my new name for the first time it all became very real. I was truly married. Right there in the hotel lobby I broke into tears like an idiot but before anyone could see the tears I turned my face and quickly grabbed the new lace hanky Aunt Maggie had crocheted for me and pretended I had something in my eye.

At the door of the room Gerry picked me up and carried me over the threshold. I was back in fairy-tale land with all the trimmings. The room had several bouquets of flowers with cards which told me everyone at the wedding knew where we were at this moment, and knew what we would be doing. I felt embarrassed but figured they were all married so what the heck.

Gerry held me in his arms and kissed me long and tenderly. I knew the time had come as the butterflies in my stomach turned to chickens. To explain what happened that night is hard. I don't understand and I really didn't even know who could help. Aunt Maggie'd told me all about men and women and how things were supposed to go but nothing happened as she said. I went into the bathroom and put on the beautiful silk night gown Aunt Maggie and I had picked out at a very exclusive shop. When I got into bed Gerry was sitting on a large love seat in front of the windows covered with red-velvet drapes. He looked funny and then I thought maybe he was a little scared too. I smiled at him and said I loved him. He went into the bathroom and came out in a nice looking pair of pajamas and got into bed.

He stayed on his side of the bed for the longest time and then reached over and pulled me into his arms and kissed me several times, then jumped out of bed and went into the bathroom where he stayed for what seemed forever. He came back into bed and told me he loved me and held me again. Eventually he made love to me, but the moment we finished he left the bed and didn't come back to bed until after I was asleep. The whole thing was so disappointing, and I felt terrible, all the butterflies were still there and I didn't understand one bit what was wrong.

We stayed for a week and had fun during the day but at night it was terrible. He made love to me one other night and then said he was sorry, and that things would be better as we got to know each other. I was beginning to feel there was something wrong with me, and I was petrified I had done something wrong. Our drive home was pretty silent. I just didn't know what to say.

Dad and the boys had moved me into my new house while we were gone, and from the way things were placed I knew Aunt Maggie had had a hand in the move. We got home on a Saturday afternoon. I couldn't wait to see the four boys, and I needed Aunt Maggie terribly. Daddy and the boys weren't at home so I rushed across the street and there was Aunt Maggie with her arms out and all her love showing in her eyes.

"What's wrong, Tazz?" She knew something was wrong as she had all my life when I was unhappy. She could read me like a book, as they say.

"Oh, Auntie, I must have done something terribly wrong." Then I shared with her what the honeymoon nights had been like and burst into tears.

Aunt Maggie didn't say a word. She just held me, then quietly she asked, "Did Gerry ever push for intercourse before you were married?" I was shocked, "Of course not, you know I was a virgin."

She then asked a hundred questions. How had he kissed? Did he do certain things? And when she was finished she just held me and said not to worry that maybe he was a virgin as well and didn't quite know the ropes.

I popped back over the street and there were my four boys. They all hugged me at once and especially Daddy. He took me into his office and sat me down on our "let's talk" davenport. All during my growing up whenever there was a discussion about school work, or actions, or anything of importance it was to this davenport I had gone. The boys shared the same davenport and when someone was in the office with Daddy there was never to be an interruption from any of the rest of us. It had to be a pretty serious thing to knock on the sliding doors which separated Daddy's office from the living room.

"So, little one, how do you like married life?" He patted my knee and had a twinkle in his eyes as he spoke. I was so emotionally wrung out from being with Aunt Maggie I just couldn't pretend so he wouldn't be worried. I burst into tears and moved into his arms that had held me safe since I could remember. I told him the whole thing and when I'd finished he said not to worry. He guessed Gerry was just new at marriage and things would get better. There was a look on his face I couldn't understand, a look I couldn't read. Almost every look my Daddy had I knew the reason. This one was new and it wasn't a pleasant look.

I went home after being teased by the boys and Gerry was waiting for me. We had dinner in the new dining room and after some T.V. went to bed. The house had four bedrooms and I was so surprised when he asked me if I would like to have my own room.

"I thought married people shared the same room, Gerry?" All at once I didn't know this man who was sharing my bed. Who was he? Not the man I had been going with. Not the man who had made me feel that I was the most special thing in the world.

"I just thought you might like some privacy, dear. Many married people have their own rooms and I would understand if you would like to have your own." By then he was standing by the window which looked down on the garden and pool.

"I'll move into one of the other rooms tomorrow," I whispered, hoping he would immediately tell me that he wanted me near him and was just asking. I thought he would take me in his arms and demand I never move out of his sight. It didn't happen, he just got back into bed, kissed me good night, turned over and went to sleep.

The next day I was moving things into the back bedroom that looked out on the mountains when I heard someone come in the front door. Aunt Maggie burst into the room before I could hide what I was doing.

"What do you think you are doing, Tazz?" She took some underthings out of my hand I'd been putting into a bureau and turned me around to face her, "What is going on in this, house young lady?" When Aunt Maggie used that tone I knew there was no getting out of a full explanation. As we both set on the bed I was going to be using from now on I confided in her the scene between Gerry and me the night before.

"Something has to be done, my dear;. I think your new husband and I are going to have a talk." I knew it would do no good for me to protest. You didn't disagree with Aunt Maggie when she set that square jaw of hers and gritted her teeth. I knew I shouldn't have told her, but all my life she'd been my shield and protector, just like the four boys and Uncle Ben. I was the baby and the only girl in the lives of six people. I'd lived under their protection all my life. This was no time to climb out on a limb by myself, especially when I hadn't a clue as to what the trouble could be.

Nothing changed that night. Gerry kissed me good night in the hall as if this was the thing to do, almost as a duty, and we both went in the opposite directions to bed. He was up and out of the house before I got out of bed. I'd spent half the night in tears. And so the routine started. He off to work before I got up. My day filled with house work, the four boys, and a daily visit to Aunt Maggie who seemed to have completely overlooked our conversation. This was so unlike her that I felt perhaps even she was blaming me for whatever I had done wrong to have turned my husband into a stranger who lived in the same house.

A couple weeks went by and not a word. I had resigned myself to the routine and figured that my life was over as far as true happiness. How could such a perfect wedding have turned out this way? One afternoon Uncle Ben drove up and popped in while I was having a cup of tea. After our regular hugs he asked for a cup too. He'd never stopped long enough in the day time to set and chat, not as busy as he was. I poured his tea and watched as he dropped several teaspoons of sugar into the cup and stir it.

"Uncle Ben, if Aunt Maggie saw you use that much sugar you'd get it," I scolded him.

"Well, my dear, she isn't watching so I'm goin' to enjoy this cup of tea my way." he laughed and put one more drop of sugar in for emphasis.

"Pumpkin, we need to talk." Whenever Uncle Ben was serious he called me pumpkin. I knew there was something wrong and became a little frightened. Whenever Uncle Ben talked seriously it was always about something bad or worse. I put my cup down and waited.

"Do you know what a homosexual is, dear?" He reached over and touched my hand.

"Sure, they talked about it in Sunday school and said Christians try not to act that way."

"You're havin' trouble with Gerry, aren't you? Aunt Maggie shared what you said the other day and I've been checking on something that has been worrying me. He stood up and started to pace, Uncle Ben was a pacer and it usually drove Aunt Maggie crazy.

"Tazz, your husband is gay, and has been for a long time. Why he married you I can only guess. As a principle of a school, and a member of the church, he needed to look proper and so he married you. Brogan and the boys don't know yet, but Aunt Maggie does and will be here before long. I told her I was stopping by today."

I was stunned. I had married a homosexual. I was living with a man who only was attracted to other men, at least that was what the teacher had said. We never talked about things like that at home. Daddy said there were some things that were best left unsaid in mixed company, and then he would always laugh and call me his little mixer. What was I supposed to do now? I had no idea how you lived with a man like Gerry.

"Uncle Ben, what am I going to do?" He was one of my protectors. he'd know.

"Pumpkin, I'm not certain just what we're all going to do? Let's wait for Aunt Maggie. I called Brogan and he's coming too. We won't share this with the boys for right now.

Uncle Ben had poured me a new cup of hot tea and told me the best thing to do was just to wait until the family had a council. By the time Aunt Maggie and Daddy got there I was a basket case. Uncle Ben told them why he had asked them to come. Daddy came unglued and Aunt Maggie just sat there with tears streaming down her face mumbling something about why her baby?

The next few hours are a little out of my memory. I felt I had been lied to and tricked. I'd gone into marriage a virgin, proud I had saved myself for the one special man that God would bring to me. How could I have been so wrong? It must have been my choice. God would never play this kind of a trick on anyone? We were all sitting in the kitchen when Gerry came home. The moment he walked in and saw all of us sitting there he knew something was wrong. He just stood in the doorway and didn't say a word. Then he walked over to me and almost whispered, "What's wrong, Tazz, is it one of the boys?"

Daddy came over and took him by the arm and asked him to sit down. He said there was something he wanted to ask him. When Daddy asked him if he was a homosexual, Gerry didn't say a word he just shook his head. I exploded, "Why did you marry me, why, why did you lie to me and spoil my whole life, oh, Gerry, why?"

Gerry looked at me and said, "I married you because I'd learned to love you and thought I could stop. I really thought I could handle it." He sat down at the table next to me and put his head into his hands and muffled out, "I'd never loved anyone until you came into my life, and I thought I loved you enough to get away." He broke into a sob and then stood up and almost yelled at all of us, "Every time I held you in my arms to make love to you I was filled with guilt that I couldn't be the man I wanted to be to you. Oh, God, forgive me, forgive me." He almost fell back into the chair next to me, and then he put his head down on the table and sobbed.

Uncle Ben went over to him and touched him on the shoulder. "Gerry were you really serious about not being gay anymore, I mean damn-gut serious?"

"Ben, there's no way out, no way out. I'll give Tazz a divorce and anything she wants. I know I don't deserve to be forgiven but

I really thought I could handle it. I really did. I want you to know I have been faithful to her. I've not touched another person since the day we got married." He looked up from the table and there was truth on his face.

My heart was breaking. I loved this man so much I couldn't stand to see him hurting. He really did love me. "Oh, Gerry, why didn't you tell me? Maybe we could have worked it out together. I just didn't understand why you kept rejecting me when you said you loved me?"

"Oh, Tazz, I wasn't rejecting you. You were so sweet and pure and giving. All I could think of was how guilty I was even getting next to you. How could I touch you and know that I was gay and had done things I won't even talk about. How could I touch you knowing all this?" Gerry got up and walked over to my Dad.

"Brogan, can you forgive me for ruining your daughter's life and yours? I'll walk out and just maybe things can go back the way they were before I started spoiling everything. There is one thing I want you to know. I love Tazz with all my heart and will for the rest of my life, even if I'm not good enough for her." He started out the door. I couldn't let him go. I loved him.

"Gerry, wait, oh, Gerry, I love you, can't we work this out someway. Oh, Gerry I love you." I put my arms around him and held him to me. He held me back so tight I could hardly breathe. "Gerry, there must be a way out of this whole thing."

I turned to the one person who was the right hand of God as far as I was concerned, "Daddy can't you make this better?" I thought if anyone could fix this Daddy could.

My office was filled with several people you already know: Tazz and Gerry Armstrong, Aunt Maggie and Uncle Ben, Brogan now a little over a century old, a rather attractive lady, and Vincent. I wondered where Nelson and Meyer were? I was introduced to the young lady as Vincent's wife, Effie, who was visibly pregnant.

"I see you're still married, Tazz. What happened in your life? I know it must be good or you wouldn't be here sharing it with me."
I was anxious to hear how the family had settled the problem.

Brogan became the spokesman for the group as I expected he would.

"We all put out heads and hearts together to help Gerry. Being a psychiatrist I knew about a homosexual counselor who was associated with a group working with ex-homosexuals. He was a Christian counselor and we got Gerry into one of his groups immediately. It has not been easy, as Gerry can tell you, but we surrounded and walked with him and I guess you'll just have to ask the kids what they think."

Gerry stood up and came over to the desk. "No, it hasn't been easy coping with such a heavy load of guilt and not always looking away when I see a handsome man or am hit on. But whenever I feel a little weak, I give one of my family a call and we go out for coffee."

He walked around the other side of the desk and continued, "You know I thought I was a Christian but I could never really believe it living an active gay life. Oh, there was a church I could have gone to that would accepted it but I knew deep down I didn't really believe what they said the Bible said. I'd been brought up reading the Bible and attending church, and every time I came to the passages about homosexuality I felt guilty, so I never read those parts. I just pretended they weren't there."

Standing up and putting her arms around Gerry, Tazz said, "Gerry gave his whole heart to the Lord about a year ago and now he really knows who he belongs to: God, me, and our daughter."

"You have a little girl, Tazz?" I asked.

"Yes, that is why Nelson isn't here. He's home playing Uncle, and Meyer felt he needed help, so they are both doing their Uncle thing. They can't gang up on me anymore, but now they have a new little niece."

Gerry held Tazz close and I could see the love and kindness that showed on his face.

"So all is well with you and yours, Tazz?" I joyfully acknowledged.

It wasn't just Tazz who answered. It seemed they all pitched in.

Brogan was the last one out of the office. He shook my hand and told me that what he couldn't fix God could so everything was always going to be alright.

10

"There Must Be a Way Out"

LOOKING BACK THERE IS ONE GLARING FACTOR that has shadowed me for over thirty eight years. Maybe even further back than that if I could put a date on the first time I felt life was a burden and that there must be a way out of my life and a way into the life I thought other people lived. Some where I must have missed something because I never felt as if I belonged to anybody or anything. Growing up was sad, as I see it now. Oh, I know I am looking back and others who lived with me and around me would perhaps not agree. But this is how I feel and after all it is me and my feelings and my life we are talking about.

My Father and Mother were good middle class, church-going, non-drinking, non-smoking, non-dancing, non-card playing, non-swearing, people. They paid taxes and blessed the country they paid them to. Neither one had been arrested or even ticketed for speeding. In fact I doubt they had bad thoughts, and if they did they definitely never said them. I never heard either one of them say anything disrespectful about another person. They didn't know how to gossip.

My grandfather, Floyd Undem, married my grandmother, Toura Vanogle, and took her into an old three bedroom, run-down parsonage in Meridian and there she had both my father, Philip, and his sister, Hazel, and then she died, I do believe, out of sheer boredom. Grandpa Undem raised the two young ones with the help of the widows in his congregation and seldom knew which widow had which child or for how long. My grandfather hardly knew his own children. Once when all the Sunday school classes sang during a morning service and the boys were in the back row pinching some of the girls, he called my father by the wrong name.

My parents were both uninteresting and grey. Mother wore either a grey or black dress and Dad wore a dark blue-grey suit, and the three of us kids sat between our parents in the third row back on the left hand side of the church sanctuary every Sunday morning. In fact if you go there today and sit in that row you will find a hymn book with my name scribbled on the back page in blood. You can hardly read the word "Philip," but you can tell its blood. Each of us boys— there were no girls in our family— made a pack to prick his finger and smear his name in blood in a hymn book to frighten away Satan and his angels. We had to do it so that our parents couldn't see us and figured if we held the hymn book with one hand and pricked our finger with the needles we took out of Mother's sewing kit we could write our names before the blood quit running. Carl, three years younger than me, pricked his finger, but Nick, two years younger than Carl, was a chicken.

Nick was a chicken all his life and Carl and I teased him for being a mamma's boy. I guess I was about nine when we desecrated the hymn books, Carl six, and Nick four. Each Sunday we'd look at the page where our blood had been sacrificed and gloated at Nick. The sissy cried one Sunday morning and told on us so we both received a whipping that Sunday afternoon. We got back at him by putting a sheet over our heads and scaring the piss out of him one night. Got another whipping with Dad's razor strap but it was worth it, since it made Nick wet his bed.

Dad was a butcher and Mom stayed at home and took care of us and most of the rest of the people in the church. Grandpa was our preacher until he had a stroke one Sunday morning on his way to church. Then a new man came who was younger and had "upstart ideas" according to Father. Mother scolded him for using such words in front of us boys. "I declare," she said, "you certainly must watch your tongue, Floyd Undem." We boys were astonished at him for saying it and for Mother scolding him. We were to always call him Father, and were not allowed to speak at the table unless we were spoken to.

Before evening grace was said we had to sit quietly and contemplate our day, looking for any sin we committed or made by mistake. If there was anything we had done incorrectly we were to confess it so Father could include it in the dinner prayer. It was always to our benefit to find something he could pray about. If we didn't find a fault then we would receive a lecture on how there was no one in this world who did not sin and if we had too much pride to confess our weaknesses then that in itself was a sin. There was no way out, it seemed, for us. We could never be good enough and if we were that was wrong as well.

Sometimes the meal got chilled waiting for Father's prayer to be finished. We hated it when Grandpa came for Sunday dinner because when he prayed it went on and on. He preached two sermons one at church and another one at our dinner table. Father always addressed him as Sir and after the prayer would commend his understanding. While we were waiting for the Amen, Carl and I would kick each other under the table as hard as we could knowing that we wouldn't dare make a sound or we'd go without our meal. The harder we'd kick the braver we thought ourselves to be. Nick sat at the end next to Mother and was too far for our legs to reach.

Contact with Father was at the table, night prayers, and morning prayers. Beside a long-meal time prayer we were always called into the parlor for morning prayers and before we went to bed we had night prayer. Never once were we sent to bed with a hug and a kiss, only a "Good night boys, see that you go straight to bed and with no conversation." Mother would mimic his words and seldom even looked up from her Bible to say it.

Father worked six days a week from eight in the morning until six each evening. Holidays were spent quietly and seldom were we allowed to play out of doors with the rest of the kids. I had to practice the piano after school and Carl the violin. Mother taught us both. She was a very good musician but seldom played except to teach us. Nick had to play the piano when he was old enough which meant my hour was after his. We spent a great deal of our time in our rooms doing home work and in the summer Father left home work for us to finish before he arrived home Monday through Friday. Saturdays we were responsible for the yard. Once a year we had to paint the fence, and each week we washed the windows on the outside of the house. Father told us that having clean windows was a good example to the neighborhood as it demonstrated that cleanliness was a Christian virtue.

At the table we were to sit straight without touching the backs of our chairs, to use a napkin correctly, and to chew each bite twenty times. If we wished something more than what Father placed on our plates, we were to ask politely. We were never to enter into a conversation he and Mother were having which generally was rather one-sided as Mother seldom spoke. If there were guests at the table we were never to ask for second helpings as our parents felt it would presume on their guests to have the children making conversation during dinner. We always had plenty of food and good clothes as Father was the only butcher in town. He had two men who worked for him, Old Billy, who cleaned up the store and put new sawdust down behind the counter where they cut the meat, and Jason Waterbury, who worked Friday afternoons and Saturdays.

Old Billy was deaf and when you wanted him to hear you, you had to stand right in front of him and make your mouth say the words very carefully because he read lips. This fascinated us boys and we took any chance we could to visit the shop. When I turned eight I worked in the shop after school which meant I'd walk home with Father usually in silence. The minute I got home and finished dinner I had to do my hour at the piano and then my school work. The only time we got to play was at school during recess and at lunch time.

None of us had the benefit of a Father who demonstrated love. He was a disciplinarian not only to us but to our Mother as well. She would simply say, "Yes, Mr. Undem," and go about obeying his directions. I never heard her initiate a conversation that didn't have something to do with the care of us boys or something about the house. She spent a lot of her day visiting those in the church who were ill and doing what she could for them. She told us boys that it was her Christian duty, and there was no way she would ever shirk that which was expected of her. I can't remember Mother smiling, nor Father, even at each other.

Father was never unkind and was always absolutely just in everything that concerned our lives. He considered fun an open door for the Devil and any type of game inconsistent with the Scriptures. We boys had to memorize a Scripture passage each week and write an essay on sin and other Scriptural subjects constantly. If we were disobedient we had to sit on a stool in the corner of the living room and read a whole chapter of the Bible which Father would assign, and then write a four page essay on what it meant. By the time I was ten or so I probably had read every book in the Bible several times. When I was punished I always hoped for the Old Testament because there were some pretty good stories in it. The King James Version was rather hard to read but I got to the point where I could do pretty well.

The problem with a disciplinarian such as my Father was I learned to think of God as just another Father who only knew how to discipline and order me around and I felt there was nothing I could do that would ever satisfy Him or my Father. Anything I did came under God's judgment and as almost everything was sinful somehow I felt I was sin itself and that I was far less than what I could ever be. As far back as I can think, I lived a double life, and I think Carl did as well. Later, when we had grown up got together and talked we were amazed at how feelings and actions we shared. Neither of us could remember ever having been hugged or loved or even told we were. Mother took her lead by Father's actions and was a stern copy of him. She saw that his orders were obeyed to the letter. Nick had a way that seemed to satisfy both our parents, and they were less strict with him than with Carl and me.

In school I was in the third grade when Carl started first. We seldom had a recess or a lunch period together. We would walk to school and, as I was helping at the store by then I walked on to the shop after school and he went home. Neither of us made friends at school because we were not allowed to stay after or visit them in their homes. We had a strict and unrelenting schedule that had to be adhered to and it didn't include any free time. Our Father felt we were put on this world to do what we were supposed to do and play was not on the schedule. People got into trouble playing and he was going to see to it his boys faced the world cleanly and righteously.

The problem with such a strict schedule was that boys need recreation with other boys and when they are limited to work and study they nevertheless find ways of making things pleasant for themselves, as Carl and I did. We shared the same bedroom and the same bed which made it easy to experiment. We found sexual pleasure as we grew a little older and started to investigate what our appendages could do. Nick was in the small nursery room off our parent's bedroom, so we were not inhibited by a tattle-tale brother. Masturbation became a routine and as we got older, other forms of sexual pleasure also became our method of escaping. Both of us talked incessantly about when we would be able to go to college and get away, but our plans always included being together.

Church camp was not allowed. Father felt one did not play with religion and so we again were cut off from being normal boys. At church we knew that masturbation and our other acts were strictly forbidden and so both Carl and I kept much of our life secret. We were the perfect family according to those at church who only saw the Sunday side of us sitting quietly together. Generally Aunt Hazel would sit with her husband just behind us.

Aunt Hazel was as strict and as uncompromising as our Father. Her husband was the town mortician, and they never had any children. Carl and I would laugh over the fact Uncle Polard was a mortician because he was as ugly as we thought any man could ever be. He had a nose with a sort of a bulb on the end, and hair that always was standing up at the back. He was also several inches shorter than Aunt Hazel. His eyes were way back in his head and when he ate dinner with us they sort of winked when he swallowed. He slurped his food. Aunt Hazel would tell him to use his napkin as if he were a child.

Aunt Hazel was no beauty so we thought they made a good pair. She was skinny and had as flat a chest as Uncle Polard did. We'd laughed because as we got older and started noticing how some women stuck out, we realized that she didn't look very much like the rest of them. She had long stringy yellowish hair which she tied in a knot at the top of her head. She had a neck at least as long as a giraffe's or so we told each other. Her shoes were very long and pointed and so our secret name for her was Aunt Witch Hazel. We'd seen a bottle of the stuff on our Mother's dresser which she used for different hurts and her face each night.

When it was time to go to high school I had to take the bus to Jackson because there was only an elementary school in Vicksburg. It was wonderful. I had a thirty-five minute ride every morning which meant I had to eat sooner than the rest and missed all the reading and prayers and was out the door to grab the bus as everyone else was coming down for breakfast.

It was hard my first year in Jackson. I'd had never had the opportunity to make friends and most of the kids I rode with had been friends all through their school year. Oh, I knew them but I had never been in any of their homes or they in mine. I never played any sports and the only thing I knew how to do other than to study was play the piano.

One day I was in the gym and there was a piano in the corner. I sat down and played some songs and before long there were several kids gathered around me all listening. I played very well and knew only hymns and things that came from the classics, but they seemed to be entranced with what I could do. One of the girls had some sheet music and ran to get it out of her locker, and that was when I was introduced to jazz and modern music and I loved it. We had a radio at home but the boys and I were never allowed to choose the program. Father listened to the news and music he thought proper and all other times it was turned off. Even Mother was not allowed to use it during the day.

I got to be pretty popular and I spent many lunch hours playing music in the gym. Kids would bring modern pieces for me to play and one day a kid brought some boogie and I went overboard. I began to make up my own pieces and write them down. I always left them in my locker and never played any of the songs I did at school during my practice time at home. Getting home later because I had to ride the bus did not alleviate my hour of practice but I didn't mind for I loved it.

The music teacher asked me if I would like to be the pianist for the orchestra and I said yes, not thinking about what my Father would say. That night, after dinner, when I told him he became quite upset and told me that I was not allowed to play unless they played music that he approved. I was so ashamed because the next day he took time off and visited my school and talked with the music teacher. I was surprised but was allowed to play and that was my first break from home and my first time away from Carl.

I'd just turned fourteen when I entered high school and was at the top of my class scholastically and as I had been since first grade. Carl and I were expected to get straight A's and heaven help us if we weren't able to or there would have been more hours at study than we already were forced to do. Nick also got good grades but he didn't seem to have to study as hard as Carl and I did. It seemed so easy for him. He would spend the time in his room drawing and painting and he still got the A's we did. He didn't like the piano and I was glad. I didn't really like Nick, even if he was my brother. He had to practice his hour a day but it never sounded like music. I loved music and had decided to major in it at college. Carl was going to be a lawyer and had started reading everything he could get his hands on about it.

Little by little Carl and I went our own ways. We still shared the same bed and still felt the urge to continue our method of sex. But during the day he had his things to do and I was in Jackson most of the day. I was a senior when I met Hayward, a new kid who had moved from Birmingham and played the trumpet as if he were made for it. We started practicing during lunch, spent our free third period in the music hall playing together. He got into the orchestra and we spent every free minute at school together.

The music hall didn't have windows in it and the doors could be locked so we started locking the doors during third period so kids wouldn't come in and bother us. We also found out there was a spark between us and one day we started spending time doing other things than music. We started with masturbation and then other things that were as pleasant. We were two musicians and two gays, and we even identified ourselves as being homosexuals.

By this time I was the church organist and played for choir practice on Thursday nights. Father was letting go of his tight reigns because I was doing exactly as he wanted me to do. He didn't have me at the shop because Carl had taken my place and when Carl went to high school Nick would step into his shoes.

Carl entered the ninth grade as I started my senior year. We rode the bus together and when he realized that Hayward and I were as close as we were, he became quite jealous. Carl played the violin almost as well as I did the piano. He was in the orchestra with Hayward and me, and it wasn't long before the three of us were a trio. We included Carl in our trio in physical actions as well as our music. Carl and I went to church, choir practice, and no one knew the real us. Everyone thought we were model boys and we were asked to many gatherings especially where there were girls of dating age. Neither Carl nor I dated and didn't want to. We didn't know much about women and didn't have time to worry about them. We weren't thoroughly impressed with the two women we knew, Aunt Witch Hazel and our mother who was more like a shadow of Father than a person in her own right.

At the senior prom I went stag and spent my time playing the piano. I towered over six feet, had dark brown hair and brown eyes, was average in looks, and wasn't interested in girls. That seemed to turn them on and made them try and see if they could date me. Rejection seems to be a key to a lot of things.

As I got older I realized some of my rejection of girls was the coldness I'd grown up with. I never remembered my mother hugging me. The only time she touched me or Carl was out of necessity or to whip me, and as far as Father went he never touched us except to whip us. The only touching and love of any kind was what Carl and I shared. I often felt sorry for Nick, but he didn't have any trouble with the girls. In fact he had them all over him. He had curly blond hair, blue eyes like our Mother and was quite a lady's man. He wasn't as tall as Carl and I were but it didn't bother him.

Carl had about the same looks as I did. He was tall, with brown hair and brown eyes. As we got older were often asked if we were twins, even with the three years difference since we were almost the same size as well.

I graduated and it was time to take off for college, and I had a few moments of sorrow when the time came for me to say good-bye to both Hayward and Carl. Hayward went back East to college and I went to Texas to the University. I received a music scholarship and was on my way. I'd written several songs and even had one published and was in the middle of adding some classical additions to my portfolio. When I got to college I found I was accepted practically before I told them who I was. I was taken into the orchestra immediately and made assistant director before the first year had passed.

It was easy to find bed partners at college since I lived in a boy's dorm. In fact that was where I found that my music and height, and my attitude gave me an edge with the teachers as well as any of the gay students. The orchestra teacher was gay and we spent time together at his apartment going over arrangements and making out. I had two loves in my life, music and men. I was very particular about my music and as far as men went it wasn't important who, just how often. Church was the last thing I cared about;. I was tired of feeling guilty so I just didn't go. My Bible was packed in my suitcase where Mother had placed it.

Every week there was a duty letter from Mother and one from Father. Carl didn't write and neither did Nick. I'd pick up the two letters and throw them on the dresser to be read later as they almost always contained the same information. Each letter was filled with directions about how to live, what to do, and not to do. I was to get good grades as honest money was sending me here to further myself in this life and in the sight of God. Each letter from Father included an assignment in the Scriptures and a long commentary on the passage which he expected me to answer. My replies informed him I was so busy with studies and I would take time to answer him during summer vacation.

To be accepted socially had been drilled into me from child-hood and I kept my homosexuality removed from anyone who made a difference in my climb to where I thought I needed to go. In the dorm the guys who were gay kept their life quiet as well, so when we did meet it was always away from the dorm and out of the view of the rest of the guys. The music teacher and I had every reason to meet at his apartment so my gay life and my social life was kept apart one from the other. I was made fun of occasionally because I didn't date, and several times I had to go on blind dates to keep up a front. I'd date the girl once or twice and drop her. I simply didn't have time and was not interested.

My every waking hour was spent living for music, either playing, studying, or arranging. By the time I was a junior I had three pieces published and thought my future was well in hand. Carl was in college in Birmingham. Nick had graduated and was engaged to be married. He planned to go into the shop with Father. Father wrote that Mother was not well and suggested I plan on coming home at Christmas instead of staying in the dorm as I had done the past two years. My excuse for staying during the holidays was that I needed to study and was playing at several places to make extra money. Money was generally a major factor in any logic with Father. His two main reasons for living was his religion and his money. The rest of us were down the line in his priorities at intervals, but none of us knew where we stood.

Graduation was exciting. Mother came as did Carl. Father and Nick had to stay and mind the shop, or that was their reason. Nick and his new wife, Lisa, could have managed, but applause was not in Father's vocabulary. Graduating at the top of my class was expected. What was surprising was the difference in Mother without Father at her elbow. She was congenial and told me how proud she was that I was at the top of the class. Carl was thrilled, but had only one day because he had finals the next week and had to get back to study.

Mother stayed at the motel for two days and we spent some very pleasant hours together. When I took her to the bus, she started to get on but turned and came back, kissed my cheek and said, "Philip, I'm so proud of you and so is your Father." Then she immediately got on the bus. I watched as she chose a seat on the side where she could see me. And as we were a little late the bus left within minutes of her boarding. I stood there for several minutes trying to understand the joy I had deep inside me from her affectionate actions. She was proud of me and had actually kissed me. It was hard to believe and it felt wonderful. I sang all the way to the car and back to the dorm.

I was taking some summer classes and continued on for my Masters in music. I planned to get a doctorate and knew I would have to do some serious composition, so I planned on living at the dorm for the next few years. Father had insisted I continue. His philosophy that nothing is accomplished until it is finished was a boon for both Carl and me. He planned on both of us to excel and with Nick taking over the shop he felt he had done his duty to the three of us boys. His remark was, "I have done my duty to you boys and I expect you to do your duty to your children as well."

The life I led for the next few years left me limited to music and whatever men were handy. Love? It never occurred to me to love any of them. They were tools. I didn't belong in their lives anymore than I belonged in the social groups I was a part of. I did what I had to do socially to be accepted, but to belong, was never part of my life. Many times I spent hours at the piano wondering what it was like to be like the people I associated with. They seemed happy and contented. Several of the boys who had lived in my dorm were married and a couple already had children.

I lived within myself except for the music which enabled me to breathe and exist. When I was playing, composing, or listening to music I never felt lonely. But the rest of the time when there was no music I was terribly unsettled and lonely. I knew there had to be a way out. I didn't know why or where. I just knew there was something missing. Why couldn't I have music and be like these people who touched shoulders day after day. My gay partners were simply a means to an end. I really didn't fit in with them either. I never went to the bars or the bath houses they kept urging me to visit. One partner told me to get on the internet because there were some great webs to watch. I did one night and was revolted at the nonsense. Sex to me was an escape, a physical necessity.

The new year had started and I was director of the college orchestra. A freshmen girl named Cassie Taylor joined the orchestra. She played the flute and was excellent. I couldn't believe a girl had such ability, especially a freshman. I usually kept the lead in any section over for thirty minutes practice. She was one of the several who loved music enough to also practice on Tuesday and Thursday nights in the music room. We would meet around seven and sometimes were so engrossed wouldn't leave until midnight when lights were extinguished.

There was something about Cassie that intrigued me and as time went on I started to date her because she would talk to me about arrangements intelligently and with great imagination. We made some new arrangements together and found ourselves more and more entwined in each other's lives. I still led a gay life but was limiting my partners to the music teacher and a couple of new guys in the dorm.

Cassie wasn't aware of the other side of my character and I had no plans on sharing it with her. She stayed that summer in her dorm to take some summer courses and I started coaching some students who needed extra help, so my summer was filled with lessons and classes. We still met on Tuesday and Thursday nights and usually I walked her to her dorm. We'd sit on the benches on the patio in front of her entrance and talk about a thousand different things. Our conversations were now including other things than music.

One night it was warm and the moon was close enough to touch I kissed her good night. From that time on it became a habit to kiss her good night and at the end of summer before classes started we became engaged. I knew I was expected to marry and as she was enough of a musician she filled the requirements. Marriage was a duty my parents demanded and when I told them of our engagement they were pleased. We would not be able to be married until I graduated and had a position, and Cassie understood.

Two years later I had a job with a junior college in Atlanta and was able to fulfill my pledge to marry her. We rented a small apartment not too far from the college and Cassie went to work teaching at an elementary school on the outskirts. I walked to class and Cassie took our car. Sex was no problem. It never had been. It was something you just did. I didn't quit my gay life on the side and had no desire to do so. Cassie insisted we attend church on Sunday which was fine as far as I was concerned. I became the choir director for both the senior and junior choirs, and started an orchestra which made me quite popular with both the senior and the youth pastor.

Even married I was still not a real part of life. I escaped into my music as I had always done, did my duty to Cassie, enjoyed her companionship, but we weren't one as the minister had said. I was one and she was one but that always made two. There was no way I could understand her when she held me at night and whispered how much she loved me. It was simply a woman thing I assumed. Yes, I cared for her, but love was something real people felt, people who were part of each other. I was on the planet but something apart from everyone else.

One night Cassie asked me why I had never said I loved her. I remembered my negligence and immediately told her I loved her and that satisfied her need. I made it a point to tell her periodically and she seemed happy with our marriage. It fulfilled a need for me socially and that was what was important or so I thought until one day during dinner Cassie informed me we were going to be parents and she hoped I would be pleased. I expected to be a father as that was part of the duty that was expected of me. I praised her and started planning to buy a house.

We found a three bedroom house that fit my income since I did not want her working once the baby came. We were an average couple. I taught college, out several nights a week at church, appeared to everyone as normal middle class married man, and that was the way I wanted it. Father and Mother came for a weekend once in a while, leaving Nick more and more in charge of the store. Nick had three children, two boys and a new baby girl. Carl had been sent to Washington D.C. on a political case, and a large firm there picked him up, so he was working at the Capitol, still not married and still living a gay life.

Nothing much changed. I went to work. Cassie planned for the baby, and at night we would play music or talk about some new arrangement I'd made. I was publishing rather a lot of music, much to be used in school orchestras and some for teaching purposes, as well as arrangements for symphony orchestras. My name was becoming rather well known in the music world and I had received a request to teach in a large University. Cassie and I replied that after the baby was born we would consider the option of moving. Everything in our house was done on a logical basis. Emotion was seldom a part of our relationship. We showed deep feelings for certain passages of music and would get rather excited over a new piece of music or an arrangement which we felt excelled.

Philip Jr. was born on a Sunday quite conveniently after church service which allowed me to direct the choir with no interruption. I was in the delivery room and held my son minutes after he arrived. He was small and rather red and cried the minute I held him. His hair was brown and his eyes were dark. I couldn't tell the color. I held him and he took my finger and held on and for the first time in my life something really belonged to me and I got a glimpse of the world of which I'd never been a part.

Cassie watched as I bonded with my son and large tears fell onto her cheeks. She whispered, "I love you both more than I can ever explain." I leaned over and kissed her holding the baby tight to me as if I might drop him. She reached out and took our son and kissed his warm little head then handed him back as they were working with her. The nurse took the baby and dressed him, placed a little hat on him and wrapped him in a blue blanket depicting a boy.

The day I brought Cassie and the baby home was exciting. Father and Mother were there and Mother took little Philip and hugged him to her then said the strangest thing to me, "Phil, don't let anything come between you and loving this baby. He is part of you and needs love something I wish I'd given you boys. It was more important for me to be the perfect mother and wife than to be a mother to you three. Don't make the mistake I did." She said it with tears streaming down her face and in sobs handed me little Philip, then put her arms around me and hugged me.

From that day on I began to change. Each morning before I went to work I held my son, and started kissing Cassie good-bye as well. She never let me get out the door with out reassuring me of her love. What started to change was a feeling of guilt I was having a hard time with. I'd not visited my music teacher since Philip's birth, but it wasn't long until I did. There was something missing or I should say something added. I felt guilt each time I was at his apartment and when I came home and Cassie welcomed me with a kiss I felt I needed a whipping like the ones Father and Mother had given me when I'd disobeyed as a child.

One Sunday morning the subject from the pulpit was adultery. Generally I studied pieces of music while the pastor was preaching. I sat at the side where I was not observed and the music stand in from of me was a perfect place to display new pieces of music or arrangements. Cassie was in the orchestra on the other side of the stage which was behind the pastor's pulpit. But I couldn't help hearing the passages Pastor Phelps was reading, passages I had ignored growing up, but that morning they made me feel sick inside. Once again I got that sinning feeling I had during my growing up years, but this time I wasn't angry or made to write an essay by Father. It was me inside, and it was me who was hurting.

The Pastor kept saying God was pouring love and forgiveness down on us and that our Heavenly Father wanted us to have a life filled with contentment and happiness. The rules were made because of love not because He wanted to punish us. I tried to take it all in but all I had ever known was an angry God, one who watched and tried to catch you so He could use His power against you. The pastor kept emphasizing the love side of God and how he even let His Son suffer death to prove His love.

I'd heard these words before but my Father's interpretations during morning and night prayers and at the table three times a day had covered up the word love with words telling me how bad a sinner I was. All at once I was alert, His Son! I had a son and I'd never let him suffer as Jesus did for anyone. No one was worth that little boy who I held in my arms and who cooed at me in recognition. He'd even smiled at me this morning when I left him in the nursery while Cassie got her flute so she could play in the orchestra. I had a lot of thinking to do it seemed.

That Sunday afternoon Cassie took a nap as she was a little tired. Phil was cutting a tooth and she had been up during the night. I picked up Cassie's Bible and reread the passage the Pastor had been preaching about. Love, how could I have missed it? The words were quite clear and simple to understand. Phil let out a little whimper and I ran to get him so he wouldn't wake his mother. I held and rocked him as I read. There in my arms was a little human being made of flesh and blood and there was no way I could ever love anyone else enough to let this precious son of mine suffer. My heart burst open and I sobbed my heart out to God. Cassie came into the room and took me in her arms, with little Phil between us, and I told her of my homosexuality. I expected her to ask for a divorce but she only said, "I love you, Philip, and I have been praying for you since the day we met. I've known for a long time, dear, and just left it in the hands of God to help you find Him."

She had known, this woman I had taken to wife as a duty and who I had been intimate with as a part of that duty. She knew and yet she stayed and loved me. So this was love, way down deep inside me I felt the warmth I'd never known in my life before the day they handed me little Philip, and now I was feeling it again. I loved. At last I knew what love was, and at last I was a part of life, real life, not just something that went along with music. It was music, real music and I had it. I was apart of it.

Cassie has just shared with me that Philip is going to have a little brother or sister around Christmas and my heart is throbbing with the thoughts of a new little child to love. All the love I missed as I grew up I am giving to my children, and even Cassie has become more than a duty. I can honestly say I love her with all my fiber. Our relationship is no longer one based upon duty. I have tried to share my feelings with Carl and my Father but they find it hard to understand, so I have started to pray for them as Cassie prayed for me. My prayer is that my Father will someday truly understand God, not just perform his traditional duty to Him.

My life changed slowly. I didn't have any problem giving up my gay life as I'd never loved any of the men I'd been with. As a matter of fact I'd never loved anyone really. Carl came the closet to what I could say was love, but even that relationship was based on what he could do for me. It took a long time to understand how to give back, in the same degree, the love that Cassie offered me. It wasn't hard to love little Philip, especially when he ran to meet me at the door and hugged me with those fat little baby arms of his and called me Daddy. I was going to make sure that he would never call me Father.

Both Phil and Cassie came for the interview. After the tape was turned off I watched them interact. Cassie had understood Phil's duty towards her but hearing it repeated in such an ardent way hurt. There was a slight amount of coolness towards Phil and I sensed she was trying to overcome some feeling that was deep inside.

"Cassie, what are you thinking right now?" I wanted to give her an avenue of expression since Phil had done all the talking.

She just looked at me, and I could see she was arguing with whether she should talk or be quiet.

"Cassie, lets get everything on the table and then leave it there. What is bothering you, dear?"

She had been sitting in a chair at the side of the desk in an office a friend had loaned us for the interview.

"Phil has never really loved me. I know that. But it still hurts to know I am married to a man who has used me. I have loved him very much. It just hurts, that's all." She lowered her head into her hands and wept.

Phil sprang to his feet and went to her. He pulled her out of the chair then held her to him, patting her hair. "Oh, Cassie. I know you're right, but there is love now and a deep one that comes from way down inside of me when I think of us. Please forgive me. I've never asked you to forgive me as much as I am asking now. Cassie, I do love you. I need you. If you ever left me I would be truly alone, oh! Cassie, I need you so." He buried his head into her hair and cried out his love for her.

"You need me, you really need me? You've never told me you needed me. I thought all you needed was your music and the baby, not me." She pushed herself away out of his arms and turned to me. "He needs me, isn't need very close to love?"

"Cassie, need is a part of love, dear, but not all of love. It seems Phil has had to learn to love and you have been the one to teach him. That is a wonderful thing to do for any person. Teaching love, Cassie, is what our Lord tried to do for the world. You have taught a human being the very thing Jesus was teaching."

She took Phil in her arms and together they stood holding each other. They were learning a new kind of love, one that would be strong enough to weather any problem they could have.

Cassie and Phil left the office holding hands. The smiles they exchanged were kind and loving. Both of these young people had almost drowned in hurt. In their torment they had helped each other swim to shore. Phil and Cassie were enjoying a new freedom that far surpassed what they had before. Love had won and they were the recipients of its joy.

11

"Wine and Roses"

I<small>T'S HARD FOR ME TO REMEMBER</small> when my life started. I'm eighty-three, and I'll be eighty-four next month. I was born in nineteen-twenty. I don't hear well, and this cane isn't just for looks. Was a beauty when I was a girl. Had all the young bucks sniffing round my heels, trying to date me. You can't tell now but if you'll look in the hall those pictures are me. I was married four times and nursed for thirty-three years. Moved here to be near my only daughter and two grandchildren. Thought I needed to, seeings as how she's alone with those two young ones. Bill, her husband you know, died from stomach cancer about seven months ago. More's the pity, he was only thirty-eight and a good man he was.

I really loved just once. Don't get all het-up, so it was a girl. We went through nurse's training together, both orphans, and both not knowing which end was up. We roomed together and bedded together before people knew all about this gay stuff. Well, they knew about it but sure didn't talk about it. A crying shame people can't keep what they do 'hind closed doors to themselves, I say.

Clara and I were the same age, even had birthdays in the same month, she was a bright carrot-top and I had black hair like my Daddy. Don't remember what color Mama's hair was. She died when my sister, Juanita, was born. In those days birthing was a risk and out in the woods where we lived it was worse. I don't much remember about Daddy either. I was nine when a tree fell the wrong way and crushed him to death. He was a lumberman.

Juanita, about thirteen months younger than me, and I were put into an orphanage run by Catholic Sisters. As far as I know there were no relatives on either side of the family tree. Mama had come from Ireland with her parents when she was eleven and Daddy from Sweden, with his parents, when he was around seven or eight. He never could remember which. I was part Irish and Swedish. There was a little German in there somewhere on my Daddy's side. He always bragged about being a descendent of some German king.

An orphanage is a sad place for a child. The sisters were kind and loving but there were always too many kids for the number of beds or clothes available, and a lot of times not even enough food to go around. Christmas was a little better. Churches would send barrels filled with used clothes and old shoes. Some of the shoes had holes in their soles. As I got older I would think to myself that people who sent shoes with holes in the soles had holes in their "soul."

Sometimes the clothes would even be ripped and the sisters would use them for rags to clean the tables and floors. The toys that came in the barrels never had all their parts. The books were missing pages, and many times there weren't enough of the right sizes of clothing so some of us had to wear stuff that was too big. There was a blue skirt the sisters had me wear. It needed a kerchief as a belt to hold it up. When they got time they cut it down for me, but I liked it big because when I went around it whirled and made me feel elegant. It had little white flowers on it and was shiny.

I can remember the sisters sitting around the little round black stove in the room off to the side of the long kitchen mending our clothing. I always had a hole in my socks. We very seldom got new things. At least at Christmas there was turkey and cranberries and always a candy cane. On Christmas there was never any school because we went to chapel early. There was singing and a special priest with a red belt and a funny little square hat would come and tell us the Christmas story about a baby named Jesus and how he was really God. It was hard for me to understand why any God would ever want to be a child.

A doll was all I ever wanted. A real baby doll that would be just mine and not part of the toys in the large box at the end of the study room. Well, it wasn't a study room all the time. We had to use it for recess and games when it rained outside. There were small desks we could use to do our school work. Some were from a school that had been torn down and were pretty beat up. We'd push them to the side of the room when we needed it for recess.

One Christmas there was a doll in one of the boxes with part of its hair gone and one arm missing. No one ever played with it so I rescued it and kept it as mine. That doll-baby, with all her faults, was mine. Everywhere I went I took her with me wrapped in one of my old ripped night gowns. Her name was Melissa, the same as my Mama's. Her eyes were open all the time and when I put her to sleep I'd turn her on her tummy and pretend she closed her eyes. One of the eyes had a little bit of paint coming off the corner and made her look a little funny, but I loved her anyway.

Juanita, being younger wasn't in the same room at night as I was. She was in the other wing and even ate at a different time. When we were first at the orphanage she had a bed next to mine and then one night they moved her. I'd been a little worried because she sure felt hot when I hugged her good night. The sisters that were on her side of the building dressed in different habits and had different kinds of hats. My sisters wore black and had hats that went way out at the side. Juanita's sisters wore white habits and had smaller hats that went up straight.

I wasn't allowed to go on that side even when I told Sister Ursula that Juanita was my sister. She was the sister who taught us and not Sister Mary who was in charge of my room side. She said I couldn't go over there because they were in something called quarantine. I had no idea what that meant. Even when you get to be ten there are still things you don't know.

One day when I was in the school room and Sister Ursula was teaching us how to do algebra, Sister Mary came and got me. I left Melissa on the seat of my desk and followed her. Sister Mary took my hand and told me we were going to see Juanita. I was so happy. At last I would get to be with my sister. I asked Sister Mary if I could go back and get Melissa, she said we didn't have time. We went through the big wide doors with a large cross on each of them and into Juanita's wing and over to a bed Juanita was lying on. I wondered why she wasn't in school. Juanita was lying still and had her eyes closed. I leaned over the bed and called her name. I wanted her to know I was there. After all sleeping in the middle of the morning was a little silly. She didn't move.

Sister Mary put her arms around my shoulders and said, "Beatrice, your sister is with the Lord. He wanted her to come see Him. She can't hear you, dear. She is dead. Now kiss her good-bye. You'll see her again when the Lord wants you to come home to Him."

I kissed her as I had been ordered. I couldn't understand. She was so cold and when I kissed her cheek she didn't move.

"Sister, what is wrong with Juanita. She's so cold and she won't talk to me?"

"She is dead, dear, like I told you. You may kiss her again if you like."

My sister was dead from diphtheria. The children kept in that wing had all contacted it. I knew later that all but three died. The sisters in white were nurses. In those days if you were a child they had you kiss the body. They felt it was a closing and a farewell that children could understand.

I can remember having nightmares for years over the coldness of Juanita's body and that she didn't open her eyes or say good-bye to me. I wondered why I had never kissed my Mama good bye or my Daddy. Way down in the very depth of my heart I dreamed they hadn't died and someday would be coming back to get me. When McGill, my last husband, died it wasn't necessary for me to kiss him to know that he was dead. Standing over his body at the funeral home I promised myself that that was the last time I would get married and I never did again. I didn't even marry Wesley and I adored him. Too many husbands and Clara, you say? Well let me tell you, any kind of loving, even for a little while, is better than being alone. Then when they die off at least you've got memories.

With Juanita dead, everything died that I belonged to. I was really alone. There was only Melissa and me. I tucked her under my arm every night and sang her to sleep. The other girls would tease me. I didn't care. She was mine and she couldn't die and leave me alone. I'd cut some ends off an old mop and glued her some hair to cover up the bald spot. I dyed the threads yellow by breaking an egg yolk into a cup when the sisters weren't looking. It worked pretty well, the strands sort of stuck together but after they got good and dry I brushed them apart. I couldn't find her another arm but I'd learned to love her that way so I held that side of her close to me. That way others would think she had two arms. The girls quit teasing me about Melissa, but I wouldn't have cared if they hadn't.

The next few years I spent growing up in the orphanage. No one ever adopted me. I was too old, too skinny and, I figured too ugly. They let me help with the babies. Some had been left on the front steps of the orphanage. There was a large bell beside the big front door that people rang to let the sisters know if there was someone there. It was always locked and only Sister Superior had the key. It was on a woven rope she wore around her waist. The rope was white and long and fell down one side of her black skirt. She had other keys and a Crucifix on the belt too.

I remember the bell ringing sometimes during the night and the next day there would always be a new little baby in the nursery. I never got kitchen duty like some of the girls because I was so good with the babies. I loved them, they were soft and cuddly and when I rocked them after I'd given them a bottle they would fall asleep in my arms. They were much better than a doll. By that time poor Melissa had been stored away in my locker. Each of us had a small box at the end of our beds the sisters called a locker. It wasn't locked so it was curious to me why it was called a locker. I was too old for dolls anyway, but I couldn't throw her away. I had to keep her. If you look in that hope chest at the foot of my bed you'll find her all wrapped up in a Japanese-silk kerchief that Pete, my first husband, brought me from Manila when he came home on leave from the army.

I was eighteen when they let me leave the orphanage and work in the local hospital helping with the newborns. The Sister Superior had recommended me. It was there I knew I wanted to be a nurse. I'd dreamt of it all my life but figured as I grew older it would never happen because you needed money to go to college and I didn't have any. When I was off duty I borrowed books from the library on nursing, memorized terms and tried to learn as much as I could on my own. Somehow I was going to be a nurse and my dream was to be a surgical one. It was a pretty hopeless dream, me, an orphan with no hopes of getting enough money for college.

The first several months I had to come back into the orphanage at night but after I'd saved enough money I was allowed to board at Mrs. Wright's boarding house on Lake Street. Some of the girls who graduated went to work in private homes as Mother's Helpers and some were allowed to work in offices. I was glad when they chose me to work at the hospital. Being in a hospital was part of my dream, and settling for part was better than nothing.

My whole life changed the day Pete Ryder came into the hospital and ate lunch in the cafeteria. He sat down at the table next to mine and kept staring at me. I'd looked good in the mirror when I growing up and knew I was pretty. Pete wasn't the first boy who had asked me for a date but the orphanage wouldn't let us girls out after nine and that put a stopper on dating. Besides when we did go out of the orphanage we had to go in pairs and who wants to date with another girl hanging around. Besides I wouldn't know what to say to a boy anyway. The only males I knew were the visiting priests who came to take our confessions and say Mass on Sunday, and once in a while, when someone was really sick, a doctor.

Pete was a good looking guy, tall, muscular, a bushy head of black hair, and a twinkle in his Irish eyes that would make any girl want to look twice. We dated for about seven months until he was out of his internship. He was six years older than me but neither of us considered the difference. Pete was going to be a doctor and that suited me just fine. If I couldn't be a nurse I'd settle for marrying a doctor. He was kept on at the hospital once he finished his internship and I was kept on helping in the nursery.

I'd had so much experience by then in the newborn nursery I was allowed to be by myself without having to get an R.N. I couldn't give meds or anything of that sort but I took care of those precious little bundles. What I loved best was when I took them to their mothers to be fed. I pretended I was once little and my mother had held me tenderly and cooed at me and then held me to her breast and fed me.

So many times I wondered what it would have been like to have had a mother. I was only about fourteen months old when she died birthing Juanita. My sister and I were brought up by an Indian lady off the reservation. Daddy had hired her because he couldn't stay with us during the day; he was out in the forest, which surrounded our cabin, working. Winona was kind and loving and for a few years we had Daddy at night. Then of course the rest of my youth was at the orphanage. I did love the sisters. Who wouldn't? They were so kind and loving. But they weren't family and I didn't belong to them.

Pete was a good doctor and said he loved me very much. Love wasn't all that important to me. Everyone I had ever loved had died and I was skittish about really loving anybody. Pete asked me to marry him and I thought it over for a day or two and finally decided to accept. I didn't feel any excitement when he kissed me but I supposed that only happened in the novels I read. I liked being with him and the idea he was a doctor had the greatest appeal.

We were married on June 6th, 1940, eight days before German troops occupied Paris and France surrendered. His parents came in from New Hampshire and his one brother from Texas. Mr. and Mrs. Ryder were pretty wealthy and very stuck up. I didn't know what to say to either of them and I knew I wasn't dressed the way they thought their doctor son's wife should be. I was thankful they left after the wedding and even thankful that Carl, Pete's brother, only had three days off work. In Texas, where he worked, he did something with a telescope, looking at the stars to give weather reports to radio stations. He was older than Pete, and had never married. I thought secretly, not sharing it with Pete that he was as stuck up as his parents and it would take a real "lady" for him to get married.

Pete wasn't like his family. He was fun and jolly, and always joking about something. I thought our new little house three blocks from the hospital was heaven. I'd never had a house of my

own. I'd walked around the rooms as if I were walking on clouds.
The clouds turned dark quickly because we'd only been married
about a year and a-half when, on December 8th 1941, Pearl
Harbor was attacked and we were at war.

Pete enlisted two days later and being a doctor they inducted
him immediately. He was sent to a place called Camp White near
a town called Medford in Oregon. He was there for three weeks
and then sent overseas to Hawaii. He didn't need much training
as he wasn't going to be fighting. I was still working at the
hospital, because they had taken so many nurses. I was doing
floor duty giving meds, taking temps, and giving enemas. I was a
nurse without a cap or degree.

Pete came home on furlough after he'd been at the hospital in
Hawaii for about a year. I was thrilled to see him and we spent
seven wonderful days together before he had to return. I never
saw Pete again. On June 4th 1944, I went to the door and there was
a Western Union telegram telling me that Pete had been killed by
a bomb that had taken out a section of the hospital and had killed
many wounded soldiers.

All I had left of Pete was a medal and I put it in the hope chest
at the end of my bed with Melissa. I should have known anything
that belonged to me would be killed or die. I received a check
from the U.S. government to replace Pete. The one thing it did
was to send me to nurses training so I could become a real R.N.
I was still alone. Pete's parents and brother never bothered to
write after his funeral. I suppose if I had given them a grandchild
it would have been different but I hadn't and that was that.

I arrived at college with the hope of actually being a nurse
exploding in my heart. I was going to be the best damn nurse this
planet had ever seen. I was going to be a surgical nurse and take
over operating on a critical patient when Dr. Kildare fainted at
the sight of blood. When we are young we have great dreams
which once in a while come true. Mine did, well not Dr. Kildare,
but I became a surgical nurse and was a good one. But a lot of
things happened while my dream was becoming a reality.

The first day I was just one of over 300 girls, some older
women, going in for a nurse's degree. The war had brought

nursing out of the shadows and put it into the drama of living. Movies that showed nurses saving soldiers, nurses as heroines, and as women fighting for our country were shown at the movie theaters. All at once the government was deciding it needed to help produce more nurses. The scholarship I was awarded and the money from Pete's insurance got me through my training, even allowed for a small car and some new clothes.

We registered and were given our dorm numbers. I carried my suitcases to Kerry Hall up to the second floor and entered room # 206. That was the first time I saw Clara. She was putting her clothes into a standing closet which separated her bed from mine. My closet, I figured, was on the other side of my bed. The room consisted of two desks, two standing metal closets, two beds with two sagging mattresses and no visible bedding.

"Hello, I'm Beatrice Sorensen," I said to my new room mate. I had gone back to my own name. I'd make it on my own and with Pete dead I felt his family could care less. In fact I kept my maiden name legally through three more marriages. When they put that cap on my head and handed Beatrice Sorensen that diploma I meant to keep it, the diploma and the name.

She turned and I was surprised. She was beautiful. Her hair was a bright red and her eyes were almost black. She jumped over my bed and hugged me, "Hi, I'm Clara Tucker and gee I'm glad you're here. I was getting a wee bit home sick." She literally bubbled. She plumped down on my bed and pulled me down beside her. "Now tell me all about you, and then I will give you the gory details about me." She sounded like she was laughing, her voice bubbling just as she did. I was completely flabbergasted. I'd never known anybody like her. Even Pete with his laughter and twinkling eyes wasn't in her league.

That was how our friendship started and it lasted for over six years and then when she was gone it stayed in my memories, and will forever. Oh, don't tell me you can't love someone all your life. Even when I knew I wasn't really a lesbian I still loved her. When I learned she had committed suicide I still remembered her bubbling voice and everlasting laughter. I never have been able to understand why she couldn't handle living?

We were in some of the same classes. We studied that first few weeks like crazy and got to know everything about each other there was to know. We clicked. It was a brand new feeling having someone know me that well. Pete had tried but with his new practice and me getting used to being married and not having enough time it never really made sense. It was hard for me to even remember what he looked like. Not having even three years with a person just doesn't give you enough time to get to know each other.

Clara was an orphan and had been raised by her maiden Aunt called Lil, short for Lilly. She loved her dearly. Her Aunt was the only family Clara had ever known. She had never known her mother or father as they both had been killed in Germany during the first war. Her father was a correspondent and he met her mother while covering the war. They had been married in Berlin and Clare was born there. She was three months old when both parents were killed by a bomb. The Red Cross brought the new baby back to the states to her Aunt.

Clara's Aunt Lil was a private secretary to the head of a large corporation and left the new baby with one housekeeper after another. When it was time for Clara to go to school she still had a housekeeper to be there when Clara got home. She was a senior in High School with only two weeks until graduation when her Aunt had a stroke and died. She left everything to Clara with no restrictions, and with no one left to direct her Clara was at odds about what she wanted to do. Clara tried two colleges. First she wanted to be a lawyer and she didn't like that, then she wanted to be a dentist and said that was a "bore." Clara always laughed at her own jokes. And now she was trying nursing school. I was determined she was going to stay with me and we were going to make it. Once again I had found someone and I wasn't about to let her go.

I knew a lot about nursing and it wasn't all that hard for me but Clara wanted to play more than she wanted to study. She had enough money from her Aunt's estate and from her Fathers insurance to do just about anything she wanted. She had her own car and clothes that were absolutely beautiful, and she let me wear anything I wanted, insisting I go with her on weekends when I didn't make her stay and study. She always picked up the tab, making me feel like a poor relative and embarrassed, but when I'd talk that way she would burst into tears and tell me the money wasn't hers either and so what was the difference whether she spent it or I did. She could come up with completely plausible theories. She believed what she said and somehow made others believe it too.

Clara was not interested in men. She was afraid of them for some reason. If a man came up to her and started talking she would always find an excuse to get away. She was beautiful and was hit on constantly. She was also asked out by men who meant well. Whenever we were out together we were always approached. She even burst into tears and ran out to the car one evening when two quite nice looking interns decided we were just what they were looking for.

I got our coats and followed her. When I was in the car I insisted she tell me what was wrong.

She frowned and said "Bea don't get nosey, you really don't want to know." Then she laughed and suggested we go for a shake at the Ice Cream Parlor which was on the way to the dorm. Our curfew on week-nights was ten and on weekends eleven. That night we only had about an hour. We got back five minutes late expecting the doors to be locked but luckily they weren't. We'd made it but just barely.

Clara was actually excited at nearly being locked out, "That was fun," she bubbled. "I wonder what we would have done if the doors were locked. Some night I'm going to find out."

Safely inside and up in our room we lit the candles she always needed, and took a bottle of wine out of the little refrigerator she'd bought and put in the corner of our room. She had decorated it by putting a long silk scarf over the top and then a large green vase filled with dried roses. We grabbed our towels and soap for a shower. The shower room was two doors down. When we got back Clara plunked on my bed and started one of her hour-long attacks on the world. She was politically a dolt, always had some crazy idea of how to solve the world's problems and I had to listen or she would pout.

There were two sides to her, the bubbling side, and the pouting side which didn't show very often but when it did it usually ended with her in tears. She either got her way by bubbling or crying. I could feel the tears coming. I was drying my hair and she took the towel out of my hand and told me to pay attention as she had to tell me something. She was actually serious and I became quiet listening to what she had to say. It seems that one of the gardeners who took care of her Aunt's property had molested her when she was about eleven. She'd been afraid to tell her Aunt because she was afraid of the man. The gardener was fired because he hadn't done what her Aunt wanted but after that she said she had always been afraid of men.

She burst into hysterics and cried as if she would never stop. I took her in my arms trying to comfort her and she hugged me. It was strange, and then she started rubbing me. That was how it started, and it never stopped all the while we were in college. We studied together, ate together, and had sex together. She said she had been a lesbian ever since she had found a friend in high school who would come and stay all night with her. She was afraid of men but not of women. Women were always kind and loving to her, just like her Aunt. She said her Aunt had women friends staying overnight with her so she figured that was the way some women were. Later when she was a little older and told her Aunt about the gardener, her Aunt was so angry she called the police and turned him in.

We were about eight months from graduating and starting to really study hard for the finals. We'd made plans to apply to the same hospital, hoping we would be hired together. If we were lucky we'd rent an apartment near the hospital and live together, even try and get the same shifts. Clara was a general duty nursing student. She didn't want the extra studies, but I'd gone further to fulfill my dream of being a surgical nurse. She was a little lazy and was curious to see what was on the other side of every hill. Clara was always moving a foot or tapping her pencil and had a hard time sitting through lectures. Me, I was a single goal gal and dreamed of being in surgery in a white gown and mask, wiping the brow of some doctor as he saved a life. That was my side of the mountain.

One afternoon in June, I had the window open trying to catch a breeze while studying when a policeman came to the open door and asked if Clara was there. He was a jock and it crossed my mind that maybe Clara, the man hater, had finally decided to see what dating a man meant. Grinning I answered she would be back in a bit, and she had gone to get a book from the library. I told him he was welcome to step in and wait. We had purchased a couple of chairs so there was someplace to plop when others came to chatter. He refused and said he would wait for her in the hall. He handed me his card. It read Sergeant J.D. Hopper.

I'd not had time to even think about men and with Clara and I being so close there hadn't been any need. I was sort of surprised when Clara declared I was a lesbian like her. Titles for sex hadn't been my first priority, and I figured having been married deleted me from that category. Clara with her usual persuasiveness explained I had to be a lesbian or we wouldn't be able to be attracted to each other. With the feelings I had for Clara guessed it had been there all the time and Pete was just an interlude until I found Clara.

I heard her coming down the hall. She flung the door open and slammed it hard, turned and looked at me as if she had seen a ghost.

"What is that policeman doing in the hall?" She was almost in a panic.

At that moment before I could answer her the officer knocked on the door and I opened it.

"Are you Clara Tucker" he asked?

She nodded and sat on the edge of the bed and began to shake. I couldn't figure out what was going on.

"Clara, what's wrong?"

The officer went over to her and asked if she drove a red Thunderbird. I interrupted and asked if it had been stolen, now I knew what this was all about.

"No, miss. Does she drive one?" Clara couldn't talk. She just sat there.

"Yes, officer, she does. It's her car. Is there anything wrong with it?"

He reached over and pulled Clara to her feet. "You are under arrest and have the right to remain silent," he said, but before he could continue she started to hit at him and tried to get past him and out the open door. He held her and finished whatever he was saying. I'd heard his speech in the movies. I never thought I'd hear it in reality for me or anyone I knew.

I demanded to know what was going on. Sgt. Hopper told me that Miss Tucker had been seen driving too fast when a lady stepped onto a cross walk and that she had hit her. Instead of staying and helping, Clara left the scene of the accident. The lady was taken to a hospital in serious condition. Clara was identified by one of the student nurses, who wrote down her license number which verified the student's identification.

The officer took Clara to the station. I followed in my own car, a little Honda. At the station she finally admitted she'd been going too fast and knew she hit the lady, but had panicked. The judge gave her two years. He said what made it worse was she was a nurse and could have helped the lady. The lawyer said she probably would only do a few months and get off for good behavior as this was her first offense. The lady didn't die but would walk with a limp the rest of her life.

I was sick. Clara wouldn't graduate and even when she got out there was a question as to whether the school would honor the credits she had earned. She had panicked and left the scene of an accident and her grades and attitude while in school was only about average. Clara was bubbling and lovable but only to those she chose. Teachers were never one of the chosen. None of them were well enough acquainted with her to much care if she ever became a nurse. I felt like holding Clara very close to me so others couldn't see her broken life. Why was it that everything I ever loved either died or was broken?

After graduation when I was wearing a beautiful white cap on my head, I was accepted at the local hospital as a surgical nurse.

I rented an apartment about five blocks away, just within walking distance, packed up my things, moved in and once again was alone. I wanted to stay close because that would allow me to visit Clara on visiting days. The woman's prison where she had been taken the day the judge sentenced her was about an hour away and every visiting day I wasn't pulling duty I went to see her.

I started on the eleven to seven shift, worked seven on and four off. One day on my way to work I saw the officer who had arrested Clara giving a parked car a ticket. I walked to work because my apartment was five blocks to the side door of the hospital. I used that door because it was where the time clock was located. I spoke to him and asked if he remembered me and Clara. I assured him how sorry I was she had panicked and tried to explain to him she really wasn't that kind of a girl when you got to know her.

He finished writing the ticket, put it under a wiper on the windshield, and then walked the rest of the way with me to the hospital. We talked for a moment or two, I said good-bye and went to work. The next day on my way to work he pulled up in his car and asked me when I got off duty. When I told him, he laughed and said he also worked eleven to seven and we had better have breakfast together and get acquainted. We had breakfast the next morning and several other mornings. It got to be a scheduled event as was his managing to drive by when I was on my way to work. He would park his patrol car and walk me up to the door. We started dating, spent time together on our days off, and little by little I stopped going to see Clara.

He was my second husband and we were married on a Sunday afternoon when a Methodist preacher had time to marry us. Neither of us were church goers so we picked the prettiest church in town and approached the preacher one morning after breakfast. Pastor Richards made us take three classes on marriage before he would perform the ceremony. We did and were married. J.D. moved in with me. He had lived in an apartment on the other side of town where he could have pets, my landlady allowed his little poodle, and we started married life, going and coming from work at the same time.

We had been married about three weeks when I finally had the nerve to tell Clara; in fact I took JD with me. We went through all the rigmarole that the prison demanded and waited in the large visiting room. They had to send a message to tell her she had visitors so, as usual, there was about a five-minute wait. The room was filled with tables each with four chairs. At one corner was a desk and two guards and on the other wall was a micro-wave and several machines filled with drinks, candy, and sandwiches. We were allowed to bring in a plastic sack with quarters and our drivers license, but we had to leave our car keys with the guard who hung them on a wall rack for that purpose.

JD and I were on our way to get a cup of coffee when Clara came through the door and saw me she ran and hugged me so tight I thought I'd break. Of course she scolded me for not being there before and then hugged me again before she saw JD.

"What the hell you doing here? Haven't you done enough to me by getting me locked up in this hell hole?" Clara had recognized JD. Neither of us had even thought about the fact she might remember him. This was going to be harder than I thought.

"Clara, he is with me. Sit down I have something to tell you." I pulled out a chair for her as JD pulled one out for me.

"What's going on here, Bea? Why did you bring him to edge in on our time?" I could see the pout side coming to the surface and knew unless she had changed tears were next.

"Clara, this is JD Hopper, my husband. We were married three weeks ago." I waited for it to sink in.

Clara stood and stared, and then very slowly turned and went back through the door she'd come in from. That was the last time I saw Clara Tucker. I tried to call, but she wouldn't come to the phone. I tried to write and she sent the letters back unopened. Finally I gave up.

JD and I were happy, I guess. There wasn't much excitement and having sex with him was a bust. There is a saying, 'wham, bam, thank you, ma'am' which covered our sex relationship quite adequately. I usually made an excuse and he usually accepted it without question. I wondered sometimes if he had other outlets because once or twice a month at our age seemed a little strange according to what I heard during lunch from the other nurses. I wasn't all that interested because I was more interested in the classes I was taking to further my career. I was bucking for a head nurse's title and was going to get it if I knew me. My career was my first priority and JD came in down the line after that somewhere.

JD was as career minded and had just made detective on the local force. I was happy for him so we celebrated, we went out the night they told him the good news and got so loaded we had to take a taxi home. Two months later I knew we had done more than get loaded. I was pregnant and getting sick every morning regularly. JD was thrilled. He didn't have any family either so having some children was pretty important to him. Me, it would interrupt my career plans, so I had mixed feelings.

One moment I was awed with the possibilities of having my own child, my own little baby to love and cuddle, the next moment I was a little angry at JD, especially the mornings I got off duty and spent urping my boot soles into the john. They would only let you nurse through your fifth month so with JD's new promotion and a larger pay check I took a leave of absence and stayed home, my very first time at being a homebody. I started reading recipe books, home beautiful magazines, and even tried attending the church where we were married. JD liked church. I could take it or leave it.

One afternoon while I was reading with my swollen ankles plopped on a foot stool, the postman rang the door. He had a package that was too big for the mailbox. I noticed that the post mark was from the prison where Clare was incarcerated. Strange, but then maybe she was relenting and it made me excited. I had to let her know about the baby. I ran to the phone and called the number in their unit and asked to talk to her. The woman on the other end asked who I was. I told her, and then she asked me to wait. It seemed forever before I heard someone pick up the receiver. "Clara, is that you?" I was so excited at being able to share my news. She loved babies as much as I did and I thought this new little person would put the two of us back together. There were times I missed her so much, simply to talk to. JD and I seldom talked.

"Is this Mrs. Hopper?" the woman asked.

"Yes, I'm Mrs. Hopper. Where is Clara?"

"It seems you weren't notified of Miss Tucker's death. I'm so sorry," she said in her clerically lifeless voice.

"No, I mean I want to talk to Clara Tucker. She's in prison there."

"I was talking about Miss Tucker. She committed suicide a week ago today."

I placed the receiver on the table and sat carefully on the chair near the phone. Somehow I was having trouble breathing. Clara committed suicide. There simply was a mistake somewhere. Then I remembered the package. I jumped up so fast the chair fell over behind me. I didn't even take time to pick it up.

The package was wrapped so securely I had to get a knife from the kitchen to cut the tape. Finally I got it open and saw what was inside: all of Clara's things with an envelope on top addressed to me. In the envelope was her will and a personal letter. The letter shared with me her sorrow at my wedding, how much I had hurt her by rejecting her, and how she just couldn't live without me. She would have been released the next week she wrote, and then, continuing in her tiny handwriting, she wrote that she couldn't face coming out and not being with me. She couldn't believe I would marry the man who took me away from her. She wrote, "I guess my wine turned sour and my roses disappeared into dust. No more wine and roses for me, Bea, dear. I read and reread the letter. She finished by saying she loved me and wanted me to be happy so she was going to go where she could be happy.

Her will granted me everything. I hadn't realized how wealthy she really was until I contacted her lawyer, had a meeting with him, and knew I was now responsible for a house in downtown Atlanta rented by a firm of attorneys, a hotel in Atlantic City managed by a corporation, and several oil wells in Texas. I was a rich woman and I'd have given every cent to have her back.

JD was ecstatic about the money and started spending it before I was even in title. His attitude wedged a small crack in our marriage. There was no sorrow for Clara, or for my mourning. The baby was due in five weeks and I was not able to get over the feeling of loss. I began to panic, everything that had meant anything to me was always taken from me. I was hysterical about the birth of the baby. Would it live or would I lose it too?

The obstetrician tried to reassure me that everything was fine and that the baby was doing well. My feet were still swelling but otherwise things were going according to schedule. JD was called to a two week convention in Washington D.C. He hated to leave me but he had no choice. I was alone and spent each day trying to get in control of myself. Everyday I walked, had lunch at the local drug store fountain, came home, and watched old movies on T.V. One day I asked some of the nurses to come for lunch. It helped a little, especially when they gave me a surprise shower. I went to church on Sunday, then came home and cried my heart out from loneliness and fear.

JD was going to be gone for two weeks, I'd gotten through the first week when one night while I was watching Tyrone Power being a swashbuckling pirate, the chair I was sitting in got all wet, the water had broken, three weeks too early. The pains started immediately. I called the doctor, a cab, and was on my way to the hospital. I'd not even called JD at the hotel I was so nervous. The cab driver got me to the hospital and into the emergency room. They immediately took me up to the maternity ward where the doctor was waiting for me.

After eighteen grueling hours a little boy was born. He lived for about three hours, there was something wrong with his little heart. It just wasn't strong enough. We buried our son and my life became a nightmare. I dreamt of the baby and Juanita and Clara. My dreams never ceased. I couldn't close my eyes that I didn't start dreaming. I wanted to join them all and one night when I couldn't take any more I slit my wrists. JD rushed me to the hospital and they saved my life. The law of our state demanded psychiatric care for any attempted suicide and I was enfolded in

the arms of a psychiatrist, and put behind locked doors and
screened windows for nearly six months.

JD divorced me. I had really expected it and didn't much care.
He didn't do it while I was under the state's care because it was
illegal, but I wasn't out but about a month when I was handed the
divorce papers. Without even contesting it I gave him what he
wanted, and soon a small nurse who worked in peds became the
new Mrs. Hopper.

Don't ask me how many months and years I nursed after that.
I became a robot. I got up in the morning, I was on days by then,
walked to work, , ate lunch in the cafeteria, went home, turned on
the T.V., watched a movie while I ate a T.V. dinner, took my
shower, put my hair up and went to bed. Once in a while I
attended church just to break the monotony. Sometimes instead
of eating at home I'd take in a show and dinner downtown. Money
was no object, I had all of Clara's, JD's alimony, and my pay
check. Once a year I hired an income tax attorney to do the taxes,
wrote a check for the I.R.S., and was amazed I had enough to
cover the amount the lawyer said they would demand.

One night I went to a show that was playing in a theater in the
not-so-nice section of town. Next to it was a bar and for some
reason I went in for a drink after the theater let out. It was a gay
bar. I'd heard of them but never had a reason to go to one. A really
nice looking man took my order and then while I was sitting there
watching what was going on, an older, rather wrinkled, and very
heavily painted lady came and sat down at my table.

"You lonely honey?" she asked, as she put her hand on my
knee under the table. "Come with me and I'll take care of that." I
was so damn lonely and had been alone for much too long, so I
went with her. From then on I frequented the bar whenever I had
a free night and started drinking heavily, and it didn't make much
difference who the "lady" was with whom I played the game. It is
an absolute miracle I didn't come down with AIDS before I shook
my head and came out of the haze.

It was on a Saturday night and for some reason I had gone
light on the booze, had an upset stomach, and was almost ready

to call it a night when a girl came in and sat at the next table. She was crying and kept dabbing her eyes with a handkerchief that was far from clean. I'd had just enough to make me verbally brave so got up and sat next to her.

"What's the matter, honey, you lonely?" They say when you are dying your whole life flashes in front of you. I wasn't dying but all at once I was the old lady making a pitch at a young girl. I'd be wrinkled and painted someday hoping for a little fun from some gal that was down on her luck, living in a room three floors up in a cold-water flat. I got up that very moment, went into the cloak room, got my coat and drove home. I never went back.

I was back to being alone and lonely. I concentrated on my career, at least I still had my job. It was a wonder I did when I counted the number of times I'd been looped and had gone to work with a hang-over. There was an opening in Santa Barbara for a head nurse. I applied, got the job, and moved out of the area I had lived in all my life and hopefully away from memories. The weather was a wonder to me. It was winter and people were walking around in shirt sleeves. The rents were atrocious but I had an adequate income so I rented a pretty nifty apartment. I invested in a new car, a convertible that let the sun and the air comb the cobwebs out of my brain. I threw away all my clothes and redid my closet from side to side with California-type clothes. I bought a membership in the golf club, took lessons, and decided it was time to carve off a few pounds.

I'd never really had fun in my life and I decided the new California gal was going to learn to live a little. I stayed away from the bars and was into sports until my tail drooped by the time I hit the bed at night. I was getting brown as a berry, feeling like a million, and working everyday. I met Clayton Forestor in a golf foursome and married him three weeks later.

He had money. I had money. He was a computer expert of some kind and did a lot of his work at home, the new one he moved me into with a view of the ocean. He told me I didn't have to work and he preferred I didn't. We were expected to do a lot of entertaining and would be traveling to Europe in the fall since some of his clients were overseas and he had to touch base with them to keep the accounts fluid. I quit work, played eighteen holes every morning, dove into the pool in the afternoon, and socialized in the evening. Clay was a lot of fun, we made love on the beach, in the car, and anyplace he felt like it.

We stayed married for almost seven years. Back and forth to Europe, South America, and even a trip to Russia. I never had time to be alone and yet I was lonely way down deep inside where I didn't go very often. We were in Mexico one weekend when I met Sam McGill. He was the senior executive in Clayton's company who was responsible for overseas problems. Clay called him his right hand man, sort of laughed when he talked about him, and said he was a goody-two-shoes. Never drank, went to church on Sunday, and had lost his wife when she was delivering their little girl. At least he isn't horning around and I can trust him, Clay kept repeating to me as if I hadn't heard it before. Clay was fun but boring and when he drank he was silly.

We were having dinner one evening when Sam walked in. Clay introduced us and I nearly fainted. He was a duplicate of my father. He sounded like my Father and walked like him. I couldn't quit staring. Clay touched my hand and brought me back out of a dream.

Later I shared with Clay what had happened. Every time I saw Sam I thought of the past. He talked nicely to me quite aware that I was his boss's wife. He was never impolite and always had interesting subjects to talk about. He'd been all over the world and in every jungle, swamp, and mountain top there was. He had the black hair my Father had, was muscular and square-jawed, with brown eyes that had no bottom. I had a feeling of contentment whenever he was near. I always felt safe near him, a feeling I'd never had in my life.

Clayton and I went back to Santa Barbara and Sam took off for Italy and some new contacts. I didn't see him until after Clay and I decided it wasn't good and settled our differences in a divorce court, still friends but tired of each other.

Clay gave me the house in Santa Barbara and he moved to New Hampshire where they were building a large plant. I heard a few months after the divorce was final that he had married again. Later I learned that his marriage lasted a little under two years. Clay got bored easily. He was a man who had to capture the enemy, and every new woman was a challenge. As soon as he won the battle, and his fascination ended, he became uninterested and needed a new challenge. I felt honored, as I laughed to myself, as he had stayed with me longer than with any other woman.

The hospital at Santa Barbara took me back and I ended up being the head nurse, having an office on the third floor and a lot of headaches. I was alone again in a big house that faced the ocean. I had two servants and a large mongrel dog that never came when it was called. Shep was some kind of collie, shepherd, lab mix. He had short and long hair, and was brown and black, and was actually quite ugly, but I loved him. I had the back yard fenced and locks put on the gates. I wasn't about to have him run out into the street and get hit.

One afternoon I was on the general ward checking the charts and recognized the name Sam McGill. He was in room seven twenty three down in the men's wing. He had a broken leg and a rather bad infection which had kept him in longer than a broken leg alone would have done. I went to the room and walked in. He was talking to the hospital chaplain, and they were going at it hot and heavy over something called predestination.

"I hate to interrupt but I had to stop in and say hello." I reached my hand out and shook his that was offered quite willingly. He was excited to see me and asked me to stop in again. I left the room and they went right back to their discussion.

I visited Sam for about three days regularly and we talked about everything in the world. He would get onto religion and I would sit there and listen. I didn't know enough about it to say much. He talked about how his daughter was growing. She lived with his sister in Washington and was almost eleven, and he had a wallet filled with pictures of a little girl with pigtails and two very large dark eyes. I was amazed at the likeness. She resembled Juanita, which I suppose was expected because of the similarity of Sam to my father. I told him of the resemblance and even brought the only picture I had and showed him. I didn't have a picture of Mama or Juanita.

Sam had a small apartment in Santa Barbara he used when he was in town doing business with Clay. He was in the process of closing it down and moving to an apartment near the new plant when he tripped carrying a box to the car. He got a nasty crack above the knee. The day before he was to be released I suggested he come and stay at my house. It was plenty big and there was a housekeeper there who could take care of him until the cast came off. After a few refusals he gave in and decided that fending for himself as yet with a cast from his hip to his ankle was a little much.

It was wonderful having someone to come home to, to talk to, and to share with. We learned to really like each other and before long were talking of the future. He wanted me to meet Cecilia and we planned on it as soon as he could travel. With our new relationship Sam felt he would prefer working for another company. He applied and before long was accepted for about the same type of position he had held with Clay. Clay would never have let our relationship make a difference. It was Sam that preferred to distance himself from Clay.

When the cast came off we visited his daughter. She was a little darling but as she had grown up with Sam's sister we felt it was not fair to disrupt her life. Sam and I were married. He stayed in the house and his only move was into my bedroom. We enjoyed talking sometimes half the night. In fact we enjoyed each other tremendously. Oh we stopped at times and had sex because it was expected. It wasn't anything spectacular, but it was nice. And wonders of wonders I got pregnant.

Sam wanted me to go to church with him every Sunday. It turned out I enjoyed it and even got busy working in the ladies-aid gathering up and sending clothes to orphanages. Believe me the clothes were clean and the shoes were practically new. There were no holes in the shoes I had anything to do with sending away. The toys were new. I went to many of the stores and purchased the ones that were on the shelves too long. I also bought dolls that had all their hair and arms. One Sunday Sam asked me if I would join the church with him, I couldn't object, and we did.

Out daughter was born healthy and with everything working the way it was meant to function. We named her Mary Sue after his mother Mary and his grandmother Susan. I didn't mind, I was so happy being a new mother he could have named her about anything and I would have agreed. I stopped working and became a full-time Mom, and I loved it.

Being a mother of a little girl I had to do some real deep thinking about where I had come from and some of the actions in my past. The sermons were getting to me about sin and repentance and Jesus and being saved. It had never made much sense to me before—I guess I hadn't given it much attention—but if this was all on the up and up then I was in for some mental changes and had better decide which way I was headed. I let the nurse watch Mary Sue one afternoon while Sam was at work and visited the pastor.

We spent over two hours in his office and when I walked out I had given my heart to Jesus, the past was wiped out, and I had a brand new life ahead. I was a mother and a wife and I was going to be just as good at that as I was a nurse. And I was.

Sam had a heart attack the summer Mary Sue was fifteen and as I stood over his open coffin I thanked him for my daughter and the happiness he had given me. I also made a promise never to marry again and to make Mary Sue's life as clean and loving and as wonderful as I could.

That next summer I met Wesley Richards at a church dinner and we hit it off wonderfully. He was tall and thin and had gleaming white hair. He was a retired missionary from Japan and was now the assistant to the pastor for seniors. We had dinner together, went to shows together, took trips to different mission fields, and used up the money that kept accumulating in the bank from Clara's investments, insurance payments from JD, alimony from Clayton who still paid it even though he was on his fourth or fifth wife, and Sam's insurance. Mary Sue was in college and engaged to a man we both adored named Bill Carroll.

Wes and I never had sex or got married. We just enjoyed loving to be together and doing what we could for our boss, the Lord. Wes died two years ago. He was eighty-six. There were so many people at his funeral they had to T.V. the service so people sitting on the lawn could see what was going on. There will come a day I'll join him and the others, I hope.

So we have covered about all of my life. I'm not much use to my daughter, Mary Sue, or with her children, Tricia, and Bill Jr., but I try. I love them dearly and that's what counts. I shared my life with Mary Sue before I ever shared it with you and she will watch little Tricia and be careful of Bill Jr. I've told her the best thing she can do for those children is to let them know they are loved. I also told her to find a good Christian man, marry him, and give those darling kids a father here on earth. They've got one in heaven but they need one on earth who can play ball and show them the correct kind of love.

I can never see a bottle of wine or a bunch of dried roses without thinking of Clara. My one sadness is that my dearest friend never knew the Lord as I do. I'm sorry we hurt Him with our actions but He forgave me for that a long time ago. Yes, I shared all of that with Wesley, and he said that everyone had a skeleton hidden in the closet somewhere, then he added with that loving kind way he had, that God shut my closet doors when I repented so they couldn't be opened, and that only He had the key.

She leaned to the side of her over-stuffed purple velour chair, not quite strong enough to sit upright. Her hair was thin, and yet rather curly, white and grey mixed equally. It was her eyes that hadn't aged; they were bright and twinkled when she looked at me. I felt special to be sitting in her 'parlor' taping her story.

The room gave off an odor of age. The curtains were limp, and the drapes had been drawn much too long. The sun had let their color escape. The folds tried to keep in step with the metal prongs that made them into proper drapes but finally had given up and let everything hang the way it had for many years. The wall paper once had bright little pink roses with spring colored leaves here and there, but now it was dry and yellowed, separating from the walls in the corners and at the seams.

The rug had worn spots in traffic areas while the furniture-covered carpet still boasted of color and depth. A large cat curled in front of a fireplace that was filled with old newspapers and a potted geranium that had never been dumped after it gave up trying to bloom.

Somehow none of these things made any difference to Bea as she told me her story. As I thought about the room later I had the feeling it was being kind to accompany her on this voyage into time. When we were finished I looked in the chest and there was Melissa. I had to take her out and see what it felt like to hold her so that her missing arm wouldn't show.

"Pretty ugly, isn't she?" Bea was grinning as she watched me. The twinkle in her eyes went a little dim and I could see memories crowding me out of her consciousness. I turned and carefully laid Melissa back in her casket and closed the lid softly. My new friend had gone to sleep. I had tired her. Quietly I picked up my things and slipped on my jacket to tiptoe out of the room. I'd reached the door when I heard her say, "Good-bye, thank you for asking me to share with you. Don't let the cat out, dear." I didn't let the cat out because it was still guarding the fireplace and the dead geranium.

12

"You Can't Go Back"

THERE IS ONE THING IN THIS LIFE THAT IS IMPOSSIBLE, and that is to go back, even for a second, and re-do what you did. You can pray for a second chance and you might get it and then you might not. I didn't. By the time I knew what made me tick I'd already gone too far and was in the midst of the consequences of my own stupidity.

Things had not been going well for some time and I'd had to take off a few days from work as I couldn't get over the flu. I was the manager of a book store in Kirkland and had to have my wife, Katie, open the store at eleven and work until one when the two clerks came on duty. We were open from eleven until nine everyday. Katie took the baby and Bobby with her and kept them in the back office. I wasn't even up to caring for them at home. Aletha was one, and Bobby had just turned four when I started to feel pretty sick. Kenneth was in first grade and could walk to school and take care of himself pretty well when he got home.

Katie finally talked me into seeing our family doctor. Chuck referred me to a Dr. Baird in Seattle since he felt what was wrong with me was beyond his scope. Chuck and I were personal friends as well as his being our family doctor. When my reports came back he cleared his throat, a habit he'd had for a long time, over the pieces of paper in his hands and told me to go see Dr. Baird. I asked him what he thought and he repeated the instructions and looked away. His actions concerned me; in fact, the way he acted I was just a little frightened.

Chuck reassured me that he was just a family doctor and these days the ones who knew what they were doing were specialists.

He felt I needed to have a more thorough check-up, after all I was nearing forty and time for a tune up. Then he laughed, patted me on the shoulder, and asked what time Saturday we planned to tee off. Every Saturday for years when it wasn't raining, we'd played early enough so that I could get to work by eleven to open the store.

I didn't play golf that Saturday morning. I was flat on my back in bed and Katie opened the store. The next week I made an appointment and drove into Seattle to Dr. Baird's office. His third-floor office was on Fifth Street. When I went in there were mostly men waiting to see him and some of them looked pretty sick. I sure hoped I wouldn't pick up any germs from waiting with them.

When I finally got into one of the little rooms and had waited some more I got a little angry at having to wait so long. Chuck's office wasn't as big and you never had to wait too long. Dr. Baird was an older man. His hair was white and I noticed he had a large scar on the right side of his cheek. I wondered how he'd gotten it. He sat on a small swivel stool in front of a cabinet and faced me.

"Bill Spencer, I am Dr. Baird," he said as he reached out to shake my hand.

"Good afternoon," was my reply.

"Bill, I have some rather disturbing news and I would like to know a little bit about you before we get into it. I read here that you are married with three children so I must know if you have had any homosexual actions in your background or are currently actively gay?"

I nearly collapsed. How did he even suspect? I was married, yes, but since I had been in grade school I'd been gay. No one knew it except a few of those I had been with. I'd gotten married because that was what I was supposed to do for society. I married Katie because she was willing and didn't demand very much of me. The kids I loved and that was another of the reasons I'd married. I had always wanted kids ever since my mother died. Two days after our Mother's funeral my dad had dumped me and Clarissa on our Aunt Clara and Uncle Baxter and then disappeared. Aunt Clara and Uncle Baxter didn't have any kids and they became our parents. I was seven when we went to live with them and Clara was nine. Aunt Clara was mother's sister and a loving and kinder person you would never find. Uncle Baxter was a clown and loved by the whole neighborhood of kids. He loved me, continually hugged me, even kissed me when Aunt Clara wasn't looking, and taught me to be gay as he was.

"Why did you ask me about being a homosexual? I'm a married man. Aren't you presuming a lot?" I retreated into blaming the doctor for poor manners.

"Bill, you have AIDS, and there is no question of how a person gets it. I'm concerned because you are married, your wife and children will know eventually, and your wife must be tested as well." He just sat there and kept fiddling with the papers in his hand. AIDS, me? I had never had sex without a condom. How? It wasn't possible, and Katie, what was I going to do. My God, AIDS was a terminal disease. I was going to die.

"There must be a mistake, Dr. Baird. There has to be." I was grasping. There had to be a way out of this nightmare.

"Bill, Dr. Thomas sent me these reports, and the tests you took at the clinic before you came here verify his findings. The reason Dr. Thomas sent you here is we treat HIV and AIDS and have programs for men and women that help; we also have support groups for you and for your family. You are aware we can't cure you but we can help to a degree." He stood up and opened the cabinet and handed me several sheets from it with information on the clinic and my disease.

There were the initials, AIDS. I knew the chances I'd taken but I was so certain it would never be me. I was careful and chose my partners carefully. I'd been with Brewer for several years. He worked at the theater a block from my store and we would meet a couple or three times a month for dinner, we always ended up at his apartment afterwards. I'd tell Katie I had book work and she never questioned me. She never questioned me on anything. She never argued or found fault, was wrapped up in the children, and if we only had sex once every couple of months she said nothing. In fact, I had sex with her mainly to have children. She would just lay there and say nothing until it was over then get up and take a shower.

I always felt as if I was just an instrument to beget kids, and that was all I really wanted anyway. I never loved her. She was my way of getting the children I wanted. I didn't love Brewer either. He was just a way of acting out the habit I had acquired as a boy. I had loved one person, my mother, and had been angry at God ever since the day when I was seven and my Dad came into my bedroom one night, bundled me up, and put me in the car. Clarissa was asleep on the seat and Mother was in the front seat moaning. Dad dropped us off at Aunt Clarissa's and took Mother to the hospital. I heard the telephone ring later on. Clarissa and I were in the big bed in the guest room and I hadn't been able to go to sleep because Clarissa was kicking and wriggling all the time. Aunt Clarissa was crying as she told Uncle Baxter that my mother died giving birth to a little girl who died too.

Dad picked us up in the morning, took us home, and spent the next few days until the funeral plastered. The day after Mother's funeral he packed us up and dumped us on the front steps of Aunt Clarissa's house with our suitcases stuffed with clothes and two boxes of toys. Aunt Clarissa wasn't home. Dad said to wait for her and left. I never saw him again and had no idea where he went or if he was even alive. Once when I got older and graduated from college as an English major I tried to find him but it was useless. There were no trails. One service I hired looked up his social security number and there wasn't a current address. It was as if he had disappeared off the planet.

"Bill, we have to make some plans." The doctor's voice broke into my memories.

"What plans? I'm a dead man. What plans can a dead man make?" I gave up at that moment. I had no future and the plans I'd made for expanding the store, adding another clerk and even a coffee corner were of no use. And the kids, what would happen to them? Katie wasn't capable of handling finances and the store and the kids. I'd give her spending money and the kid's allowances, well, the two older ones, and she charged everything else.

I'd given her a check book once and she got it all messed up so I took it away and took over everything else.

"You aren't entering the mortuary tomorrow, Bill, and there are many things you can do. As far as how much time you have in a way depends on how you live it. There are many things we can do to help but you must realize there are also some things you must do immediately, and one is to have your wife come in and be tested. There are some things you are going to have to learn to do; ways of living, especially with your wife, and you also must have the men you have slept with tested. Everyone you have been with must be notified. Here are some cards for this clinic. Have them all come in. It is imperative we start treatment as soon as possible if they have it. After all one of them gave it to you." He patted me on the shoulder.

"I am having you meet with a consultant on the second floor before you leave, and I will want to see you again in a month. The consultant will tell you what is necessary and give you some prescriptions I want you to have filled and take regularly. He will also give you a schedule of when you are to come in and when the support groups meet. I suggest you follow his directions carefully. You must tell your wife immediately and get her to come in. She will be a part of your support group as well as your children. I'm sorry to have to be the bearer of such sad news but that is part of being a doctor." He opened the door and motioned to his nurse.

"Miss, Larson, will you please make appointments for Mr. Spencer for next month and also send him downstairs to start his treatments and support groups."

"Bill, Miss Larson will take good care of you. Just follow her into her office there to the left."

I don't remember much of the rest of that day. It was going from one office to another and meeting people who were kind and gracious and kept telling me there was hope but that I must be certain to do what the doctor had scheduled. It was after four-thirty by the time I was back in the car and headed home. I had no idea what I was going to do. It had started to rain and the five o'clock traffic was getting backed up. Some joker had slid into someone on the bridge and I was forced to sit there, the rain pounding the top of the car. Finally I turned off the motor and watched the waves beginning to lap up on the side of the bridge. The storm was picking up and sheets of rain made visibility poor.

Katie. What was I going to tell her? And the children. How could I face them, their Dad dying of AIDS? And what would people think of me at the shop? Church, now that was going to be the hardest. I was a deacon and taught third grade boys. I couldn't face it. All the people who thought I was an upstanding citizen and a good father, how could I face them? The driver ahead started his motor and the smoke from it alerted me to start mine and creep ahead. It was after six before I pulled into the driveway. Katie was in the kitchen, the baby in a roll-away crib next to the kitchen table, and I could hear Ken and Bobby in the play room arguing over who got to ride the rocking horse their Aunt Clarissa had given them for Christmas.

Uncle Baxter had died the year I graduated from college. Aunt Clarissa lived in an apartment not too far from our house so she could help Katie with the babies and see me more often. I'd learned to love her almost as much as my mother but there was always a hurt inside of me when I thought of my mother. I missed Uncle Baxter but others had taken his place. My Dad had been replaced many times by older men. I was young and had curly blond hair, large blue eyes, and was "a looker" as Aunt Clarissa would say.

Uncle Baxter never found out he was not my only partner. My second grade teacher, a youth director at church camp, and Uncle Baxter's lawyer were all my close men friends. I needed them. I needed to be accepted by as many men as I could. I always had this little feeling inside of me that I'd show my Dad I didn't need him. Each time I gave out my favors I gloated that this man wanted me and would never have left me. The sad thing is they all did, except Brewer.

Brewer, I had to get to him and tell him. Maybe I'd lose everybody and die alone. I hung my jacket up in the front closet, yelled a hello at Katie, and went straight up to my office. I had taken one of the upstairs bedrooms and made it into an office so I could bring some of the paper work home. I didn't dare use the phone so I got onto the computer and hoped Brewer would be on his at his home or even the one in his office. He managed the theatre and saw that the systems were set for showing the movie on time. He also managed the help at the popcorn and candy counter. He was a partner in the theater with several other business people in town.

Local business men had built the theater when I was in high school and it was still going. Brewer's parents had owned a share and when they retired they signed it over to him. He was always at the theater so the board of directors made him manager and he had been the manager ever since he left high school. He'd never gone to college. He said there wasn't any use since he was doing what he wanted to do. He tried to talk and walk like Humphrey Bogart and had pictures of him all over his office, even an autographed picture. He had gone to Hollywood one summer and tried to meet as many stars as he could. There were several other signed pictures but he treasured the one of Bogart.

I couldn't get an answer and decided after dinner to make an excuse to go to the office and make-up some of the paper work I'd missed being gone. There was a small knock on the door, I knew it was Katie.

"Come in, Katie,"

"Bill, what did the doctor say? I have been worried." She sat in the small rocker at the side of the desk and folded her hands like a child who was waiting to be scolded.

"Oh, it wasn't much, just a hang over from the flu. He gave me some pills and said I had to go back in a month to check it. When is dinner?" She obediently rose and answered, "It is ready. I'll get the children."

That was Katie, no questions and no visible signs of feelings. I often wondered if she had any except for the children. I would put off telling her as long as I could. But there were those nagging, insistent words of the doctor to get her tested. I'd talk to Chuck and have him bring her in for a test, something about seeing if she had the flu too, or something. That way we could find out if she had been infected and if she wasn't maybe I could carry this thing on for as long as I could. Maybe I could even keep everyone except

Brewer and Chuck from knowing about it. That was my answer. I'd work it out. I'd always worked everything out before so why not this? I had a plan. I'd keep everyone out of it except Brewer and Chuck.

The next day I contacted Chuck and told him what Dr. Baird had said. Of course he already knew, and told me how sorry he was. He never said a thing about my being gay. He just said he would call Katie in and test her. He warned me my plan wouldn't work and I should share it so my family could be a support. I was getting angry and knew I'd damn well do it my way and nobody was going to tell me different. I had lived my life my way and I didn't care what others thought. Well that wasn't actually true. I'd done all the right things. I'd married. I was a good husband. I paid for everything, wasn't it debt, and certainly had treated everyone fairly and owed no one anything.

When I told Brewer he ducked his head and said he suspected he had it too as he hadn't been feeling good. The son-of-a-bitch had given me AIDS and he didn't give a damn. He'd been playing around with other men and all the time he'd told me he hadn't. I hated his guts. I felt like killing him, a feeling which was new to me. Extremes were not the way I lived. I was careful and cautious and like Katie did all the right things at the right time, well, except for my secret life of being gay, but I excused that as just one of those things that happen. Of course, even my gay life was scheduled and there was no excessiveness in any of my relationships. I used the men and I knew they used me. If I broke up with a partner I just went out and found someone else. What difference did it make? They were all built the same way and once I had what I wanted and they had what they were there for, it was over. Life was scheduled and if you were half-way intelligent you could direct your life with a safe and sane schedule.

This whole thing was not planned and I needed to be in control. Uncle Baxter had taught me to be in control as he was. Aunt Clarissa had no hint of his other life. He'd told me men had the right to do what they wanted to and women were not to control them. Aunt Clarissa controlled him, or so she thought, and Uncle Baxter said that was as it should be. "Let the little woman think she is running the show and then go do what ever the hell you want to do, just don't let her know." I did what I wanted with my life and now that there was a screw up, I was still going to schedule what future I could.

Chuck tested Katie and she was clean. At least there was no need for me to tell her now. I went to the appointments at the doctor and turned down the support groups. Why did I need such nonsense that was for men who didn't have a backbone. I'd gotten my self into this mess and I was going to get myself out somehow. They were discovering new things all the time and I was feeling a lot better with all the pills I took everyday. I hadn't missed a day at the store for several months. I moved into the guest room and told Katie we should wait until Aletha was at least two before we had any more children. She took my move as she did everything, calmly and with little or no feeling. I wondered if there was any feeling in her.

I watched Katie carefully. For some reason I had to know what made her the way she was. I hadn't known any of her family. We met at college and it was simply a matter of necessity for me to marry so I picked her. She seemed to feel the same and we were married by the Justice of Peace on spring break, went back to our respective dorms, graduated, and then I moved her back to Kirkland. We bought a house not too far from the shop and our married life began. One night after dinner while we were having coffee she announced in her whispery voice she was pregnant. She suggested we turn the guest room into a nursery. I agreed and for several months she spent her days fixing, painting and preparing for the baby. It was rather matter-of-fact the night she woke me and asked me to drive her to the hospital where twelve or more hours later my son Kenneth was born.

I had asked Katie several times about her parents and she would say, "I don't wish to talk about my family." When Kenneth was born I asked her if she would like me to phone her family. She said no, so I didn't mention it again. Her maiden name was Waterhouse. She was born in Wichita and was three years my junior. It occurred to me that she might need her family, so one night as we were having our coffee I told her I had to have the address of her next of kin for the new insurance forms I was filling out. I had a paper and pen in hand and figured she would oblige as she always did.

"Just write deceased. If family is needed there is always Aunt Clarissa and you are quite capable of handling any emergency." She picked up her coffee cup and put it to her lips without drinking, then put it down, got up and left the room. I was utterly amazed. She walked out on me, something she had never done in all of our time together. Now my curiosity was pricked past endurance. I followed her out of the room and said with my 'obey me' voice, "I'm sorry, Katie, but I must have some background on your family."

"Bill I have no intentions of talking about them. The matter is closed." It was at that moment we had our first fight.

"Damn it, Katie, what is there about your family that you won't talk about them. I demand an answer. Come back in the dining room and sit down and let's talk this thing out." I took her arm and literally dragged her back to her chair. She sat and folded her hands in her lap and closed her mouth tightly like a child who didn't want to take a spoon filled with medicine.

"Katie, I need to know, and especially for the children. They have to know where their grandparents are if they are alive. Now quit being stubborn and tell me where your parents live."

She sat there for quite a long time and then said, "My parents are dead. They were mountain climbing in Switzerland and were killed in an avalanche. My father was a geologist and my mother went with him wherever his company sent him. I was three when they were killed. They'd left me with a baby sitter at the lodge when it happened. I was brought up by my Uncle who was never married and treated me as if I were there for his use in everything. His name is Frank Waterhouse. He was my father's brother and he lives in Dallas. He owns the Waterhouse Emporium on the main street. I have the address up stairs but if you have any feelings for me at all, which I doubt, please do not contact him and let him know where I am." She closed her mouth and just sat there, all the color had faded from her face and there were tears on her cheeks. I had never seen her cry, even when she was birthing the children she had never made a sound. What had she said? She doubted if I had any feelings for her?

"Katie, I have no plans in contacting your Uncle. Why didn't you ever tell me how you were treated growing up. I would have understood."

"Would you, Bill?" She stood and started to take the dishes off the table and carry them into the kitchen, leaving me standing there without an answer to her accusation. Now I knew why she was so unrevealing. She'd been used by her Uncle and then I'd used her for my own goals of children and nothing more. I'd never told her I loved her, never treated her with any compassion. Sexually I had treated her as a duty with no kindness of any kind. I figured she owed me children because I paid the bills and saw to it they had plenty of whatever they wanted. She was a tool, just like the clerks at the store, like Brewer, and anyone else who was a necessity in my everyday associations. I had liked it that way. That way I didn't owe anybody anything.

I felt cheap. Somehow she had made me feel shoddy and ugly and I didn't like my reaction. She was comparing me to her Uncle and I didn't like the assessment. She gave all of herself to the children. They adored her but were polite to me. My own children were polite to me, and a little afraid of me. At dinner Ken and Bobby sat as quietly as their mother, and when I got up from the table and went into my office I could hear the three of them laughing and talking to each other. Before it hadn't bothered me but now I was feeling angry. I wasn't the type to get angry;. I was intelligent and could figure out a problem without getting emotionally involved. I didn't like the mood I was in. I felt like I was being left out somehow, and I was. I was in control but it seemed as if Katie really was in her quiet stubborn way, and I didn't quite know what to do with this new transfer.

I never contacted her Uncle, simply put his name and address in the address book in my computer and ignored it. It was time for my third monthly visit to Dr. Baird. He took more tests and changed some medication and told me he was not at all pleased with my progress, something about my blood count. This didn't make much sense to me but it explained the loss of weight and some very sleepless nights. I was getting pretty thin and my appetite was gone. I had to make myself eat but there were days I couldn't. I'd sent my suits out to be tailored and thought I was getting by with my secret. One Saturday morning Chuck asked me to have a cup of coffee before I left the proshop for the store.

"When are you going to tell, Katie, Bill? You are getting pretty thin and from your game today pretty weak as well."

"Are you at that again?" I was angry. "I'm fine and have no intentions of telling her or anyone else and you sure as hell can't, you know all that doctor-patient stuff." I thought I had him, but he kept on.

"What are you going to do when you can't get out of bed and go to work? Are you making plans to have someone to take over the store?"

"Chuck, lay off. I'm still able to handle things and I sure as hell don't need a doctor telling me about my business. I have to go, see you next Saturday." With that I got up, went to my locker and changed to go to work.

On the way to work I started to think what if I didn't make it? I'd never really contemplated on not getting better, I knew I could lick it so why was I upset? Something in the back of my mind told me I was kidding myself and the day was getting closer when I wouldn't be able to go to work. Already I was getting so tired by the end of the day I could hardly make it home for dinner. I had to face reality. I wasn't ready to die. I wasn't even old yet and my kids were just kids, not going to college, I hadn't even seen Kenneth graduate from sixth grade. I pulled off the side of the road near the park and got out of the car and took a walk in the trees. Die, I was going to die before I'd even lived a full life. There was only so much the doctors could do. He'd told me that and I had ignored him.

All at once I was angry. I clenched my fists and raised them and screamed at God. How dare He do this to me? I gave to the church, taught Sunday school, took my family every Sunday, and followed all the rules. All the rules? There was a bench in a small grove and I sat there trying to get in control. All the rules, the words kept clamoring in my mind. So I hadn't followed all of them, but good God, no one was perfect, I thought. Lip service was the word that crossed my mind. My relationship with God was doing my duty, filling the social expectancies for mature men, and doing a damn good job. Angry I left the grove and drove rather fast the rest of the way to work. I wasn't weak-kneed and this kind of thinking was pathetic as well as not very intelligent. I was just weak because of all the medicine the dumb doctor was forcing me to take.

The following Saturday I didn't feel like playing and I missed several Saturdays in the following months. Work was getting to be almost all I could handle and then I caught the flu. I was in bed for nearly a week. Chuck came by one day when Katie was out with Bobby and Althea. I guess they had gone to the park. I'd finally decided to train a new man to manage and he was doing quite well so I thought I'd just spend a couple more days resting and get a little stronger before I took back the reigns

"So how're you doing?" Chuck slapped my shoulder and grinned his one-sided smile. I was sitting in the recliner watching T.V.

"Going back to work Monday. I guess I beat this flu. Many others down with it? I hope the kids don't get it makes it too hard on Katie to have them sick. See Katie on your way in? She and kids are off to the park, I think."

"No, I didn't see Katie."

Want a cup of coffee. I think there is some in the kitchen. Throw it in the micro to get hot." I was glad to see him and something other than the chatter and nonsense the T.V. afforded.

"I had a cup at the office. Came over to talk to you Bill. We've got to get to the bottom of what is going on."

"Good God, Chuck, are you going to start preaching or did you come for a visit?" I was getting angry. Why didn't he just tend to his own business?

"Bill, when are you going to tell Katie? You have got to get things in order. You aren't going to get over the flu, Bill. You are dying and you have got to face it. I'm your friend. Let me help. I'll tell Katie if you like."

"Chuck, I thought we had this settled. I'm not telling anybody, least of all Katie. I don't want the kids to know their Father died of AIDS. You call me your friend, then if I do kick the bucket,

which I don't think is going to happen—I feel much better today—
you can tell them it was a heart attack or something." There, that
was the answer. Chuck was a doctor and he could fix it.

"Bill, I can't do that. You know I can't. You have got to tell
Katie, don't you think you at least owe that much to her. You
haven't given her much as far as love now, have you?"

"What the hell, she been crying on your shoulder?"

"You know better than that. Katie never talks to anybody
except those kids of hers. She doesn't join in with the women in
church and only worked in the nursery because Althea was in it.
She's very shy and withdrawn. There is something bothering that
lady and I think it is lack of love. I've never seen you touch her. It
is a wonder there are any children the way you two treat each
other." Chuck sat down on the couch facing me and leaned back
with his legs out into the room. Whenever he had a chance he
relaxed.

"Why do we need to go over this again, Chuck? I'm not going
to tell anyone and you can't, so that is the way it is going to be. I
stopped teaching the kids at church. I told them I didn't have
time. Fact is I haven't even gone for the last several Sundays.
Katie takes the kids. It gives me time to rest with no noise in the
house."

"Bill, let me tell Katie. You have to let her know before she
finds it out some other way. You will get a bill in the mail, Dr.
Baird's office will call, the support team will drop by, something
is going to happen, and that is a chicken way for her to find out.
You have always been a fair man, and this is not fair, and not very
complimentary to you." Chuck sat up straight and looked me in
the eye.

"Maybe it won't happen and she won't have to find out,
Chuck." I was getting tired and I wanted him to leave.

"Bill, think. She's your wife. She needs to know. Man, get
some guts and do it." Chuck stood up and all six feet two of him
leaned over me. "Bill, you're more of a man than this." I knew he
was right but how could I admit that I'd been sleeping with
Brewer and her at the same time. How she missed getting it was
a miracle. It was a good thing we seldom had sex. "I'll tell her if

it will help." Maybe it would be easier hearing it from me and then I can explain just what it is."

Chuck touched my shoulder and squeezed. I could tell how it hurt him as there was nothing much there but bone. We'd been good friends. He was the one person in the world who hadn't wanted anything from me, and I'd never asked him for anything. I didn't want to owe anybody anything. I would have to tell Katie myself. I couldn't owe Chuck for that kind of a favor.

"I'll tell her, Chuck. I'll tell her. She will probably leave me but then she hasn't any money so maybe she will stay because she needs my money. I certainly haven't given her anything else."

"Bill, what about you and God? You've been a good church-goer. Have you talked to the pastor?"

"No, and that is one I'm not going to do. Katie yes, anyone else, no, and that's final."

"O.K. just so you let Katie know what she is in for. I'll call you later. I have to make rounds at the hospital." Chuck left and let the screen door bang. I needed to fix that hinge.

That evening when she was finished with the dishes and after she'd put the kids to bed, she came in and sat on the couch to watch T.V. with me. I turned it off and told her I needed to talk. She sat there as usual, her hands folded and perfectly motionless.

"Katie, I don't know how to tell you this, but it isn't the flu that has made me sick. I have AIDS. I've been gay for a long time and Brewer at the theater gave it to me. He also has it and has gone back east to be with his sister. I'm not going to get well and there are some things we need to take care of. I know this is a shock and I really think I owe you an apology. I'm sorry I haven't been a better husband. I really am."

She sat there not moving a muscle. Even her eyes were motionless. She was still for the longest time and then she said in that whispering voice of hers, " I know Bill. I've known for a long time about you and Brewer. Once when I was pregnant with Kenneth I thought I'd go to the office and see you. You weren't at the office. The new girl at the counter said you had gone to dinner with Brewer so I went over to the theatre. The girl in the box-office, not knowing I was your wife, told me you had gone home with Brewer and made some remark about two queers making out. I knew then why our marriage was really in name only. And I knew when you got sick and have been getting weaker that you had AIDS. What else could it be?"

"You've known it all this time and never said a word?" I couldn't believe what she was saying.

"What was there to say, Bill? You never loved me. You only married me to have children." Tears fell onto her cheeks and all at once something inside of me exploded. This woman had lived with me for over ten years knew she was living with a homosexual and never was less than a good mother and a faithful wife. Never once had she been bitter towards me. Never once had she thrown it up to me. Never once had she even hinted at it. She had gone to bed with me knowing it was only to give me children. She was really living almost a celibate life at her young age while I was getting what I wanted when I wanted it.

"I had my religion and my children," she said. "I suppose we can't have everything in life. It had to be enough and I made it suffice." She still had her hands folded in her lap and hadn't moved an inch through all this. The woman was made of iron, and I thought I had control. I looked at her. She had long brown hair, braided and circled at the top of her head. Her face was oval and her skin was clean and delicate. She had large brown eyes almost the color of her hair and the hands folded in her lap had long beautifully shaped fingers. She was beautiful. There was something about her that was ethereal and quiet. There was peace in this woman who I had lived with for over ten years. All I ever had seen was a machine that gave me children and kept the house.

I realized that I owed her something and there was no way I could ever pay it back. I would leave her well taken care of with insurance, the store, the house, and a good bank account, but that wasn't enough to pay her back for what she had given me. I'd never been man enough to see the need and the beauty of this woman.

It was my mother sitting there. My mother who went everywhere with my father. She lived in tents, scaled mountains, took samples of water from rivers filled with slime, got malaria, and had my sister and I on the trail following a man who had more interest in his work than his wife and two children. At seven you remember a lot of things. You remember eating out of tin cans, going to the bathroom in the woods and using leaves, freezing at high altitudes, and being frightened by native people who wore paint on their faces and shook rattles at you. I remembered my mother's hands, long and slender and folded in her lap like Katie's while my Father ranted about some new rock formation. I'd never put it all together, the feeling of rejection by my Dad and the feeling of hurt when I was old enough to see my Mother lying on a cot cold one moment and burning up with malaria. Some native would be taking care for her instead of my Dad. He would be out chipping off a rock someplace or taking water samples, or bending over his fold-up desk writing endless journals with an oil lamp hanging on a pole to see.

I'd treated Katie as my Dad had treated my Mother, but I'd killed myself instead of Katie. I remembered my Mother reading the Bible to Clara and I and having us memorize small passages she hoped we'd never forget. I can remember Dad laughing at her and her myths. When we were living with Aunt Clarissa and Uncle Baxter, we went to Sunday school because Aunt Clarissa took us each Sunday. Uncle Baxter stayed home and informed that when he wanted to read a fairy tale he'd choose Pinocchio.

I went to church because it was what a man did when he had a family. I taught Sunday school because of the prestige it gave me. I read constantly and was a well informed teacher and the kids liked all the extras. I threw in about the times and the surroundings, but I skipped over most of what the Bible really said and just emphasized the stories. I liked being popular, especially when the kids told their parents what a neat teacher I was.

Katie asked if there was anything else I wanted to tell her. She thought she heard the children and needed to see if they were all right. What else was there to say to this woman who knew my secret?? She left the room, and after she checked on the kids she went into her bedroom and left me alone in the living room.

Alone. I'd never felt so alone in my whole life. I knew what being alone meant at that moment. I knew what it was to have lived a selfish life, lived only to satisfy my self, to do just what I wanted, to take and take and never really give back. Me owe people? Hell I owed my Mother, Aunt Clarissa, Chuck, Katie, even the kids. Me, who never wanted to owe anybody anything in this life owed more than I could have paid off if I had been able to live for decades.

At that very moment I wanted to live. I wanted somehow to make it right for Katie, Chuck, and even my kids who really didn't know me at all. I'd been the same kind of Dad to them that my Dad had been to me. But it was too late. I'd made a schedule for my life all neat and tidy and it had turned into shambles. You can't go back, there is no way you can turn back the clock and redo life. Once you have spent the second, the minute, the hour, years, you cast them into cement and they are there to stay. I'd even planned my relationship with God. In a way it was funny, me scheduling God?

The next morning I called Chuck and told him I'd told Katie and that she'd known it for a long time that I had been with Brewer. Chuck asked if he could come over, and I said since when did he need an invitation.

When Chuck came over later that morning he didn't knock. He never knocked. Katie was in the kitchen cleaning up, Althea was in her playpen, and Ken and Bob were in the yard arguing as usual. Katie had treated the morning as if nothing had been said between us the night before. She asked me what I would like for breakfast, graciously made it, and then brought it into the living room and sat it on the coffee table in front of the recliner. I was getting weaker and weaker, and had a hard time sitting on the hard chair at the table. There was nothing left on my butt but bone. I'd just finished a cup of coffee when Chuck popped in. He called in a 'hello' to Katie, and then came straight to the couch and plopped his long body down as usual.

"So you told her, and she knew? How long has she known?"

"Since before Ken was born."

"And she's lived with you all this time knowing about Brewer?" Chuck was startled and then ran his hands through his hair as he often did when he was upset. I'd seen him do those same actions trying to decide whether to use a driver or a wood on a par three.

"What are you going to do now, Bill? I think you ought to tell the pastor. You might be surprised at the help he could give you. I also have to ask if you are you ready to meet your Lord?"

"No. What is the use of even talking about it, after the way I have lived? I used Him the same way I've used everyone else. Forget it, Chuck. Forget it. I don't want to talk about it so change the subject."

"O.K. I have to run. I have a slew of office hours today. I'll check with you tonight."

He slammed the door and the hinge still needed fixing. I guess it would never be fixed. I didn't have the strength these days to do much of that.

Althea was asleep and the boys were in their room watching the comics, the Chipmunks and Popeye and a few others. They were allowed to watch T.V. for about an hour and then it got turned off. Lately there hadn't been much for two boys to watch that Katie and I approved.

Katie came in and asked if there was anything she could get for me. She dusted off the piano with her apron and straightened my pillows for me.

"Katie,' I asked, "why have you lived with me all these years knowing what kind of a man I am?" I had to know. There had to be a reason. I couldn't understand such actions.

She sat down on the couch folded those hands together and very quietly said, "Because, Bill, I love you and hoped someday things would change." She never moved, that was her way of handling things I realized.

"You love me? How could you love me, for God's sake after the way I've treated you?" I didn't understood what she had said.

"Yes, the day I met you in college I fell in love with you and wanted to be your wife, and when you asked me for a date and we were married I realized my dream. Even though I knew you didn't love me I thought I could somehow win your love. I failed, but I had a part of you in each one of the children and so in their love I have realized another part of my dream. I'm sorry I wasn't whatever you needed to gain your love. When I realized you were gay I knew it was never going to happen."

"Katie, I'm sorry. If I had it to do over I would change. There is one thing you must know. I never loved any of the men I was with. It was a habit and they were simply the tools with which I could continue my habit. I know that doesn't help but it is true. I've never really loved anyone but my mother, and now that it is too late I have learned what it is to love, and I know in my heart I love you."

She sat there and then said quietly and kindly, "Thank you, Bill. That means a great deal to me."

There is no dramatic end to my story. I have shared it with you and hopefully it will be read by someone who can identify with me and learn what I learned too late. You can't ever go back and redo what you have done in your life. Once you take a step the print in there and the moment is gone. Probably by the time your book is published I won't be here to read it. Chuck has stayed my friend and will be with me until the last. Katie takes care of me but there is no emotion, even though I have tried to show her how much I am learning to care, she can't accept it. Ten years of hurt can't be wiped away in a few months. It takes time and I don't have time.

And my relationship with God? I am trying to get that straightened out as well. It is hard to break a habit of manipulating people and God. I have a way to go but I read the Bible daily and have asked the pastor to help me. My prayer is that God will give me time to learn to understand his schedule and how it is that forgiveness takes only a few words. It still seems very one-sided to me. Making up for nearly forty years of doing religion my way takes some understanding.

It is too late for me to give Katie the happiness she so deserves. My other prayer is that someone reading this book will start changing and begin to give kindness and love to his wife and family, before it is too late. I'll not have time to become friends with my children. I'm trying to show Ken and Bob the kind of love I should have given them from the time they were born, but there won't be enough time, I'm afraid.

Don't let life spoil your living. Live your life for others. Don't just take from them as I did, because you always owe those who love you, so be certain you pay that debt with love, a lesson I learned too late.

I had to visit with Bill in his house; he was too weak to come to me. Katie and the children weren't there, but Dr. Chuck came in as we were taping and sat, or I should say, sprawled over the couch as we finished. Every once in a while Chuck would interrupt and say that Bill was being too hard on himself, but Bill would continue hardly breathing as if he had to get every word out before it was too late.

Bill was a shadow of the man I imagined he'd been. His arms had scarcely enough skin to cover the bones, and his lips pulled back from his teeth because he'd lost so much weight. Chuck kept running his hands through his hair and changing positions, his long legs always seeming to be in the way. You could tell the sorrow Chuck felt for his friend.

"Bill, have you been able to convince Katie how you have come to feel about her?"

"No, or I should say I have no idea, we don't talk. There isn't any reason, I can't make it up to her and there isn't enough time left to convince her. I would try very hard if I had the time. It is hard to change when you haven't the time."

"Chuck, isn't there anything that can be done medically these days?"

"Sorry to say, no. It's hell to be a doctor and not be able to cure your patient. It's hell!" He stood and walked to the door. "See you later, Bill, got a baby coming and better get there." He slammed the screen door which I could see hadn't been fixed.

"Where are the children and Katie, Bill?" I wondered why they were missing.

"I sent them to the park. I didn't want Katie to know I was sharing this. She may have worried about the kids finding out. Glad you aren't going to use my name. I'd hate for the kids to know."

"Thank you for sharing, Bill. I'm very sorry you are ill." I left the room hurting for the man I'd just met. I was also hurting for the children and for Katie whom I will never get to know.

Two weeks ago Chuck called and told me Bill had passed away. I'd asked him to keep me informed of Bill's progress. Chuck said that Katie was doing quite well taking over the store and he would help her as much as possible, but his schedule was pretty filled. The new manager had agreed to stay and was helping her as well.

I asked Chuck how she was doing personally and he told me there was no way of knowing as she was not the type to share with anyone.

My heart went out to this lonely lady who kept her hurts all bottled up inside. My prayer was that someone would come along who would sense her need and bring happiness into her life.

13

People Who Help

THROUGHOUT THE WORLD homosexuality is either accepted or rejected. Rejection takes the form of kindness or cruelty and from this many organizations have been formed to reach out a hand to gay and lesbian individuals.

The organizations listed in this chapter are there to help, several are international. The complete list of every currant service could not be indexed as it would have taken too much space. We have tried, however, to list the major ones throughout the U.S.

If you are looking for someone to understand where you are at this moment and need to talk telephone numbers have also been offered. You do not need to suffer in silence. There are individuals out there who are happy to talk with you and share their own walk with you.

If you are trying to decide which is the right pathway for you share your feelings with some of these people. Let them help you take the rocks out of your road or make you aware of the rocks you will encounter in your walk as a homosexual. Each one listed has run, walked, or stumbled down the homosexual highway; you are not alone!

Beyond Imagination
919-833-6201
P.O. Box 28294
Raleigh NC 27611-8294
life@beyondimaginations.org

Beyond Imagination exists to bring God's healing and re-demptive power to those who struggle with homosexuality and other sexual addictions. By coming along side those who struggle—offering them love, compassion, encouragement, ex-hortation and an understanding of the issues—our hope is that the struggler will grow spiritually, emotionally and mentally. Our desire us that their minds be renewed and that they gain strength to resist temptation. Ultimately, we hope for them to develop a passionate relationship with Jesus Christ, released into their callings as men and women of God.

Beyond Imagination is a not-for-profit Exodus member Min-istry.

Cross Ministry
919-569-0375
P.O. Box 1122
Wake Forest, NC 27588
info@CrossMinistry.org
www.crossministry.org

Cross Ministry (a speaking, teaching, and writing ministry) conducts its 1-day conference, *More Than Words* across the country. Its focus is "walking: versus "talking" people out of homosexuality. Issues addressed include: If a friend says, "I'm gay"; Just how tolerant was Jesus? Loving and reaching the gay community; Debunking the 'gay' gene; What's a parent to do; Counseling the homosexual; Untwisting 'gay' theology; and They didn't teach me this in the seminary.

Founder-Director, Tim Wilkins is a graduate of Southwestern Seminary. He has spoken for the Billy Graham Association and regularly appears as a guest on radio and TV; Cross Ministry has been featured through numerous mediums-The Washington Times, SBC Life, CNS News, Janet Parshall's America, Family News in Focus, USA Radio, and Concerned Women of America.

Tim Wilkins has written for such publications as AFA Journal, Baptist Press, Light, Christian Single, and Preaching. Wilkins is a member of the National Association for Research and Therapy of Homosexuality, Conference of Southern Baptist Evangelists and is endorsed by the North American Mission Board.

While Cross Ministry upholds the biblical truth that homosexuality is sin, it also advocates an aggressive, compassionate
and redemptive response to those affected by homosexuality.

Exodus International
888-264-0877
P.O. Box 540119
Orlando, FL 32854
http://www.exodus-international.org

Exodus is a nonprofit, international Christian organization
promoting the message of freedom from homosexuality through
the power of Jesus Christ.

Since 1976, Exodus has grown to include over 100 local
ministries in the USA and Canada. They are also linked to other
Exodus world regions outside of North America, totaling over
135 ministries in 17 countries.

Within both the Christian and secular communities, Exodus
has challenged those who respond to homosexuals with igno-
rance and fear, and those who uphold homosexuality as a valid
orientation. These extremes fail to convey the fullness of redemp-
tion found in Jesus Christ, a gift which is available to all who
commit their life and their sexuality to Him.

Exodus is the largest Christian referral and information
center dealing with homosexual issues in the world. Each year,
over 1,000 "ex-gays," pastors, therapists, spouses, parents and
other interested persons come together for a unique gathering of
instructions and celebration. Besides powerful; worship and
inspirational messages, dozens of workshops are presented on
counseling, relationships, sexual struggles, societal issues, support for family and friends, ministry development, and various
other topics. This five-day conference is held annually in late July,
in different cities throughout North America.

First Stone Ministries
405-236-HOPE
1330 N. Classen Blvd., suite G-80
Oklahoma City, OK 73106-6856
http://www.firstone.org/main_frame.htm

First Stone Ministries is dedicated to the healing and restoration in all areas of brokenness. We specialize in leading those caught in homosexual life-style and other areas of sexual brokenness to freedom in Christ Jesus. We are dedicated to the healing of the homosexual, and other wise sexually-broken, and wounded.

The definitions of – Sexual Brokenness: Devastation brought by out by behavior outside of God's original intent of sexuality. These include adultery, promiscuity, homosexuality, lesbianism, sexual abuse, molestation, prostitution, pornography, transsexuality and transvestitism.

Freedom from homosexuality is not a method, but a person. Jesus Christ; therefore we are dedicated solely to the purpose of brining the life of Christ to people who desire to live their lives more like Jesus Christ and His examples given in scriptures. We minister freedom through a personal and intimate relationship with Jesus Christ as Lord.

First Stone Ministries has been a member of Exodus International since 1976, which is a network of ministries to the sexually broken in the United States and Internationally. Since its founding in 1976, First Stone Ministries has been an independent nondenominational, Christ centered, parachute organization. Prior to 1991 First Stone was only a part-time ministry; however we are now a full-time ministry with ordained ministers and counseling staff. We are governed by a Board of Directors.

Our services include individual biblical discipleship by appointment. Day and evening hours are available. Several groups to minister healing, restoration and education to all who have been hurt by sexual brokenness are available. Support groups include, homosexual strugglers, spouses, parents, families, friends, and those who are impacted by AIDS.

We are a ministry and there are no fees for our services. We are supported by donations exclusively. We are a nonprofit 501-3© organization, so all donations are tax deductible.

Fresh Word Ministries
812-475-8560
1425 Green Meadow Rd.
Evansville, IN 4715-6055
freshwordministries@yahoo.com

The Fresh Word Ministries Recovery at Home Mentoring Program

The man whose life has become unmanageable needs a program, which will help to regulate his life in such a way that it will bring it back under control of the Holy Spirit. The requirements help to provide the structure that the man so desperately needs. Daily homework-material is specifically designed to bring the man in sexual sin to true repentance and teach him how to live in daily victory over sin.

Weekly disciple sessions (one thirty-minute telephone) or (one hour face to face) sessions per week throughout twelve weeks is offered. A man will find three Christian men to help him walk through the recovery process by praying for and with him while holding him spiritually and morally accountable on selected goals which the man attempts to reach for six months.

Healing Presence Ministries
303-903-9886, 303-905-9886
P.O. Box 566
Littleton, CO 80160-0566
rob_winslow@msn.com

Healing Ministries was founded in 2000 by Rob and Lois Winslow and is a non-denominational ministry in Denver, Colorado. Our purpose is to assist others draw close to God and enjoy His love and acceptance. Rob, a former homosexual struggler, found his healing and freedom in a life of intimate relationship with Jesus Christ. Now he and his family facilitate this experience for others who desire a vital, living relationship with God. Two programs are offered.

The Living River is a 25 week program designed to develop relationship with God and other Christians in a safe, confidential environment. The program consists of quieting our hearts before Him in worship, participating in stimulating, interactive teaching and getting to know one another in a small group setting of healing prayer. Topics include; Getting to the Roots, Come Back to Love!, Getting Real with God, Who am I?, Voices of the Hear, Peeling the Onion of Self, Suggestions to Ignore!, Temptation, Addiction, Alive Inside!, Abuse, Let if go!, Restored to Wonder, True Masculine, True Feminione, Walking Out the Adventure, Friendship, Dating, Marriage Preparation, Being Married, Family.

There is a minimal charge for materials.

Wild At Bat is a free softball team for men who are embarrassed at their lack of skill at sports. Our games are open to all men who have attended a brief workshop explaining our philosophy of encouragement, positive comments and pressing forward to improve. Our goals are to work through our embarrassment and become more skilled and confident. In a safe place we can practice without shame and overcome limitation together. Gentle mentoring in skills is provided.

Homosexuals Anonymous
610-921-0345
P.O. Box 7881
Reading, PA 19603
HomosexualsAnanymous.com

Homosexuals Anonymous (H.A.) is a Christian fellowship of men and women who have chosen to help each other to live free from homosexuality. The purpose of H.A. is to support individuals seeking freedom. Group support is available through weekly H.A. meetings. Guidance is received through the shared experiences and growth of others. Strength is acquired by training the faith responses through the 14 steps.

H.A. is a non-sectarian and works inter- and nondenominationally.

H.A. does not endorse or oppose any political causes. It is not a crusade against "gay" organizations or movements. It does not wish to engage in any controversial issues that would draw member's energies away from the goal of maturing in their relationships with those around them and rediscovering their true identity through a restored relationship with God through Jesus Christ. Homosexuals Anonymous, a Christian fellowship, holds the view that homosexual activity is not in harmony with the will of God and that the universal creation norm is hetero-sexuality.

Love In Action
901-767-6700
P.O. Box 171444
Memphis, TN 38187
info@loveinaction.org
www.loveinaction.org

Love In Action was started in 1973 by Frank Worthen. At 43, Frank rededicated his life to Jesus Christ after spending 20 years pursuing homosexual behavior. With a testimony tape and a newspaper ad Frank gave a message seldom heard before. "There is a way out of homosexuality."

With close to 30 years of research and experience, Love In Action has gained worldwide recognition a leading authority on healing from sexual brokenness. We are used as a referred by ministries, Focus on the Family and The 700 Club. We are also a member of the referral listings of Exodus International.

Under the direction of Rev. John Smid, Love In Action has developed the reputation as a forerunner in residential recovery ministry. Our move to Memphis, Tennessee in 1994 has opened up the doors needed for the program to evolve into a professional recovery treatment center.

In recent years the staff at Love In Action has effectively refined its residential recovery tools for broader application. This pivotal step has stretched the focus of the ministry. Love In Action's program (The Source) is committed to anyone seeking recovery from all types of sexual brokenness (adultery, fornica-tion, emotional dependency, homosexual behavior, etc.) Love In Action has also evolved to offer counsel and support to individu-als not struggling with sexual brokenness through our Radical

Living, Serenity Garden and Family and Friends Programs. As time progresses Love In Action intends to keep broadening its focus to include more and more resources for you.

Mastering Life Ministries
904-220-7474
P.O. Box 351149
Jacksonville, FL 32235-1149
Staff@MasteringLife.org

Mastering Life Ministries is an interdenominational, non-profit Christian ministry. It exists in order to target areas of life where people are caught and deceived into unhealthy, dysfunctional life-styles that separate them from the power and blessing of God, and to equip the Church to redemptively minister to such people.

The primary focus is sexual sin and brokenness, and related issues such as intimacy with the Father, performance orientation, anger management, etc. The tools of the ministry include film, television, and radio as well as seminars and publications that communicate the truth of Jesus Christ.

Metanoia Ministries
253-627-1054
P.O. Box 1353
Tacoma, WA 98401-1353
www.metanoiaonline.org

For over 20 years, Metanoia has served as a ministry proclaiming freedom from sexual brokenness in the Puget Sound area. Metanoia is a member of Exodus International and NARTH (National Association for Research and Therapy of Homosexuality).

Having personally struggled with sexual addiction and homosexuality, Pastor Rob's journey of healing has been the foundation of his commitment to providing hope and healing to men, women, and young people struggling with or affected by sexual and/or relational brokenness. He and his wife, Jackie, have been married since July 1995, they have two children.

Rob has delivered a powerful message throughout the U.S., including interviews with *MTV News* and *The London Times*. He is the author if the program, *Beginnings: Hope and Healing for Families and Friends of a Gay Loved One*.

Prodigal Ministries Inc.
513-861-0011
P.O. Box 19949
Cincinnati, OH 45219
prodigal@goodnews.net
http://w3.goodnews.net/~prodigal/

Prodigal Ministries Inc. is an organization whose goal is to assist people desiring to come out of homosexuality. Prodigal Ministries is a Christian organization. These two characteristics sometime drag us into controversy we neither seek nor enjoy. Because we are Christian it is sometimes assumed that our attitude and approach is the same as other more vocal Christians whom the media is sensationalizing and highlighting.

We are not about condemning, attacking, labeling or insisting that others believe as we do. Prodigal Ministries is about giving respect and unconditional love to every person regardless of their sexual orientation. We desire the utmost good for all, and conclude that God in His Word did not ordain homosexuality, but He had a greater redemptive restoration in mind for all. We believe that fully accepting/affirming the pursuit of the homosexual lifestyle is not the only intelligent, enlightened position or option.

We are not persuaded by the theories presented today that homosexuality is genetic, in-born or in any way unchangeable destiny. We believe that hurtful development conditions may leave someone predisposed towards a same-sex attraction. We believe that by caring for, ministering to and mending the wounded places in a person's emotions, belief system and relational abilities a person can obtain a heterosexual identity and orientation. Change is not immediate nor all or nothing. Change is not that way for any of us regardless of our issues. Growth and healing are with some issues a life time process.

We are not a political action group. We do not seek our ends by political means. We, as citizens have placed ourselves peacefully within the community to assist individuals whose choice is to change.

We are a member of Exodus International.

Truth Ministry
864-575-2321
P.O. Box 5781
Spartanburg, SC 29304
info@truthministry.com

Truth Ministry is an Exodus affiliated ministry based in the Upstate of South Carolina. We are non-profit, non-denominational, Christ –centered organization whose mission is to help people who struggle with homosexuality be free to live in sexual and relational wholeness according to God's design.

As a ministry, our desire is to shed light on the complicated issue of homosexuality. We hope that men and women will find comfort and help, both through a personal relation shop with Jesus Christ, and through godly love demonstrated by God's people. We know that there is hope to live in this freedom because we have experienced this change in our own lives.

We offer one-on-one counseling, support groups (including a Living Waters group), an annual conference, and many resources for men, women, and family members with loved ones who struggle with same-sex attractions.

14

Medical Problems Related to Homosexuality

SEXUALLY TRANSMITTED DISEASES (STDs) are also known as venereal diseases, diseases which spread from one partner to another
through sexual activity. There are twenty or more diseases that
can be transmitted sexually. Some are caused by bacteria, some
by viruses, and some by parasites.

There is no truth to the belief which holds that certain STDs
are related only to homosexuality. STDs are present in both
genders and are passed on with no particular proclivity towards
all sexes or ages. And, against popular belief, people can transmit
STDs even if they have no visible or physical symptoms. Some
STDs, such as syphilis and genital herpes, can be identified by
genital ulcers or sores. Others, like gonorrhea and Chlamydia,
inflame the urethra or cervix and are accompanied by a genital
discharge.

If you have a condition characterized by genital sores and
inflammation, whether sexually transmitted or not, this can
encourage HIV transmission. It can cause a person with an STD
to be infected with HIV. If you are a sexually active person and
experience pain or burning during urination, genital discharge,
sores or a rash in a genital or anal area, or pain during sexual
intercourse, you should see your doctor. Scientists have identified three ways that HIV/AIDS infection spreads: sexual relationships with an infected person, contact with infected body fluids,
and transmission from an infected mother to her child before or
during birth or through breast feeding

STDs are the most common type of infectious disease throughout the world, with the United States rating the highest in the industrialized world. It is estimated that nearly 15 million new cases of STDs are annually reported in the U.S. The World Health organization estimates that in 1995 over 333 million new cases of curable STDs occurred. In the U.S. STD's are higher among teenagers and young adults; people under the age of 25 count for two-thirds of the new cases. The southeastern U.S., and certain ethnic groups have higher rates of STDs. Rates are also high among populations of men who have sex with other men.

According to the American Social Health Association it is estimated there are 65 million people in the United States with an incurable STD, and there are approximately 15 million new cases of STDs every year, of which a few are in fact curable. They find that two-thirds of all STDs occur in people 25 years of age or even younger, and one in four new STD infections are in teenage youngsters.

STDs are generally associated with socioeconomic factors. Lack of good health care, especially among the working classes and heavily-populated poor sections of the country, increases the possibility of contacting an STD. Behavioral factors, such as having a large number of sex partners, also affect the chances of contacting a STD. Cases of Chlamydia and herpes have risen in the U.S. over the past ten years, possibly because of improved detection methods, but syphilis infections have decreased in number.

Most STDs can be "silent" showing no noticeable symptoms, which make testing very important in sexually active people who are not limited to one partner. Social stigma and lack of public awareness regarding STDs restrains honest discussion between doctors and health care providers and individual who needs to be tested.

Doctors, schools, or clinics are required to report only four of the STD's, syphilis, chlamydia, gonorrhea, and hepatitis B. These must be reported to the state health department and the CDC for statistical purposes. Hepatitis B is 100 times more infectious than HIV. More than two-thirds of Hepatitis B infections are transmitted sexually, which is linked to chronic liver disease, including cirrhosis and liver cancer.

Other than HIV, STDs, cost more than eight-million each year to treat. It is also estimated that one in four Americans have genital herpes and of those 80 percent are unaware they have it. At least one in four Americans will contact an STD at some point in their lives.

Herpes is the most common of the STDs in the US, with nearly forty-five million people having this relatively harmless lifelong virus. It is estimated that over one-million people are infected with herpes each year. However, more than five-million people are infected with HPV (Human Papilloma Virus) each year, exceeding the number of other infections. More than half the adults ages 18-44 have never been tested for a STD that is other than HIV/AIDS. It is quite understandable these statistics are more than likely quite shy of the real count..

Because of the fear of HIV transmission, the recent emphasis on safe sex—and the use of condoms, has reduced the risk of some STDs. Because STDs can spread from contact with lesions on the skin, which may exist on areas of the body that are not covered by a condom, condoms are not completely effective. A sexually active individual should always check a partner for sores, discharge, or other symptoms, however since most STDs do not have visible symptoms, sexual promiscuity is dangerous

STD risk factors are similar so a person who contracts one disease should be tested for others. Sexually active people should routinely have themselves checked for STDs because early detection allows early treatment and may prevent serious consequences. Bacterial STDs such as chancroid gonorrhea, syphilis and chlamydia can be treated with antibiotics and are completely curable if treatment is started early. It is also imperative that the sexual partners an individual has be treated at the same time to keep from passing the infection back and forth.

Herpes, AIDS, and genital warts—all caused by viruses and are not curable—can be treated but remain in the body for life. Syphilis, AIDS, genital warts, hepatitis, herpes and even gonorrhea have caused death. Some of the complications of these diseases lead to related conditions such as pelvic inflammation and cervical cancer, and may also cause complications in pregnancy.

Sexual contact is not limited to intercourse; it includes kissing, oral-genital contact, and the use of sex aids. There really is no such thing as safe sex. The only fool proof method is abstinence or having sexual relations with one partner and if possible with one partner for life. It is also recommended for partners to be faithful. If one has multiple sexual partners each brings to the relationship all the people he has been sexually active with during his or her lifetime.

As there are many different STDs, it is well to be educated as to how they are transmitted, what you can do, if anything, and to be aware of the symptoms. We will treat HIV/AIDS as one unit even though many experts believe that integrated programs to prevent and manage the diseases together are more effective. As we are only stating some of the facts of medical problems associated with homosexual activities we will not be giving medical advise so integration is not necessary as a needed part in this chapter.

STDs are linked in several ways with HIV. STDs and HIV are spread by similar types of sexual activity by people who come together in behaviors that transmit HIV are also more likely to contact STDs. People who contact STDs also put themselves at danger for HIV and in all cases should be tested regularly. Regions and populations in the U.S. with the highest STD rates also tend to have the highest rates of HIV. STDs increase the risk of contacting HIV. High STD rates are also associated with high HIV rates in some populations of men who have sex with men and may act as a predictor of an impending rise in HIV incidence.

Having a STD makes it easier to become infected with HIV due to various biological mechanisms. A person, who has an STD that causes genital ulcers, syphilis, chancroid, or genital herpes, is more likely to contract HIV from an infected person because the open sores can serve as a portal for HIV to enter the body. Also there is more of a chance to contact HIV because people with certain STDs', epithelial cells lining the genital and urinary tracts do not function as well. With the increased number of white cells present needed to target STD infections it makes an added opportunity for HIV.

The presence of an STD makes it more likely that a co-infected person will transmit HIV, as the virus can be transmitted through an open genital lesion which may come into contact with a partner's vaginal, anal, or oral mucous membrane during sexual activity. HIV is detected in the fluid secreted from most types of genital ulcers in men and women with HIV. HIV positive persons with inflammatory STDs such as chlamydia or gonorrhea are more likely to shed HIV in their semen and cervicovaginal fluids and to have greater amounts of HIV in these fluids compared to HIV positive people without STDs. STD symptoms may be more severe, last longer, and be harder to treat in people co-infected with HIV. Herpes lesions may also be more severe and longer lasting and outbreaks may occur more frequently in people with HIV/AIDS as well as people co-infected with HIV are more likely to develop multiple genital warts and warts that endure for a longer time.

Here is a partial list of STDs:

HIV/AIDS:

Human immunodeficient virus or HIV is a virus that attacks the immune system and results in Acquired Immunodeficiency Syndrome, or AIDS. (This subject is addressed later on in the chapter.)

CHANCROID:

This bacterial STD usually causes soft abrasions located on the genitals and is widespread in some areas of the U.S. Chancroid lesions begin as elevated bumps that fill with pus and develop into sores. Usually there is only one ulcer, but in some cases there may be more. Men are more likely to have painful lesions than women. In women Chancroid often presents no evidence of the disease. The soft, tender chancroid lesions can be distinguished from syphilis ulcers, which are typically firm and painless. Symptoms usually appear 3-10 days after exposure to the bacteria. About one-half of people with chancroid also have painful, swollen lymph nodes in the groin, usually on one side; these enlarged glands may fuse into a mass called a bubo. Some people also experience genital discharge, painful urination and defecation, or pain during intercourse.

Prevention: Abstaining from vaginal and anal sex with an infected person is the only 100% effective means of prevention. Latex condoms can reduce but does not eliminate the risk of contacting this disease.

CHLAMYDIA:

Chlamydia is the most common of all bacterial STDs, with an estimated 408 million new cases occurring each year. One in twenty childbearing aged women may be infected. Transmitted by vaginal and anal sex and, chlamydia is highly contagious. As many as 85 percent of cases in women and 40 percent of cases in men of chlamydia are symptomless, untreated chlamydia can lead to serious complications in women.

Each year this STD causes as many as 500,000 cases of pelvic inflammatory disease, an infection of the female reproductive organs that can cause infertility or an entopic pregnancy. Babies born to mothers with chlamydia may be infected with chlamydia conjunctivitis or pneumonia.

Chlamydia symptoms are similar to those of gonorrhea and can include pain or burning during urination; inflammation of the urethra, cervix, or rectum; pain and itching of the penis, vagina, or anus; and a whitish discharge from the penis or vagina. Symptoms begin to appear in two or three weeks after exposure to the bacteria. Women may also experience lower abdominal pain. Men may suffer swelling or pain in the testicles.

In as many as two-thirds of the cases, especially in women, chlamydia shows no visible symptoms. Because of this regular testing is extremely important in those who are sexually active.

One strain of chlamydia is prevalent in tropical climates but is rare in the U.S. This strain is characterized by swollen lymph nodes in the groin. Chlamydia can be diagnosed by genital fluid, a DNA amplification assay or a recently approved urine test.

Because gonorrhea and chlamydia commonly occur together, a combination antibiotic treatment is often given to combat both infections. If chlamydia is left untreated it can cause pelvic inflammatory disease (PID) in women and epididymitis in men.

Chlamydia can be transmitted to newborns during birth causing conjunctivitis (eye infection) or pneumonia.

Prevention: Refusing to have vaginal or anal sex with an infected person is the only absolute way of not contacting this disease.

GONORRHEA:

Gonorrhea, another bacterial STD, multiplies in warm, moist areas of the body. It is estimated that over a million people, contact gonorrhea each year. According to the U.S. Health Department statistics there was a 9% increase in 1998—to 132.9 cases per 100,000 people—after a twelve year decline.

Gonorrhea is transmitted by vaginal, anal, or oral sex, and may affect the urethra, vagina, cervix, rectum, pharynx (throat), or eyes. Symptoms typically appear 2-14 days after exposure and include pain or burning during urination or defecation. Symptomatic of this disease is a yellowish or greenish pus-like discharge from the penis, vagina, or rectum. There may also be some swelling and tenderness of the vulva a sore throat or a false urge to urinate or defecate. An estimated 10% of men and up to 80% of women have no symptoms.

In pregnancy, gonorrhea can cause premature labor, miscarriage or still birth. Gonorrhea can also cause serious infections in infants who contract the disease from an infected mother during delivery. Complications from gonorrhea can include arthritis.

Prevention: Abstaining from vaginal, anal and oral sex with an infected person is the only known way of not contacting the disease. Condoms can reduce but do not eliminate the risk of contacting this disease.

HEPATITIS B:

This virus-induced liver disease infects approximately 200,000 Americans each year. It is transmitted by vaginal, oral, and especially anal sex. One can also be infected by sharing contaminated needles, and piercing the skin with a contaminated instrument such as those used in dental and medical procedures, or by receiving contaminated blood or blood products through transfusions. The hepatitis B virus is found in blood, semen, vaginal secretions and saliva.

Many people with Hepatitis B have no symptoms; others experience fever, headaches, muscle aches, fatigue, loss of appetite, vomiting and diarrhea. This viral STD can damage the liver, putting one at risk for cirrhosis and liver cancer. Symptoms of liver involvement include dark urine, abdominal pain, yellowing of the skin and the whites of the eyes. There is no known cure. Most infections clear up by themselves within 4-8 weeks. Some individuals, however, about 10% of the cases, become chronically infected.

Hepatitis B is the only STD that has a vaccine. Many health officials recommend the vaccine for children, adolescents and young adults; it is not widely administered, largely because of the stigmatization of STDs and the cost of the three-part vaccine.

Pregnant women can transmit the disease to their unborn children. Some 90% of infants infected at birth become chronic carriers and are at risk of liver disease and liver cancer. They are capable of transmitting the virus. Infants of infected mothers can be given immunoglobulin and vaccinated at birth, potentially eliminating the risk of chronic infection.

Prevention: Refraining from sex with an infected person, particularly when blood, semen, vaginal, or anal fluids are likely to be exchanged; is the only way to prevent being infected with Hepatitis B. Sharing needles of any kind while using drugs is also a way of contacting the disease.

HERPES:

Genital herpes is caused by a simple virus (HSV). HSV, type 2, is classically associated with genital lesions and HSV type 1 with oral lesions, (cold sores). Both types are able to infect either area of the body. HSV-2 is quite common; it is estimated that 45-60 million people are infected in the U.S. and that over a million people are infected each year. Consequently it is thought that

20% of U.S., adults may be infected with HSV-2. Approximately two-thirds of the people who are infected do not know they have genital herpes because they have no symptoms or that their symptoms are so mild they go unnoticed.

Symptoms generally appear twenty-six days after exposure and last about two to three weeks. The disease is distinguished by blisters on the genitals, inside the vagina or rectum, or around the mouth. Symptoms also include itching or burning sensations, and discharge. They are sometimes accompanied with flu-like symptoms such as swollen glands and fever. After the first infection the virus can reactivate and cause a new outbreak of sores. The rate of recurrence and severity can differ from person to person. The blisters break open and cause painful ulcers. The sores usually dry up and will probably scab over and heal without scarring after 2-7 weeks.

Studies have shown that HSV is present in the genital fluids of people with herpes, even when they do not have active herpes lesions. Even after genital herpes lesions heal, the virus is not eliminated; instead it takes up residence in nerve endings and may be reactivated periodically. Outbreaks are associated with emotional stress, illness, exposure to ultraviolet light, menstruation, and a weakened immune system. Itching and tingling in the area in which the outbreak will occur, pain in the groin or buttocks, and sometime melancholy can occur before an outbreak.

A person can spread the disease during an active outbreak but the virus can also be transmitted when there are no symptoms showing. HSV is present in genital fluids. Outbreaks are usually milder in later episodes and the frequency often decreases over time. Herpes can be transmitted from a mother to her newborn especially if she is experiencing her first episode. It may also lead to miscarriage premature birth, eye and nerve damage, mental retardation and even death in a newborn.

Prevention: Abstaining from vaginal, anal, and oral sex with an infected person is the only way of preventing sexual transmission of genital herpes. Condoms will not eliminate the risk of contracting the disease during sexual activity since it is still possible to be infected by coming in contact with sores anywhere in the genital area.

GENITAL WARTS:

Genital warts, human papillomavirus (HPV), are caused by a virus related to the virus that causes common skin warts. It is one of the family of over 60 strains of virus that cause warts. Various so-called "low-risk" strains are associated with common warts or genital warts. High-risk strains are associated with cervical, anal, or penile dysplasia abnormal precancerous cell growth) and cancer. Many people are co-infected with both high-risk and low-risk strains. HPV is one of the most common STDs. It is estimated that 5.5 million new HPV infections occur in the U.S. annually, with a cumulative total of 30-40 million cases. The virus is spread by direct skin-to-skin contact with an infected person and may occur even if the person shows no symptoms.

Genital warts become visible from a few weeks to several months after exposure. They begin as tiny bumps, which are not painful or itchy, on the penis, scrotum, vulva or anus, inside the vagina or rectum, or on the cervix. They frequently happen in clusters and if untreated grow into large fleshy masses. The growth of genital warts is more rapid in a pregnant woman and in people with compromised immune systems. Many people with HPV infections have no visible symptoms. No cure has been found for HPV and the virus remains in ones body for life.

Prevention: As with other STDs sexual contact with a person carrying the virus puts you in a position of being infected. Multiple partners, anal, vaginal, and oral sex is costly when it is with a partner who is carrying the HPV virus even though there may be no visible symptoms. Don't trust your eyesight; know with whom you are sexually active. Has he/she been tested? Have you?

SYPHILIS:

It is believed that syphilis was introduced into Europe in 1493 by crew members returning from Christopher Columbus's first expedition to America. By the 16th century syphilis had become a major public disease. The bacterium responsible for syphilis was identified in 1905. In 1943 penicillin was shown to be highly effective against syphilis and is still the preferred treatment for the disease.

Successful treatment and concentrated public-health action have diminished the number of reported cases in the U.S. from 106,000 in 1947 to 25,000 in 1975. This steady reduction ended in 1998 when the number rose to 38,000 reported cases. Most cases of syphilis in the 1970s involved homosexuals, but the increase in the 1980s occurred in the heterosexual population. This increase of congenital syphilis then caused a high rate of morbidity and mortality in infants. Individuals with AIDS are more likely to develop serious forms of syphilis and suffer relapses after treatment that in most cases would be cured. It is estimated each year that there are over 120,000 new cases of syphilis.

There are three stages to the progress of syphilis. The first symptoms usually appear ten days to six weeks after sex with an infected partner. A chancre (painless sore) appears on the genitals or in the vagina. Fluid from the chancre is extremely infectious. In the second-stage, which appears about six weeks later, a skin rash, painless mouth ulcers and broad wart like lesions, which are also highly infectious, appear accompanied by flue-like symptoms. Headache, fever, and enlarge lymph glands are sometimes observed.

Generally the infection remains in a level stage after these symptoms disappear. If left untreated the disease lapses into the latent stage, which can last twenty to thirty years, during which it is not contagious and has no symptoms.

When the final stage, tertiary syphilis does occur it may produce hard nodules, called gummas in the tissues under the skin, the mucous membranes, and internal organs. The bones are often affected, as well as the liver, kidney, and other visceral organs. About one-third of people who reach this stage of tertiary syphilis will develop severe complications, which can result in mental illness, blindness, heart disease or death.

Prevention: Abstaining from vaginal, anal, or oral sex with an infected person it the only 100% effective means of preventing the transmission of syphilis. Latex condoms can reduce but not eliminate the risk of contacting the disease. It is possible to contact syphilis even if one uses a condom by the sores in the genital area. It is important to avoid sexual or any physical contact with the infectious sores (chancres), rashes or mucous patches caused by syphilis.

General Rules for STDs:

The only 100% effective way a person can protect themselves from STDs is to avoid sexual contact with anyone other than a life-time faithful partner. If you realize this and yet insist on being sexually active with more than one partner, especially with partners who have not been tested and with whom you do not use a condom (and condoms are never 100% safe), it would be well to read the following suggestions. They might save your life.

First, and of course, have a monogamous relationship with an uninfected partner.

Consistently use a condom and use it correctly.

If you are a drug user be certain your needles are clean.

Control STDs to decrease vulnerability to HIV infection and to reduce your infectiousness if you are HIV infected.

The younger you are when having sex for the first time, the more susceptible you are to being infected with STDs.

The risk of being infected with an STD increases proportionately with the number of partners one has sexual relationships with over a life time.

Have regular checkups for STDs even if you have no symptoms.

Learn the symptoms of STDs.

Avoid having sex during menstruation.

Avoid anal intercourse, but, if practiced use a condom.

Do not douche because it removes some of the normal protective bacteria in the vagina and increases the risk of getting some STDs.

Most STDs are treatable so do not be too embarrassed or scared to ask someone for help. The earliest you seek treatment the easier it is to treat and it will keep you from causing physical damage that may not be reparable.

ASHA provides free information and keeps lists of clinics and private doctors who provide treatment for people with STDs. ASHA has a national toll-free telephone number: **1-800-227-8922**.

The phone number for the Herpes Hotline is **1-919-361-8488**.

ACQUIRED IMMUNODEFICIENCY SYNDROME (AIDS):

(Statistics have been gathered from the USA Public Health Reports, and the World Health Organization Centers for Disease Control and Prevention, and American Social Health Association)

AIDS was identified in 1981 among homosexual men and intravenous drug users in New York and California. It wasn't long after that evidence of AIDS was found among heterosexual men, women, and children in Africa. From there it developed into a worldwide epidemic and has now infected every country in the world. Over 35 million adults and 1 million children worldwide in 2000 were living with AIDS. The World Health Organization estimates that from 1981 to the end of 2000 about 21.8 million people died as a result of AIDS, with 4.3 of those children under the age of 15.

In the U.S. nearly 40,000 new HIV infections occur each year. Over 30% of these infections involve women, and 60% in ethnic minorities. In 2000 about 800,000 to 900,000 U.S. residents were infected with HIV, and about 300,000 people had full blown AIDS. In Canada about 4,200 new HIV infections occur each year, with 23% of those infected being women. In 2000 over 40,000 Canadians were reported to have AIDS.

In the United States Caucasians made up 60% of AIDS cases, with blacks and Hispanics numbering at 39%. By 2000 the numbers were reversed: 38% of reported new cases were Caucasian, and 61% were blacks and Hispanics. In the US female AIDS patients accounted for 30% of the cases in 2000. African and Hispanic women accounted for 82% of these cases.

Ellison and Duesberg write in 1944:

> By any measure, the war on AIDS has been a colossal failure so far. In the thirteen years since the first AIDS cases were

diagnosed, our leading scientists and policymakers cannot dem-
onstrate that their efforts have saved a single life. This dismal
picture applies as much to the United States as to Europe and
Africa. No scientist or doctor has stepped forward to claim credit
for discovering an AIDS vaccine, nor is any vaccine expected for
several years, at minimum.[1]

To the question of who gets AIDS, Andres Tapia gives these
answers in a small pamphlet written in 1988:

> Here is the breakdown for people with AIDS in the United
> States:
> Homosexual and bisexual men: 64%. The practices of anal
> sex and multiple sexual partners account for the high incidence
> of AIDS among male homosexuals and bisexuals.
> Intravenous drug users: 18%. These people transmit the
> virus by sharing blood contaminated needles. Over 60% of
> heroin addicts in New York State are believed to be infected with
> the virus now. Because addicts are a very isolated group, they
> will be difficult to reach with education on prevention.
> Homosexuals and IV drug users: 7%. Some drug abusers are
> also male homosexuals, who can then spread the virus further
> through sexual contact.
> Heterosexuals: 4%. Cases of AIDS acquired through hetero-
> sexual contact are increasing rapidly. In March 1986 only 1% of
> all AIDS cases were heterosexuals. In 1991 they are expected to
> be 9% or more[2]

Notice the difference in the statistics from the August, 2003,
The Commission:

> The day is fast approaching when it will take stepping over
> bodies to ignore AIDS on the mission field. More than 60 million
> people have been infected with HIV since the epidemic began
> two decades ago. In 2001 it claimed over 3 million lives.
> It is projected that between 2000 and 2020 in 45 of the most
> affected countries, 68 million people will die prematurely as a
> result of AIDS. The greatest toll will be in sub-Saharan Africa
> where 55 million of those deaths are expected.
> In many countries AIDS is erasing decades of progress in life
> expectancy. For example, the average life expectancy in sub-
> Saharan Africa is currently 47 years. Before AIDS, it was 62

years. In Botswana, the life expectancy from birth has dropped below 40 years, the lowest expectancy since before 1950.

But Africa is not the only continent where AIDS is having an impact. Increase of incidence is being felt in Europe, South America, China and India.

By the end of 2001, 13.4 million children worldwide under the age of 15 ha lost a mother, father or both parents to the disease. The number is expected to jump to 25 million in 2010[3]

AIDS is transmitted by vaginal, oral, and anal sex; infected blood or blood products; sharing drug needles with an infected person; and from infected mother to infant in utero, during birth, or while breast-feeding. Within one to three weeks after being infected with the HIV spores most people experience flu-like symptoms including fever, sore throat, headache, skin rash, loss of appetite, weight loss, fatigue and enlarged lymph nodes. The symptoms usually disappear within a week to a month. During this phase HIV reproduces rapidly in the blood. The virus circulates in the blood throughout the body, particularly concentrating in organs of the lymphatic system. Typically a person can enter a stage of system-free symptoms and the virus can remain dormant for years. However, it continues to weaken the immune system, leaving the individual increasingly unable to fight other infections. No existing medical treatment can totally eliminate HIV from the body once it has integrated into human cells.

AIDS is the final stage of a chronic infection caused by the human immunodeficiency virus. There are two types of this virus: HIV-1, which is the major cause of AIDS worldwide, and HIV-2 found mostly in West Africa. On its exterior HIV carries a protein arrangement that recognizes and connects only with a specific structure found on the outer surface of certain cells. HIV attacks any cell that has this binding structure. White blood cells of the immune system known as T-cells, which coordinate a wide diversity of disease fighting mechanisms are especially vulnerable to HIV attack. Particularly susceptible are certain T cells known as CD4 cells. When HIV infects a CD4 cell it seizes the genetic tools within the cell to manufacture new HIV virus. The newly formed HIV virus then leaves the cell destroying the CD4 cell in the procedure.

It is dangerous to one's health to lose CD4 cells because these immune cells help other types of immune cells react to attacking organisms. An average count for a healthy person is over 1,000 CD4 cells per microliter of blood. A person who has contacted HIV, the virus progressively destroys CD4 cells over a period of years, thus lessoning the cells defensive ability and deteriorating the immune system.

Many people with AIDS develop cancers. The destruction of the CD4 cells impairs the immune functions which halt the development of cancer. Kaposi's sarcoma is a cancer of blood vessels caused by a herpesvirus. This cancer produces purple lesions on the skin which can spread to internal organs and cause death. B-cell lymphoma affects cells of the lymphatic system that fight infection and perform other vital functions. Cervical cancer is more common in HIV, infected women that in women free from infection.

A variety of neurological disorders are common in the later stage of AIDS. Collectively called HIV associated dementia, they develop when HIV or another microbial organism infects the brain. The infection produces degeneration of intellectual processes such as memory, and sometimes also causes problems with movement and coordination.

HIV transmission takes place most commonly during sexual contact with a contaminated person including genital, anal, and oral sex. The virus is in the infected person's semen or vaginal fluids. During sexual intercourse the virus gains admission to the bloodstream of the uninfected person by passing through openings in the mucous membrane, a protective tissue layer that lines the mouth, vagina, and rectum and through the breaks in the skin of the penis. In the United States and Canada, HIV is most commonly transmitted during sex between homosexual men but the incidence of HIV transmission between heterosexual men and women has rapidly increased. In most other parts of the world HIV is more commonly transmitted through heterosexual sex?

AIDS is a threat to the survival of millions, especially in the Third World, where health resources and social standards are relatively poor and education is lacking. Of the 40 million people who contracted AIDS by 1998, 90% live in less developed countries, and two-thirds of those, nearly 35 million live in Africa, with more than half of these being women. The transmission of AIDS in Africa predominates in heterosexual sexual relationships. Girls are 6 times more likely to be infected with AIDS than boys of the same age. AIDS, in Africa, is the leading cause for the death of their youth and young adults as it is in the U.S.A. in poor urban areas.

The rates of HIV/AIDS infections were lower in Asia than in other areas, but have increased in recent years. It wasn't until 1992 that India reported any cases and by 1999 the AIDS population had increased to over four-million adults. At the start the infection in India were primarily in prostitutes, but spread to the general population in less than five years. China reported that by 2002 they had 850,000 HIV infected people. The rising drug use in China has augmented the HIV numbers to range from 44%-85% in the areas where drug users are concentrated. There is also a growing sex industry in China with 4 million prostitutes five out of ten who never use a condom. In rural areas of China people regularly sell their blood and people who buy the blood do not use sterile needles and also reuse contaminated needles which spread AIDS.

In the Caribbean and Latin America there are nearly 1.8 million people diagnosed with HIV infection or AIDS. Mexico reports over 150,000 people have been infected which makes the disease the third leading cause of death in men aged 20-34.

Prevention: Abstaining from sex with an infected person, especially anal sex where body fluid, blood, semen or vaginal secretions are likely to be exchanged is the only 100% effective means of preventing the sexual transmission of HIV. Latex condoms can reduce but not eliminate the risk of contracting the disease during sex. Avoid illicit IV drug use and sharing drug needles. Even petting can be a source of infection. According to the US Center for Disease Control, even "Open-mouth" kissing is considered a very low-risk activity for the transmission of HIV. However, prolonged open-mouthed kissing cold damage the

mouth or lips and allow HIV to pass from an infected person to a
partner and then enter the body through cuts or sores in the
mouth. Because of this possible risk, the CDC recommends
against open-mouth kissing with an infected partner. One case
suggests that a woman became infected with HIV from her sex
partner through exposure to contaminated blood during open-
mouth kissing.

The Use of Condoms:

> The question is do condoms work; the answer is "maybe."
> Whenever I talk to young people about AIDS I find the same
> thing: they think that using a condom will prevent them from
> getting HIV. The truth is that it may reduce the risk, but I
> wouldn't trust my life to a condom. Condoms are unreliable. If
> one hundred coupled use condoms, up to fifteen of them could be
> in clinics each year asking for abortions. When taken out of the
> packet, holes were found in up to thirty-two out of one hundred
> condoms of the least reliable makes.—The British Standards
> Institute actually permits three out of one hundred to have holes
> in them when they leave the factory. In the U.S., government
> standards are much higher, tolerating only four condoms out of
> every thousand to have leaks. But even with this high standard,
> condom users still experience a failure of 5-15 percent, which is
> the percentage rate of women who have an unwanted pregnancy
> while using this method of birth control over one year's time. A
> leading medical journal puts the failure rate much higher at 13-
> 15 percent per year.[4]

We are led to believe that condoms are effective when used
correctly and consistently, but the question is how effective are
condoms when having sex with an STD or HIV infected partner?
You can cut the probability of contacting a disease by properly
using a condom and by using condoms responsibly, but there is
still a chance that you will contact the disease.

Simple instructions are needed; correctly removing it from
the packet, checking to see if there are holes in it by blowing it up
like a balloon, putting it on correctly, using all the way through
the course of sexual contact, and then removing it correctly. The
key words here are "using it correctly."

Homosexual men are using condoms more that they used to. This is not surprising since their chances of sleeping with an infected person may now be up to one in three in the United Kingdom or one in two or greater in parts of the Untied States. However, there is a condom which reliably withstands the rigors of anal intercourse [5]

Contacting HIV/AIDS or STDs follows a very familiar pattern. People with the most partners also are more likely to have used drugs and or alcohol and practiced sex with someone they did not know well and were less likely to use a condom. Therein is the pattern repeated, the more partners an individual has the more likely they are to have sex with people who themselves have many partners and the more likely they are to have been under the influence of drugs or alcohol during sexual encounters.

Dr. Socarides writes:

A study by the San Francisco Department of Health in 1991 found that gay men between the ages of 17 and 25 consistently engaged in high risk sex with numerous partners, mostly strangers, and without the benefit of condoms, to boot. The younger they are, the more they persist in having a great number of partners-and rarely with protection———I tried to learn all I could about the disease. Eventually, the medical school at Columbia came out with some guidelines that counseled "safe-sex"- that is, the use of condoms. But I knew that condoms weren't safe. I started telling my patients to avoid most of their favorite sexual pathways. "The safest sex," I said, "is about two and a half feet away from your partner."[6]

Men who have sex with men are more likely to be found in larger metropolises and shun rural areas. The breakdown reads that in larger cities an estimated 9% have sex with men where in the smaller towns 2% do and in the rural areas the count diminishes to around 1%.

In the late 1970s, in gay communities in cities like New York and San Francisco, HIV silently made its inroads. It was a time when some gay men in these cities went to bathhouses, having impersonal sex with strangers and exploring their new-found sexual freedom. When the Centers for Disease Control and Prevention began questioning gay men with the new disease in 1982, its investigators found that men who had AIDS had twice as many sexual contacts as men who were uninfected, that they were twice as likely to visit bathhouses, and that their partners were far more likely to have more partners of uninfected men. Some of the men interviewed in the early 1980s reported they had on average 1,100 partners in their lifetimes and some had had many more. These numbers may sound implausible, but with anonymous sex in bathhouses and clubs, a man would be the receptive partner for anal sex with a dozen or more partners in a weekend.[7]

Summary:

The bottom line is that condoms are not 100% safe. They lull the society into a sense of false security which allows sexually active people to increase their behavior patterns and being out of control contact, at some point, the virus they thought they were safe against.

But shockingly and frighteningly, yet consistent with the concentration of AIDS cases among high-risk populations, epidemiologists estimate that 30 percent of all twenty-year-old homosexual males will be HIV-positive or dead of AIDS by the time they are thirty. This means that the incidence of AIDS among twenty-to thirty year-old homosexual men is roughly 430 times greater than among the heterosexual population at large.[8]

Homosexuals and heterosexuals found a new lack of social-sexual restrictions as the dawn of sexual freedom exploded in the world. And with this new freedom came a cloud of plagues which may very well destroy a large part of the population. Sexually active individuals currently applaud their freedom to extend their sexual desires in any way they wish to be active. Restraints have been removed, Pandora's Box has no lid, but time will count the cost!

15

History of Homosexuality

THE TERMS SODOMY AND HOMOSEXUALITY, the one very old and the other very new, refer to the attraction of one individual for another of the same gender. The term comes from the Greek, *homo*, meaning "same"; not, as some say, from the Latin, *homo*, "man." The relationship between those living in a homosexual relationship usually, but not always, leads to sexual contact. Males living in same sex relationships are said to be *gay*; females, lesbian*s*. The word, *lesbian*, comes from the Aegean island of Lesbos where the poet, Sappho, was a teacher. In Victorian England and in the New World, sodomy referred to as an act not to be mentioned. The term, *homosexual*, was created in the late nineteenth century by a German psychologist.

Slang, colloquialisms, scientific language, and distasteful comments have created a confusing sense of this activity, making it difficult to categorize the different ways people refer to acts between same-sex individuals. Today people prefer to use the terms *gay* and *lesbian*. In English the term means "happy, cheerful, jolly," but has denoted male homosexuals for many years. Gay, in this context, was used in Victorian England as a tag to demean a prostitute.

The ancient term was "paederasty." In Greece and Rome this term did not receive the negative reactions it often does at present; it merely referred to one variety of love with no negative connotations. It is necessary to understand the Greek attitude towards the male gender to understand the ancient usage of this term, and to realize that actions which fall under our present term did not have the same meanings they often do now.

However, when we talk of the Greek love of boys it is never a question of boys as we currently use the word, but always of sexually mature young men who had reached puberty. Sexual intercourse with boys, as we use this term today, was punished, and frequently severely, in ancient Greece. This is parallel to countries with a southern European climate where early maturation seems to be prevalent: countries such as Spain, Southern France, Greece, Italy and Northern Africa.

Same-sex relationships are one of the most ancient and universal forms of sexual behavior. These relationships were not studied scientifically until early in the 20th century, and only since WW II has extensive data on the subject been available. From 1948 to 1953 Kinsey conducted a large-scale systematic appraisal of the incidence and social correlates of homosexuality. He disclosed that 37 percent of U.S. men and 13 percent of U.S. women had at least one overt homosexual experience. There are no comparable statistics for other countries. C.S. Ford, a U.S. anthropologist, and F.A. Beach, a psychologist, reported homosexuality in 76 out of 190 primitive societies. Out of this number 49 societies (64 percent) considered the relationship normal. But even in societies which condemn the practice and punish it with harsh sentences, even execution, it is clear that some form of homosexuality has always occurred.

Homer speaks of a Phrygian royal boy named Ganymede and how Zeus carries him off because of his beautiful figure. Homer also tells of the extensive trade in boys by Phoenician shipmasters to fill the harems of wealthy pashas. The paedophilia spoken of in ancient Greek writings, however, was a voluntary relationship based upon mutual affection and received Greek societal acceptance. Reading Greek mythology one has a sense of the ethereal attraction of a beautiful body with emphasis upon the young male body. Many of the Greek gods were pedophiles if the current meaning of the word is insisted upon. The ancients looked upon the love of a man for a boy as a compliment to the youth, and youths not being cared for by an older male "guardian" felt it to be a loss.

Tobias Schneebaum has studied the Amakaeri people of the Peruvian Amazonian rainforest and found that homosexuality is the norm and that heterosexuality only occurs for the purposes of reproduction. This also seems to be the case for some Polynesian tribes.

In many civilizations today heterosexuality is the norm or is looked on as the type of sexual relationship to be desire. In some North American tribes gay people are regarded as special individuals. Gay men of the Crow Indians are believed to have mystical powers and are often chosen as shamans and healers. Many tribes in Africa accept homosexuality as a normal way of acting, so do the Aborigine people in Australia.

Modern controversies with regard to homosexuality tend to revolve around whether same-sex lovers are psychologically abnormal. Must their sexual preference be thought abnormal or not? At one extreme it is assumed that homosexuals are psychologically sub-normal human beings. On the other same-sex lovers are as normal as anyone else.

When we look at records concerning sodomy and homosexuality, particularly early records, we must rely a great deal on ecclesiastical records, legal documents, artistic suggestions, the prose and poetry of the time, and opinions expounded by medical personnel. Most of these records reflect the social pressures in force at the time of their authorship. There is also the problem of relying on ancient documents when homosexual behavior is seen as a threat to the stability of the society, financially or politically.

Obviously this book is not primarily a history and there clearly is insufficient space to mention every historical record available. Consequently a brief brush with the most relevant history must suffice.

The history of homosexuality in the past has been influenced by the prominence of male same-sex attractions, and lesbianism has been removed to the side or ignored. The way in which history tends to ignore the female, must be understood. History leans towards the male; societies have viewed females, for the most part, as second class humans. Thus a woman's feelings, desires, passions are usually eclipsed by the desires and passions of men. Women have three positions in most societies: subservient wives, mothers, and prostitutes. And as most historians are male, one can understand the lack of historical coverage for lesbians. But when brought to light lesbian acts were often seen as being equivalent to those of male sodomites and were punishable by execution in some countries.

Stating facts alone is sterile. To be humane historians must include the variables which pattern the society under the microscope. Fairness demands a writer must unearth plausible reasons why a given society made certain laws, ignored some of the laws, and enforced others.

Thus the written record of homosexual behavior originated with pagan religious worship of a variety of male gods. These pagan gods were associated with war and fertility and to appeal to a god for a good crop, fertility rites were practiced by individuals and tribes. The pagan gods were similar to people: they had the same desires, and were capable of changing their minds, making mistakes, and copulating with each other. A tribe's or a clan's survival was based upon its ability to obtain favors from the gods.

As ancient pre-historic matriarchal societies gave way to patriarchal ones, reverence for the womb switched to reverence for semen, with a rise in phallic worship. In many pagan cultures the initiation of boys included acts of sodomy. Some primitive societies thought that semen didn't occur naturally but had to be placed in a boy by an older man through sodomy. Sexual relations between men and boys was an accepted process in which masculinity was established and passed on in a society.

> Most likely, additional homosexual practices became a part of polytheistic worship as a successor to masturbation. Evidence suggests pagan priests orally stimulated the sexual organs of the worshippers in order to facilitate masturbation in ancient mid-eastern cults. If one believed that having sex with a god would bring fertility, it was easy to also believe that, if a man added his maleness, through his semen, to a male god, fertility would be multiplied all the more. Male gods could plant seeds and were therefore seen as more productive than the female gods to some.

When a man ejaculated his semen into another man's anus at a shrine he was depositing more male power to the gods. With the additional strength of the semen of many men, the god could then insure a bountiful crop, a larger herd, and many children to care for the field.[9]

Babylonian

Ancient Babylonian cities were known for their Ziggurats, shrines created as phallic symbols and used for sexual worship. Such towers multiplied as Babylonian worship spread. The custom of worship at these towers included masturbation, spilling the semen on the ground, which to them was female so that fertility would occur. To prohibit masturbation was in fact a way to forbid a Babylonian form of wórship. Mutual masturbation and homosexual acts played an important part in many of the early pagan practices a well. We see a remnants of phallic Ziggurats in the Maypole dance, totems, Egyptian architecture, and Mayan culture.

Oriental

Homosexuality was known throughout the Orient and was accepted to different degrees. It was a normal ordinary act in Confucian China. Hindu writers, regarded same-sex attraction as common, and did not look on it as a problem. The Samurai in Japan revered the devotion between male warriors as a virtue, and sexual relationships between Buddhist masters and disciples was also expected and accepted.

Greek

In ancient Greece homosexuality and bisexuality were accepted as natural in most areas.

In his *Sexual Life in Ancient Greece*, Hans Licht writes:

The first beginnings of the Greek love of boys are lost in prehistoric times even in the darkness of Greek mythology,

which is completely saturated with stories of paedophilia. The
Greeks themselves transfer the beginnings to the oldest times of
their legendary history.[10]

Plato (428-348 BC) wrote in his *Symposium* that pairs of
homosexual lovers would make the best soldiers. In his discussion of love, heterosexual love is inferior to that of the attraction
between people of the same sex. Phaedra's speech in the *Symposium* describes gay love as "heavenly" and heterosexual passions
as "vulgar."

The Greek emphasis on athletic prowess and military su-
premacy demanded the perfection of the male body. Every Greek
male from twenty to forty nine was inducted into military duty
unless he was physically unable, and the major cities of Greece
insisted upon athletic training as a part of their military pre-
paredness. A beautiful male body was a means of gaining recognition and honor. The Dorians, a linguistically distinct Greek
people traditionally acknowledged as the conquerors of the
Peloponnesus, were the most warlike and exercised in gymnasiums naked. This led to the view of gymnasiums as "the place
where men go naked." While exercising, young men would be
watched by the older males who appreciated their nudity as.

The gymnasium in Greece was the center in which upper-
class citizens passed their leisure time. Male nudity was the most
popular Greek form of art and statuary, and painted vases generally depicted the most beautiful men of the time. The gymnasium
was the place where men gathered and spent time in discussing
philosophy and politics. Male friendships rapidly became homosexual love affairs. And though homosexuality occurred in all
known ancient societies, the Greeks were unusual in that they
honored it as a necessary aspect of male hierarchical social
order.

The Hellenic love of boys follows from Greek ideals concerning gender. There is a basic difference between the ancient ideas
with regard to gender and our twenty-first century concepts. A
woman in Greece was looked at as a mother of a man's children,
and as the head of his house. Men were seen as the center of

intellectual thought and logic. Boys were educated, but girls were not expected to be on the same mental level as their brothers. Male education lasted longer and was more intense than a modern boy's education. It was the custom, especially in the Peloponnesus, Crete, Sicily, and southern Italy, that every man take some boy or youth under his guidance. The older man was to act as a guardian and friend and teach a boy the manly virtues. The man was responsible for the boy and shared whatever blame or praise the youth's actions received.

The older man was also responsible for the youth's physical growth and excellence. He was to be trained to perfection in mind and body. Greek boys were pushed to excel in all attributes for the beauty and strength of the body.

> Homosexual "lover" relationships were parallel in some ways to ancient heterosexual "lover" relations, but exhibited a number of notable differences. They were prominent throughout ancient history, not just at a few points, and often constituted the same-sex equivalent of marriage, at least in the sense that they were the most common and typical relationship among the group in question and generally set the tone for other interactions. In fourth-century Athens, they were similar to heterosexual marriage in that an age difference of nearly a generation was the cultural ideal for both homosexual and heterosexual relationships; in that entering into such a relationship constituted a sort of "coming out" as a young adult (like the bride's entering adult society through marriage); and in that the older person played the role of educator and protector, comparable to that of the husband in heterosexual marriage.[11]

In the *Iliad* (an ancient Greek epic poem attributed to Homer) beauty of young boys is glorified. The beauty of Nireus was more beautiful than all the other Greek youths. Many Greek poems exclaimed the beauty of youths and were not ashamed to pay honor to boyish magnificence.

In Greek art women are represented as a type of male youth. Even the Sirens were often painted as quite boyish. Vases were inscribed with the Greek word for beautiful boy and the inscription, beautiful girl, is quite rare. Frequently a vase painter wanted

282 _You Aren't Alone_

to pay tribute to a boy who was his preference. The names of favorite boys are also inscribed on graves.

Popular among ancient theories as to the cause of homosexuality is that it was learned from cross-cultural contact. Herodotus (484?-425 BC), a Greek known as the father of history and born in what is now Bodrum, Turkey, was insistent the Persians learned homosexuality from the Greeks. This idea was attacked by Quintus Curtius Rufus, a Roman historian of the first century A.D., who asserted that homosexuality was not known among the Persians.

Male prostitution in ancient Greece was abundant. In the temples beautiful boy prostitutes were more popular than girl prostitutes. Many Greek authors wrote that boys and youths were to be had everywhere for money or gifts.

Boys could be hired by contract for long periods of time. There are several documents which record that in Greece and Athens as well as other harbor towns, brothels accommodated the client with boys who were to be had alone or with girls. These young people were sometimes prisoners of war and sold for a price relative to their beauty. Many times boy prostitutes in these public houses, if especially beautiful, cost much more than the girls. Also free youths could be found in public brothels earning money by selling their bodies. Boy prostitutes were visited by their lovers in the public houses and went with them to their homes to be used by the master of the home or for the festivities of the guests.

In contrast to the Christian era where sex was subjugated, mortification of the flesh was a road to eternal blessedness, angels were sexless, and doctrine separated the sensual from the religious, we need to see that the Greek attitude towards sexual desire or gratification was treated as a natural and a normal means of complementing the beauty of the body.

The Greek gods were also continually looked at through sensual eyes. The sky, the earth, and the sea were Greek gods and had sexual experiences with gods and goddesses. The character of the Greek gods was certainly not moral; they were not bothered by death, nor did age wrinkle their beauty. Each had time to enjoy living to the fullest and moral codes rarely inhibited them. The gods did what they desired. They were an answer to the mysteries of life that beset the imaginations of the Greek poets and philosophers.

According to Greek mythology, Zeus—the supreme god of light, the father of gods and men, and a seducer of mortal women—sanctioned the love of boys, and did what ever pleased him from the ethereal heights of Mt. Olympus. Apollo, a beautiful lover of manly youth, was worshipped as a god, and applauded the homosexual actions of the Greek society. His statues can be found beside Heracles and Hermes in many Greek gymnasiums. Helios, the all-seeing sun god, was never timid in acquiring young boys to satiate his desires. And most of the rest of the Greek gods and goddesses found no problem in bedding down with each other without much care as to whether the object of desire was married or of the same sex.

Roman

Homosexuality in ancient Rome was influenced by Greek religion, mythology, and life styles. The Roman gods were similar to those in Greece. It is believed that fourteen of the first fifteen Roman emperors were homosexual. For Romans sexual attitudes had more to do with property and the authority males exerted over their wives and children than with moral considerations.

It has to be understood that Roman law and especially Roman polytheism attached no moral difference to homosexual eroticism and heterosexual eroticism. An adult male in the Roman society had sexual relations with both sexes. Gender was a matter of preference as long as one followed the societal rules of propriety.

According to Ovid a Roman poet, (43 B.C.-17 A.D.), the idea of homosexual intercourse was not an offense against marriage. If a husband compensated himself with the love of boys, he was not deemed to be unfaithful to his wife.

Roman legal restrictions on sexual relationships were seldom an issue. Proven adultery was risky for a woman, but seldom is there reference to punishment. Marriage in the upper classes was generally arranged by a father as a political and economic benefit to his family. Divorce was common in early Rome and a legal marriage was necessary for inheritance.

The concept of faithfulness and chastity were relevant only to married or marriageable women and vestal virgins; the emphasis was on the legitimacy of the children as well as the fear of cuckolding the husband. The male's sexual morality was as he chose. As a male he was allowed to follow his own sexual proclivities without sanctions from his wife or society. Wives sometimes employed slaves of both genders for their husbands' use.

It seems that infidelity with a male or female was only frowned upon if a man's sexual life did not conform to that of his peers. He could have sex with a man in the Roman baths, his wife, and even a brothel prostitute, male or female, but he had to keep each separate and in their place. One could enjoy any type of sex if one were a male but only if that person had no control over him.

Homosexuality was not illegal in Rome because the government taxed homosexual prostitutes and even decreed a legal holiday for them. If there had been a law against homosexuality, Cicero (106-43 BC) a Roman statesman, scholar, lawyer, writer, and staunch upholder of republican principles would no doubt have been aware of it. Cicero mocked several male citizens because they had been male prostitutes when young, but there is no suggestion that such actions were illegal. In fact, when he defends Cnaeus Plancius, who had taken a male lover into the country for sexual purposes, Cicero writes, "this is not a crime."

Legal action was taken against homosexual practices only if the act was a sexual assault on an unwilling Roman citizen. The gender of the person assaulted was not an issue. If the individual was a Roman citizen he or she was protected by that fact. The mitigating factor wasn't whether the individual was homosexual or heterosexual; assault was the issue.

A famous case tells of a young Roman who, enslaved because of an outstanding debt, was cruelly beaten by his master when he would not indulge in a homosexual relationship. Roman citizens were angry when they found out about this case, not because of the older man's sexual interest in the young boy, but because the man had beaten a Roman citizen.

The right of a Roman citizen was of major importance and not to be violated. Being a Roman citizen was to be desired. Even Paul deferred to being a Roman in the book of Acts.

> "Paul said to the centurion who was standing by, "Is it lawful for you to scourge a man who is a Roman and uncondemned?" and when the centurion heard this, he went to the commander and told him, saying, "What are you about to do? For this man is a Roman." And the commander came and said to him, "Tell me, are you a Roman?" And he said, "Yes," and the commander answered, "I acquired this citizenship with a large sum of money," and Paul said, "but I was actually born a citizen." Therefore those who were about to examine him immediately let go of him; and the commander also was afraid when he found out that he was a Roman, because he had put him in chains. (Acts 22:25-29 NAS)

One difference between Greek and the Roman sexual practices was the education of young boys. Greek fathers allowed the teacher not only to educate his son but to have a man-boy love relationship with him. Roman fathers accepted the responsibility of educating their sons, but sexual relationships between a father and a son were not allowed nor sought after. It wasn't until the third century A.D. in Rome that laws were enacted to regulate aspects of homosexual acts, which included statutory rape of minors and gay marriages. John Boswell writes:

> Polybius, a historian of rare objectivity and unparalleled reliability, records that during the heyday of the Republic—two centuries before the Empire— "moderation" in sexual matters was virtually impossible for young men in Rome, since nearly all of them were having affairs with courtesans or other young men. There is no hint of disapproval based on gender; what Polybius criticized was the fiscal extravagance of the "many men who have spent a talent (about $2,000) for a male lover or 300 drachmas for a jar of caviar from the Black Sea." Homosexual prostitution was common under the Republic, and Cicero states

that Clodius always had a number of male prostitutes with him."[12]

One point must be addressed; the cruelty that existed extensively in later Roman culture. Cruelty was the manner in which Roman royalty lived. Otto Keifer writes:

> Since I have been engaged in the study of Roman civilization, it has seemed to me quite inexplicable that a nation whose predispositions were so pure and upright should have been suddenly influenced by some singular and mysterious force so as to develop into something very different—a brutish, immoral, and cruel nation. On the contrary, I have found it unceasingly clear that a nation whose development led it from a rough and primitive sensuality towards the unmistakable signs of lust for cruelty must always have possessed at least these characteristics which were evidence of its inclinations. My point, then, is that cruelty and brutality were original Roman characteristics, and not later importations into an originally different and "better" disposition.[13]

The underlying cause of the cruelty was a need for power. The basic drive in the Roman society was to excel in conquest as well as in personal fitness and beauty. The ambition was to dominate, to demand that everyone be subservient to Roman philosophy and religious beliefs. Cruelty is a symptom of that need for power. "Romans, remember: thou shall rule this world," was Virgil's way of declaring their destination.

The Roman Empire approved male prostitution because it involved slaves and foreigners, but by the late fourth century this validation no longer existed. The dignity of the common citizen along with that of the slave had been changed by Christianity and Roman domination weakening. Caracall in 212 granted citizenship to most of the empire making it difficult to devalue slaves and prostitutes, now residing as citizens.

Christianity

From the foundation of the Republic in 509 BC Roman power maintained authority over much of Europe and from the middle of the 1st Century A.D. the polytheistic religion of Rome and the monotheistic law of the Christians came into conflict. The moral codes with respect to man-boy love and lesbianism, accepted by the Romans but rejected harshly by the Jews, were gradually rewritten by the early Christians.

Christianity was emerging and the Roman Empire was losing its position as a world power. The Empire didn't tumble at the blowing of the horn, as did Jericho, but with each successive Emperor the roof began to leak. Punishments were increased death penalties were given for less and less serious crimes, and even Roman citizenship lost its traditional protection. When the pockets of the general public were stripped and when punishment was allotted to commoners for crimes committed out of necessity to live, rumbles started.

Roman cruelty, commonplace by the time Christians demanded a place at the table, was at the height of its popularity. The Christians were persecuted for many different reasons. More than likely one of the important causes the new religion was persecuted stemmed from their belief in one God and the moral code demanded by its doctrines. Even upper-class Romans who confessed Christianity were beheaded, burned at the stake, crucified, eaten by wild beasts, and all of these were before audiences as daily entertainments.

When half of Rome burned in 64 AD, under the Emperor Nero, Christians were targeted as scapegoats. Persecutions of Christians continued until Emperor Constantine, a Christian convert, ended them in 313. Goths, under Odovacar deposed emperor, Romulus Augustus, in 476, which ended the power of the mighty Roman Empire.

It wasn't until the sixth century that homosexuality was outlawed in the Roman Empire, partly because of the influences of invading peoples, but mostly because of the spread and the influence of Christianity. Christianity was a popular religion and encouraged banning female and male prostitution from the empire. Christianity also helped bring about a new legal barrier against the brothels and homosexuality, but not all of the early churches adhered to the same attitudes.

According to John Boswell, Saint John Chrysostom (347-407 AD)—a famous preacher and early Church Father, biblical interpreter, and archbishop of Constantinople—considered homosexual attraction perfectly normal even though he preached against it publicly.

> Despite his violent rhetoric against homosexual practices, Saint John Chrysostom himself obviously considered homosexual attraction perfectly normal and constantly juxtaposed homosexual and heterosexual desires as two faces of the same coin. In complaining, for instance, about sinful motivations for entering the temple of the Lord, he mentions in terms of equal likelihood a man's desire to view the beauty of women or of young men who frequent the sanctuaries; and in warning parents about the difficulty of restraining the sexual desires of adolescents, he emphasizes that the danger is twofold, sin the "beast" of lust may impel the youth either to being debauched by men or to debauching women.[14]

Middle Ages

From the fall of the Western Roman Empire in 477 to the fall of Constantinople and the end of the Eastern Roman Empire in 1453 stands the Middle Ages, an age when the removal of the strong central government of Rome left Europe in turmoil. The once mighty Roman Empire was broken up into small kingdoms. In many districts rule was by local lords, each of whom had authority only over the area surrounding his castle. The country was bending under the weight of poverty, and the lack of wealth caused a decline in learning.

After the destruction of the Roman Empire and the emergence of the Catholic Church attitudes on homosexuality began to change. Christianity officially agreed that homosexual practices were sinful; however, very little is written about the enforcement of this belief, even among the priests and monks.

Through out the Middle Ages it was believed that crusaders brought homosexuality into Europe from the east and spread it throughout the country.

Efforts in the early Middle Ages to reduce homosexuality proved ineffective. The churches officially forbid sodomy and male prostitution as early as the third century, but with little effect and in the East taxes on male prostitution were collected by the emperor until the sixth century.

Charlemagne, the great warrior-king established Europe as a Christian power. When he discovered that some of the monks were sodomites he chided them and demanded they turn aside from such actions, as he could not permit it in any part of his territory. He threatened sentencing them, but no civil legislation against homosexuality was ever instigated during his reign.

The early medieval church, some writers argue, seemed to have a proclivity for punishing homosexual behavior through the use of penances. Pope Saint Gregory III charged a 160-day penance of fasting for lesbians, and a one year sentence for male homosexual acts. Most of the sexual provisions in the penitentials referred to men, but the Penitential of Theodore listed a penalty for female homosexuality of penance for three years. The penance for homosexuality, however, was insignificant in proportion to such things as not eating fish on Friday, or for a priest caught hunting.

Masturbation, homosexuality, and bestiality were more severely punished for a priest than for a layman and more for men than boys. Penalties for men who were married and committed sins of masturbation, homosexuality or bestiality were worse than those for a single man.

A wave of tolerance extended until the twelfth century, and it seems that the practice was especially prevalent among the titled. The writings of Bernard of Morlaix tell us that gay people were numerous in cities, the countryside, and even in holy places. During the twelfth century homosexuality was widespread in most European countries and in the Christian clergy. Many twelfth-century English manuscripts include gay literature and the well-known homosexual life style of Richard, duke of Aquitaine, and Philip, king of France, for example, was widely condoned.

Renaissance

The Renaissance roughly dates from 1400 through 1600. The term, "Renaissance" is the French word meaning 'rebirth'. During the Renaissance the absolute authority of the Church in religion was being disputed by various heretical sects. Confidence in the Bible and personal study with simpler worship services was beginning to emerge, and the development of printing by Johannes Gutenberg in 1454 allowed books, especially the Bible, to be produced more cheaply, increasing the spread of knowledge.

The Reformation began in Germany when Martin Luther, an Augustinian monk, nailed his 95 Theses to the church door at Wittenberg in 1517. When brought before the Church officials he refused to recant his findings and was excommunicated. By 1519 the Reformation gained power in Switzerland led by Ulrich Zwingli and the new religion called Protestantism began to gather followers protesting against the abuses of the Roman Church. These Protestants, claiming the Bible forbids it, did not sanction homosexuality.

Henry VIII outlawed homosexuality in England in 1533. The penalty was death and loss of property. The Spanish Visigoths punished homosexuality by castrating offenders. France punished homosexuals by three different methods: the first offense cost a man his testicles, the second his penis, and the third got him burnt at the stake.

The New World

Immigrants to the New World brought with them the views of the European Protestant Reformation. In 1566, in St. Augustine, Florida, a military man received the death penalty for homosexual acts. Sodomy laws in the New World can be found in the settlement at Jamestown as early as 1607, and as the number of colonial settlements increased each created its own laws and each included sodomy as a capital offense. The colonies in New England were adamant against anything that even breathed sexuality. In 1779, Thomas Jefferson proposed a bill to drop the death penalty for the crime of sodomy and to replace it with castration.

Puritans and Quakers looked on sex as a necessity, but ignored any pleasure where it was concerned, and punished homosexuality severely because they saw it as a crime against marriage and the family. As the major economic unit in agricultural societies the family needed protection. With a high infant mortality rates and numerous deaths among young children, multiple children were a means of survival. And thus homosexuality was banned as "infertile" sex. For example in 1646 John Winthrop, Governor of the Massachusetts Bay Colony, stated during a trial that "Spilling or spending male seed in any kind of non-procreative activity was considered a sinful waste, because it put the future of the colonies in jeopardy." However, only 20 cases of sodomy are recorded concerning male colonists from 1624 to 1740, and of these only four received the death penalty. The laws were even more lenient with lesbians because their actions didn't include "seed spilling" as in the case of males.

Colonial pastors preached against the "sin of Sodom" and warned their parishioners that homosexuality was a one-way path to hell. For settlers uneasily positioned on the raw edge of a vast continent, the metaphor of an angry God destroying Sodom and Gomorrah was a fearful threat. The language of the colonial sodomy statues was taken from the Bible. In Connecticut, the law repeats *Leviticus* 20:13: "If a man also lie with mankind, as he lieth with a woman, both of then have committed an abomination: they shall surely be put to death; their blood shall be upon them." It must also be noted, however that sexual acts other than marital heterosexuality, such as adultery and fornication, were also subject to severe punishment.

It was only in the New Haven colony that death for "filthiness" between women was the law, though there is no record of a sentence ever being carried out. Lesbian sexual acts were seen as contrary to what women were for, childbearing. The duty of women in the colonies was to produce more citizens, and not to do so was looked on as undesirable. In many cases mutual love was not considered the prerequisite for marriage, but whether a woman was "built for babies."

The American Revolution demanded the separation of church and state. Individual states still had sodomy laws on their books; however, penalties for this crime gradually lessened in severity until jail time and loss of property became the norm. Even as late as 1961, all 50 states had some form of sodomy law on their books. Today, such laws can still be found in southern, Bible-belt, states but they were seldom carried out unless there was a question of guardianship of minor children. However a recent Supreme Court ruling now makes such laws unconstitutional.

Current

In the late nineteenth century, medical science added to the condemnation of sodomy as a crime by its designation of homosexuality as a disease. Diagnosing homosexuality as an illness American physicians varied however as to whether it was acquired or congenital. Remedies listed were castration, lobotomy, electroshock, aversion therapy and for women hysterectomies.

The immigration of German and Austrian psychoanalysts in the 1930s, and their analyses of homosexuality as an illness supported American physicians. This caused more than half the states to enact "sexual psychopath" laws. Selective enforcement singled out male homosexuals as a way of committing them to mental asylums. These laws allowed courts to give undetermined sentences in mental institutions as punishment for active homosexuals. By the middle of the century only murder, rape, and kidnapping held heavier sentences than consensual homosexuality.

World War II changed America's view of homosexuality. Great numbers of the young men from small towns entered the military and migrated to larger cities for wartime employment. In the larger cities and in the sex-segregated forces it became easier for gay men and women to meet and to form relationships outside the supervision of families and small home towns. It is said that the war was a nationwide "coming out" for the gays. The findings of Alfred Kinsey's studies on human sexual behavior established that homosexuality was neither rare nor abnormal, but a prevalent pattern in human society.

America's attitude about homosexuality has changed over the last century. This is likely the result of gay activist movements, changes in the laws, and media coverage. Homosexuality is no longer whispered about; gays no longer hide in closets; and to be a homosexual does not subject one to punishment by the state. The controversies now are whether it is a sin to be an active homosexual, whether a gay person should be a second class citizen, and whether gays should be allowed to adopt children, be Scout leaders, teach children, be members of a church, and be married.

Each person has to decide where they fit in this dialogue. Each must decide where they belong in this changing society. No civilization ever survives without change. Change strengthens or weakens a society and history becomes the toll keeper.

16

Religious Attitudes Towards Homosexuality

The subject of homosexuality is not new in religious debates. Nearly all religions, ancient or current, strongly disagree over the issue. Some incorporated the practice into their worship, and some excluded it, calling it a sin, excommunicating those who practiced it from the religious community or by killing the perpetrators.

The term, "homosexuality" does not, of course, exist in ancient writings. Lying with one of the same sex was, in general, the way of describing an action which has been with us since the beginning of civilization. Written history has included the attraction between same-sex lovers in prose and poetry.

To understand how the different approaches to this issue are, we will look the beliefs various religions have accepted. Even within a given religion, however, there exists wide diversity. Moreover doctrines do not necessarily report reality. What is written or spoken is not always takes place in the general public; it is often the same in religious circles. Written doctrines of a given religion or denomination, may not be what is understood or preached by a follower.

Presently, we have a conflict between scientists and theologians. Science today demands an answer, an entity in a Petri dish, repeated occurrences to prove their findings, and the media to enhance their importance. Scientists trying to prove a point sometimes go against their own rules but believe all things have an answer and are out to discover the solution. Religion, they say, is a far cry from reality; consequently, science is determined to find a gene-link to establish that homosexuality is a normal function of the body caused by genetics, as is hair-coloring and buckteeth.

Are we limited to certain sexual actions? Are we born heterosexual, homosexual?

> The sexual impulse doesn't come from chromosomes, and it isn't our chromosomes that help us decide what kind of sex we like. That decision comes from the part of the brain called the human cortex, which is the repository of our feelings, memories, dreams and dreads as well as our reason.
>
> No, men and women aren't born homosexuals. Neither heterosexuality nor homosexuality is in the genes. These orientations come about in the process called growing up with a sense of self-identity, or gender-identity. In a normal family, boys and girls come to their identities as boys or girls very quickly.[15]

Societies and religions are known to change their "cast in stone" doctrines. Time has a way of dealing with man's intelligence and frail ability to walk a perfectly straight line.

> The attitude if the American Psychiatric Association was well defined when, on December 15, 1973, its trustees decided to drop homosexuality from the association's list of mental disorders. When put to a vote among the entire membership of the association, only about 65 percent voted, and of that, 60 percent sustained the action of the trustees. The wording was then changed to categorize homosexuality as a "sexual disorientation disturbance."[16]

Each generation looks at the subject of homosexuality through the eyes of society, family, their peers, and for some their religious leaders. Living in a vacuum or in a secluded cave is not possible. Social groups demand certain sexual actions are accepted or rejected.

Homosexuality (a term we will use as it is understood in our currant era to mean individuals who are attracted to members of the same gender) is mentioned in the Bible, in the Book of

Mormon, in the Qur'an, and in nearly all sacred writings of different world religions.

Baha'i

Baha'i is a religion founded in Iran in the middle of the 19th century by Mirza Hoseyn'Ali Nuri also known as Baha'Ullah (Arabic for Glory To God). Members of the Baha'i faith believe that Baha' Ullah and his predecessors are manifestations of a god who, in his essence, is unknowable. The Baha' faith believes that the founders of the world's great religions are manifestations of god and agents of a progressive divine plan for educating the human race. Baha' Ullah's objective was to overcome the disunity of religions and establish a universal faith.

Baha'i believes in an oneness of humanity and its members devote themselves to the abolition of racial, class, and religious prejudices. Baha'i teaching is chiefly concerned with social ethics. The religion has no priesthood and observes no formal sacraments in its worship.

Membership in the Baha'i community is open to all who profess faith in Baha' Ullah and accept his teachings. Every Baha'i is under obligation to pray daily; to abstain from narcotics, alcohol, and any other substance that affects the mind; to practice monogamy; to obtain the consent of parents prior to marriage.

The Baha'i faith teaches that there is only one acceptable form of sexual expression and that is between a married man and woman. They view homosexual feelings and behavior as improper and contradictory to their god's plan for humankind. They see homosexuality as a difficulty an individual must overcome, and they believe that through prayer, counseling, medical treatment, and personal discipline a gay or lesbian person can become heterosexual in sexual matters. However, if a lesbian or gay cannot change they are expected to remain celibate for life.

It is noted in the sacred text of Baha'i written by Prophet Baha'Ullah in 1875 that "Ye are forbidden to commit adultery, sodomy and lechery." The Baha'i House of Justice wrote on Mar. 14, 1973: Baha'i teachings on sexual morality center on marriage and the family as bedrock of the whole structure of human society, and are designed to protect and strengthen that divine institution. Thus Baha'i law restricts permissible sexual intercourse to that between a man and the woman to whom he is married."

However the Baha'i Faith is experiencing conflicts. It's National Spiritual Assembly has been requested to rethink the Baha'i position towards homosexuality and bisexuality. The group may well bend under the external pressure being brought to bare on this subject. Discrimination, against homosexuals, also might increase the growth of the Faith in those countries in the world which openly oppose homosexuality.

Buddhism

Buddhism, an Asian religion and philosophy founded by Siddharta Gautama in northeast India about the 5th century BC, plays an important role in the East. In the 19th century it began to spread to the west.

The teachings of the Buddha Gautama, as transmitted orally by his followers always, are prefaced by the phrase *"Evam me sutam"* (Thus have I heard); therefore it is difficult to say whether these dialogues relate what Gautama actually said.

Buddhism became a great missionary religion and in due course nearly died out in its native India. The Mahayana school, which developed an ostentatious cosmology with many semi-deities, is to be found in China, Korea, and Japan. The Therevada School, a more severe sect of Buddhism, thrives in Ceylon, Burma, and Southeast Asia. Zen is in principle a Mahayana sect but more closely resembles the Therevada School. All have their proponents in the West.

Gautama, called the Buddha the (Enlightened One), discovered that a life of luxury and a life of extreme asceticism are of no use in gaining spiritual freedom. Thus he propounded the "Middle Way." His teachings, however, have undergone many transformations during the years.

By this 'middle way' there is no god though many have understood Buddhism to be a search for enlightenment. Buddha did not refute the existence of God completely, but said the uncertainty of His existence "tends not to edification." Those seeking enlightenment needed, he said, to concentrate on their own spiritual pathways rather than depending on an outside support. Gautama did not claim holiness or a divine source for his teachings; rather he saw himself as a model for the other monks. He is said to have compared his teachings to a raft that should be left behind once the other side of the river is reached.

Buddhism begins with an examination of the world of appearances especially man. Buddhism as Hinduism sees the cycle of reincarnation measured in pain. Buddha taught that life was not permanent in any sense. He taught that all creatures including mankind are illusions, that there is no "self," only a series of occurrences that appear to be individualized. The notion of 'no self' is a difficult concept and needs a great deal of effort to try and understand it completely.

Overall Buddhism does not condemn homosexuality, and many Buddhist countries do not have social or legal prohibitions against it. The Dalai Lama, the leader of the Tibetan people revered by millions of Buddhists worldwide, is ambiguous on the subject. In general Buddhists prohibit oral, manual and anal sex for both homosexuals and heterosexuals. That is, its not so much partners who are prohibited, but inappropriate sexual uses of organs.

Homosexuality is not mentioned in any of the Buddha's discourses. It is assumed that it is meant to be evaluated in the way that heterosexual conduct is. If there is mutual consent and no adultery involved, and if the sexual act is accompanied by love, respect, and warmth, it would not be breaking one of the Precepts. Zen Buddhism does not make a distinction between heterosexual and homosexual sex. It encourages sexual relationships that are mutually loving and supportive.

From the Theravada school all sexual relationships are considered matters of personal mutual consent. If a relationship promotes the happiness and well-being of both parties, then it is positive and acceptable. Many Buddhists believe that sexual orientation is as much outside a person's control as race and gender are. They feel that gays and lesbians should have the same civil rights and benefits as all other persons.

Buddhists countries had no legal statutes against homosexuality between consenting adults until the colonial era when the British instigated them. Thailand still has no such laws. Buddhists are urged to follow the Five Precepts which prohibit killing (including animals), stealing, illicit sexual relations, wrong speech (including gossiping), and drugs or alcohol

Islam Religion

In the seventh century A.D. Muhammad—thought to be the last prophet in a line that includes Abraham, Moses, the biblical prophets, and Jesus—founded a strict, monotheistic religion in reaction to the polytheism and lawlessness of existing Arab cultures. The term, "Islam", translated means 'surrender'. A believer accepts the idea he must surrender to the will of Allah (Arabic: "god"), who they believe is the creator, sustainer, and restorer of the world.

The will of Allah to which they must submit is made known through sacred scriptures known as the Qur'an. The Qur'an mostly is a series of short teachings and is intensely revered by Muslims as the final word of Allah, the culmination of what was only begun in the Bible. These scriptures were revealed to Muhammad, whom Muslims believe to be the messenger of Allah. Centered in Islamic belief is the view that, as the last of the prophets were tokens the Qur'an abolishes all previous revelations it replaces all earlier sacred texts.

The Islam faith is thoroughly monotheistic and demands strict adherence to certain essential religious practices. Taught first to a small group of followers it spread rapidly through the Middle East, then to Africa, Europe, India and China. Muslims reject the title Muhammadism for they believe Muhammad was only a carrier of the truth and not divine in any way.

There are different sects in Islam: Shi'ite, Sunni, Sufi are the best known. Shi'ite Muslims believe that religious leaders should also be political rulers, whereas the majority of Muslims, the Sunnites, believe the two should be separated. Sufis teach a demanding path of self-denial which concludes with unification with Allah.

Stephen Cory tells us that:

> Muslims see the universe as created by the deliberate act of
> a personal, omnipresent God. The universe is not considered an
> illusion in any way and is basically good, being given for the
> benefit of man. Muslins respect for the world order led to the
> development of sciences in Arab countries long before develop-
> ments in Europe.
>
> Muhammad did not produce miracles but simply pro-
> claimed the message of Allah. Thus the presence of God in the
> world is seen not through supernatural signs but through the
> wonderful order of nature and the one great miracle, the Koran.
> Muslims generally do not expect miraculous deliverance from
> suffering in this life but believe that food deeds will be rewarded
> in the next life.
>
> Man is considered a sort of vice-regent, in charge of creation
> under the authority of God. His purpose-and the goal of Islam-is
> to make a moral order in the world.
>
> Man is endowed with *tagwa,* a sort of divine spark mani-
> fested in his conscience that enables him to perceive the truth
> and to act on it. Conscience is thus of the greatest values in Islam,
> much as love is the greatest value to Christians.
>
> But Islam is in no way pantheism. Man may cultivate his
> *tagwa* and so live according to the way of Allah, or he may
> suppress it. Man thus deserves or is undeserving of God's guid-
> ance.[17]

There is no doubt that in Islam homosexuality is sinful. Islam
believes that humans are not homosexual by nature and that
people become homosexuals because of their environment. There
are five references in the Qur'an to gay and lesbian behavior.
These references to homosexuality seem to imply that this behavior did not exist before it first appeared in Sodom One passage
links the destruction of Sodom to the sin of homosexuality.

There are two main references in the Qur'an to homosexuality:

> We also sent Lot, who said to his people: "Why do you
> commit this lecherous act which none in the world committed
> before? In preference to women you satisfy your lust with men.
> Indeed you are a people who are guilty of excess. (*Qur'an,* 7:80-
> 81)

Do you have sexual intercourse only with males of all creatures of the World and neglect the wives whom Allah has created for you? Nay, you are a sinful people indeed. (*Qur'an* 26:165)

The Hadith, a collection of sayings of Mohammad, also seems to emphasize the attitude that homosexuality is a sin. Orthodox Muslims claim that the Hadith literature contains the authentic sayings of Mohammad, where as many liberal Muslims doubt their authenticity.

The treatment for homosexuality in Muslim countries varies. The Hanafite School, located mainly in Asia, teaches that no physical punishment is needed. The Hanabalites, located mainly in the Arab world, teach that severe punishment is warranted. The Sha'fi school of thought requires a minimum of 4 adult male witnesses before a person can be found guilty of a homosexual act.

To summarize Islamic beliefs on homosexuality:

Homosexuality is considered sinful within Islam.
Homosexuality is a profound mistake.
Humans are all naturally heterosexual.
Homosexuality is caused by environmental factors, particularly near the time of puberty. People can control their thoughts and steer themselves away from homosexuality.
Homosexuality is a chosen sexual orientation; any homosexual can become a heterosexual.[18]

Hinduism

Hinduism is the religion followed by about 70 percent of the seven hundred million people of India. In other countries, with the exception of the Indonesian island of Bali, Hindus represent only minority populations. The word "Hindu" is derived front the Sanskrit word Sindhu ("river"-more specifically the Indus.) The early sacred literature of Hinduism was titled Veda, meaning *'knowledge'*, and is also known as Sruti, which means *'that which is heard.'* These texts are an impressive collection originally oral in character, that grew into its present form over nine or ten centuries between 1400 and 400 B.C.

During the fourth century B.C., Aryans, the people that developed Greek culture, conquered much of present-day India. Their pantheon of gods, similar to that of the Greeks, combined with indigenous Indian traditions of meditation to form a loose combination of beliefs and practices that came to be known as Hinduism. "Orthodox" Hindus can be either pious worshippers of a god, atheists, self-negating ascetics, or men of the world.

The English term, Hinduism was coined by British writers in the first decades of the 19th century, and became familiar with the publication of such books as Sir Monier-Williams' *Hinduism* (1877), a word designating religious ideas and practices distinctive to India. Since the 19th century Hindus have reacted to the term, Hinduism. Preferring the term, Veda or Vedic Religion, to embrace an ancient textual core and the tradition of Brahmin learning that preserved and interpreted it.

Hindus typically focus their worship of the One on a favorite divinity; they do not insist there is anything exclusive in their choice. Thus a range of deities is worshiped, though many Hindus worship Vishnu and Shiva. Vishnu is regarded as a special manifestation of the preservative aspect of reality, while Shiva is regarded as the manifestation of its destructive aspect. Another deity, Brahma, a masculine creator, remains in the background. Brahma, Vishnu, and Shiva constitute the so-called Hindu trinity. This conception was an attempt to harmonize the conviction that the Supreme Power is singular with a reality that a plurality of gods were worshiped in everyday practice.

Brahman is seen by many Hindus as a personal loving God who desires the salvation of all men. More usually, however, he is described as a supreme impersonal being completely above all creation and uninvolved with life on earth.

Of the many gods or incarnations of gods that are worshiped by Hindus, some are amoral; their freedom from the usual restraints necessary to humans is often celebrated and they are often represented with sexual imagery. Many cults worship a complex variety of gods, all of whom are usually seem as manifestations of the one supreme being, Brahma.

Hindus accept the doctrines of transmigration and rebirth, and believe in *karma* (action), a belief that acts in an earlier life condition a being in subsequent lives. The whole process of rebirth is called Samsara, a cyclic process which has no clear beginning or ending and encompasses lives of perpetual serial attachments. Advaita Vedanta which believe in complete identity between the inmost self and the impersonal, ultimate 'god,' is the most common form of Hinduism in the West. Jainism probably represents the most ancient, pre-Aryan elements of Hinduism. The Sikh religion attempts to unite elements of Hinduism and Islam.

The Hindu view of homosexuality is confusing, and the Hindu Veda is conflicting. The Bhagavad-Gita says that all people are eternal souls, and that we are not our bodies Hindus believe that one must act in accordance with one's true nature, like spiritual souls. Any action that is based on gratifying the senses of this temporary body will drag a believer further into the illusion that they are their bodies.

Furthermore the *Manusmritis* (another Hindu scripture) specifically rejects homosexuality. It is punishable by fines, whipping, and even loss of caste. In some cases a woman can have her head shaved or two fingers cut off and then be paraded around on the back of a donkey. Kama Sutra Vatsayana, writes that homosexuality is allowed by the holy teachings and that upper caste Hindus and Muslim rulers practiced homosexuality prior to a British takeover of India.

Christianity

Christianity is a religion which traces its origins to Jesus of Nazareth, whom it believes is the only begotten Son of God, the Son of the Yahweh of the Bible's Old Testament. Christianity numbers one-third of the earth's population, with a substantial population on every continent. Over 2,000,000,000 people are in some way identified with the Christian religion on the planet. The primary commandment is to believe in God and to love him, and the second commandment is to love one's neighbor as oneself. Christianity has reached out with its message to individuals all over the world.

In the following Apostles Creed the summary of what the traditional Christian belief covers is well stated.

> I believe in God, the Father Almighty, the Creator of heaven and earth, and in Jesus Christ, his only Son, our Lord:
> Who was conceived by the Holy Spirit, born of the Virgin Mary, suffered under Pontius Pilate, was crucified, died, and was buried.
> He descended into hell.
> The third day He arose again from the dead, He ascended into heaven and sits at the right hand of God the Father Almighty,
> Whence He will come to judge the living and the dead.
> I believe in the Holy Spirit, the holy catholic church,[19] the communion of saints, the forgiveness of sins, the resurrection of the body, and life everlasting.
> Amen.

The many Christian denominations, sects and new religious movements vary from conservative to liberal attitudes toward homosexuality. The present issues tend to be whether a church will allow known acting homosexuals to become members with full privileges, consider homosexuals for ordination, allow them to hold positions of power, and allow them to be married.

On these issues modern protestant denominations widely disagree. As liberal denominations slowly change their attitudes towards a more all-embracing posture, conservatives ones become stricter and less tolerant. Mainline denominations such as the Presbyterians, Episcopalians, Methodists, and Lutherans are actively debating the question. Conservative denominations are standing firm in their belief that the Bible does not allow such actions to be accepted by the church. For example the Southern Baptist Convention has expelled three congregations who, having conducted a study of homosexuality that led to the view that the denomination's beliefs were invalid, welcomed gays and lesbians as members.

A glossary, "Lexicon on Ambiguous and Colloquial Terms about Family Life and Ethical Questions," prepared by the Vatican's Pontifical Council for the Family, covers issues such as sexuality, condoms, abortion, birth control and genetic manipulation for the Roman Catholic Church. According to The Data Lounge on July 14, 2003[20] this glossary has caused a great unleashing of anger. It states that gay people are not normal and that anyone who allows gay marriages are individuals with "profoundly disordered minds." And according to Pope John Paul II, "homosexual acts are against nature's laws and the church cannot silence the truth, because this would not help discern what is good from what is evil."

Views of homosexuality in Christianity come in part from the Mosaic Law:

> Thou shalt not lie with mankind, as with woman kind: it is abomination. Neither shall any woman stand before a beast to lie down thereto: it is confusion. Defile not ye yourselves in any of these things: for in all these the nations are defiled which I cast our before you. (Leviticus 18:22-24)
>
> If a man lie with mankind, as he lieth with a woman, both of them have committed an abomination: they shall surely be put to death; their blood shall be upon them. (Leviticus 20:13)
>
> There shall be no whore of the daughters of Israel, nor a sodomite of the sons of Israel. Thou shalt not bring the hire of a whore, or the price of a dog, into the house of the Lord thy God for any vow: for even both these are abominations unto the Lord thy God. (Deuteronomy. 23:17, 18)

Michael Cosby tells us that:

> For the Jews, Gentile idolatry and Gentile sexual immorality were almost necessarily connected in a cause –and-effect relationship: If people worshipped idols, then of course they would be immoral! Adultery, incest, prostitution, and sexual worship of gods and goddesses were used as stock examples of Gentile perversion, but homosexuality occupied a special place of abhorrence for the Jewish people. The position of the Mosaic Law is abundantly clear.... For Torah-loving Jews; homosexuality was a ridiculously sinful practice.[21]

In the New Testament, Paul's view of homosexuality is in harmony with the position uttered by Jewish authors of ancient times:

> Don't be mislead, neither the immoral nor idolators nor adulterers nor effeminate men nor sodomites nor thieves nor drunkards nor robbers will inherit God's Kingdom. (1 Corinthians 6:9)
>
> God abandoned them to their degrading passions. There women exchanged natural relations for unnatural and the men too in the same way gave up natural relations with women and were consumed with passion for one another, men committing shameless acts with men and receiving in their own person the penalty for their perversity. (Romans 1:27)

In brief, like the Old Testament Christianity condemned male and female homosexuality as immoral, but also placed it in exactly the same ethical level as adultery, theft, idolatry, and alcoholism. Homosexuality is designated as sin according to traditional Christianity and therefore must be treated in accordance with the precepts of the Bible. Sin is forgivable and God has the ability to keep a repentant individual from returning to it.

Notes

[1] Bryan Ellison and Peter H. Duesberg, *Why We Will Never Win the War On Aids*, (Inside Story Communications, 1944) p. 1

[2] Andres Tapia, *The AIDS Crisis*, (New York: Intervarsity Press, 1988) pp. 5-6.

[3] Bill Bangham ed. *The Commission*, (Richmond, VA. Southern Baptist Mission Board, 8-2003) p. 7.

[4] Dr. Patrick Dixon, *The Whole Truth About AIDS*, *(New York:* Thomas Nelson Publishers, 1989), p. 90.

[5] *Ibid.* p. 95

[6] Charles W. Socarides M.D., *Homosexuality A Freedom Too Far, (Phoenix*, AR. Adam Margrave Books, 1995) pp. 191, 206.

[7] Robert T. Michael, John H. Gagnon, Edward O. Laumann, and Gina Kolata, *Sex In America A Definite Survey (,*Boston, New York, Toronto, London: Little, Brown and Company, 1994), p. 209.

[8] Jeffrey Satinover, M.D., Homosexuality and the *Politics of Truth*, (Grand Rapids Michigan: Baker Books, 1996), p. 57.

[9] Robert J. Buchanan, *Homosexuality in History, (*Durham, NC: Grace Community Church), p. 2.

[10] Hans Licht, *Sexual Life in Ancient Greece*, (New York: Dorset Press, 1993), p. 449.

[11] John Boswell, *Same-Sex Unions in Premodern Europe*, (New York: Vintage Books, 1994), p. 56.

[12] John Boswell, *Christianity Social Tolerance, and Homosexuality, (Chicago*: The University of Chicago Press, 1980), p. 72.

[13] Otto Kiefer, *Sexual Life in Ancient Rome*, (New York: Dorset Press, 1993), pp. 64-65.

[14] John Boswell, *Christianity, Social Tolerance, and Homosexuality*, (Chicago: The University of Chicago Press, 1990), p. 160.

[15] Charles W. Socarides, M.D., *Homosexuality A Freedom Too Far*, (Phoenix, AR.: Adam Margrave Books, 1995), p. 27.

[16] Paul D. Morris, Ph.D., *Shadow of Sodom*, (Wheaton, Ill.: Tyndale House Publishers, Inc., 197), p. 10.

[17] Steven Cory, *The Spirit of Truth and The Spirit of Error*, Chicago: (Moody Press, 1977) p. 1.

[18] *"What is Islam's View of Homosexuality"*, http://www.islamic.org.uk/homosex.html

[19] The holy catholic church means , the universal church, it does not refer to the Roman Catholic Church.

[20] The Data Lounge, http://www.datalounge.com/datalounge/news/record.html?record=20644

[21] Michael R. Cosby, *Sex In The Bible*, (New York: Prentice-Hall, Inc., 1984), p. 147.

Glossary

Abstinence: Not participating in sexual intercourse.

Adultery: Voluntary sexual intercourse between someone other than one's spouse.

AIDS: (Acquired Immunodeficiency Syndrome) the late stages of the illness triggered by infection with human immunodeficiency virus (HIV).

Anus: Opening of the large intestine

Aphrodite: The goddess of love and beauty in Greek mythology.

Aphrodisiac: Exciting sexual desire.

Bacterial STDs: Diseases such as syphilis, gonorrhea and Chlamydia respond effectively to antibiotic treatment, yet they remain epidemic in the population.

Balanitis: Inflammation of the penis or clitoris.

Benign: Not cancerous; does not invade nearby tissue or spread to other parts of the body.

Biopsy: The removal of a sample of tissue that is then examined under a microscope to check for cancer cells.

Birth Control: Any instrument, pill, or method that prevents a female from getting pregnant.

Bisexual: An individual who is sexually attracted to either sex.

Bladder: A hollow organ that stores urine.

Brothel: An establishment in which prostitutes are available for hire.

Butch: Slang for the female who takes the part of the male role in female homosexual intercourse.

Cancer: A term for diseases in which abnormal cells divide without control.

Candida: A group of yeast-like fungi, in particular Candida albicans, that infects the mouth as well as other mucous membranes in the esophagus, intestines, vagina, throat and lungs. Oral or recurrent vaginal candida infection is an early sign of immune system deterioration.

Castration: To deprive a man of the testes: to deprive a woman of her ovaries.

Carcinoma: Cancer that begins in the lining or covering of an organ.

Cervix: The narrow part of the female's uterus which extends into the vagina.

Chancre: A painless, oozing sore which appears in early stages of syphilis, usually on the sex organs.

Chancroid: A highly contagious sexually-transmitted disease. It appears as a pimple, chancre, sore or ulcer on the skin of the genitals. The lesion appears after an incubation period of three to five days and may facilitate the transmission of HIV.

Chemotherapy: A method of treating cancer with drugs..

Chlamydia: The fastest spreading STD in the US, chlamydia infects as many as four million men and women each year. As many as 85% of cases in women and 40% in men are symptomless. If undetected and untreated chlamydia can lead to serious complications in women.

Circumcision: The removal of all or part of the foreskin from a penis, female, removal of the clitoris.

Climax: The response of the body to sexual stimulation. A man discharges semen through the end of the penis upon having a climax (orgasm).

Clitoris: A female organ located above the opening of the vagina; a small bulb that, when massaged, leads to excitement.

Cohabitation: Living together without being married, a couple having intercourse as if they were legally married.

Coitus: (Sexual Intercourse) the natural conveying of semen to the female reproductive tract.

Cold Sores: Otherwise known as "fever blisters" and herpes type-1 infection.

Coming Out: Letting other people know that you are homosexual.

Conception: Fertilization of an egg by sperm.

Condom: Male: A sheath made of rubber, plastic, or animal gut that is rolled over the penis before intercourse to protect against sexually transmitted disease and or avoid conception. Female: a condom that lines the vagina.
   Are not 100% safe.

Contraceptive: Voluntary prevention of conception or impregnation. Oral, suppository, or physical means of preventing pregnancy.

Copulating: To engage in sexual intercourse.

Crabs: A slang term for sexually transmitted lice that infect the pubic area causing itching. They are very contagious.

Cunnilingus: Oral sex performed on a female. (Fellatio: oral sex on a male.)

Cyst: A sac or capsule filled with fluid.

Dermatitis: Inflammation of the skin.

Diaphragm: A devise inserted in the vagina to prevent pregnancy.

Dildo: Sexual aid shaped like a penis used by lesbians.

Douche: A means of washing out the vagina, usually with a douche bag.

Dysuria: Painful or difficult urination. May be due to a STD.

Effeminate: Unmanly: having unsuitable feminine qualities.

Ejaculation: Discharge of semen form the penis at orgasm.

Embryo: A term for a developing baby during the first eight weeks after conception.

Encephalitis: A brain inflammation of viral or other microbial origin.

Endometrium: The mucous membrane that lines the uterus.

Erection: A penis aroused and hardened so it can be inserted into a vagina for sexual intercourse.

Erotic: Arousing sexual feelings.

Eunuch: Castrated human male.

Exhibitionist: A male or female who gains sexual excitement from exposing their sex organs in public. Slang: flasher.

Fallopian Tubes: A hollow tube leading from the ovaries to the uterus through which an ovum passes on the way to the uterus. Fertilization generally takes place while the ovum (egg) is in this tube.

Fellatio: Oral sex performed on a male.

Fertilization: A sperm entering and egg. At this point conception has taken place.

Foreplay: Sexual activity that usually leads to more intensive sexual activity such as intercourse.

Foreskin: The fold of skin that covers the head of a male's penis at birth. The head or glans of the penis is exposed by pulling the foreskin back.

Fornication: Sexual intercourse between a spouse and an unmarried person. Sexual intercourse between unmarried people.

Fricatrice: She who rules the penis

Gay: A man who has sex with a man.

Genitals: Male and female sex organs.

Gonad: Biological term for a sex gland, either ovaries or testes.

Gonorrhea: A sexually transmitted disease often characterized by a burning feeling during urination and discharge of pus from the urethra. An estimated 1.1 million American men and women each year contract gonorrhea. Many people who are infected show no signs of the disease.

Gynecocracies: A social system ruled by women..

Gynecology: The branch of medicine that involves care of the female reproductive system and breasts.

Hepatitis: Inflammation of the liver caused by microbes or chemicals. Often accompanied by jaundice, enlarged liver, fever, fatigue and nausea and high levels of liver enzymes in the blood.

Hepatitis A: Is acquired through ingesting fecally contaminated water or food or engaging in sexual practices involving anal contact. Injection drug users who share unclean needle also are at risk.

Hepatitis B: A virus-induced liver disease that infects approximately 200,000 Americans each year. The hepatitis B virus is found in blood, semen, vaginal secretions and saliva. This highly contagious virus is spread through sexual contact, sharing contaminated drug needles, blood transfusions, and piercing the skin with contaminated instruments.

Hepatitis C: Another virus-induced liver disease. It appears to be more common among heterosexuals and injection drug users that B.

Herpes: A viral sexually-transmitted disease characterized by painful blisters which may reoccur.

Heterosexual: A person who is attracted to the opposite sex.

HIV: Human Immunodeficiency Virus. It is estimated that 600,000 to 900,000 people in the U.S. are infected with HIV, the cause of AIDS. A virus transmitted by blood, semen, and vaginal secretions of an HIV infected person. Both men and women can pass HIV to a sex partner. The virus can also be passed from person to person by sharing needles. There is no way to get rid of the virus once a person is infected.

Primary HIV Infection: The flu-like syndrome that occurs immediately after a person contracts HIV. This initial infection precedes seroconversion and is characterized by fever, sore throat, headache, skin rash, and swollen glands. Also called acute infection.

Homosexual: Males who are attracted to males are referred to as gays, and females attracted to the same sex are called lesbians.

Hymen: A fold of skin which often partially covers the opening of a vagina. During first intercourse its rupture may cause a small amount of bleeding and pain.

Immune Deficiency: A breakdown or inability of certain parts of the immune system to function, thus making a person susceptible to certain diseases that they would have not contracted with a healthy immune system.

Immunity: Protection against disease.

Impotence: The inadequacy in a male to achieve or maintain an erection for sexual intercourse.

Incest: Sexual activity between close relatives, such as a father and daughter, or brother and sister.

Intercourse: Sexual contact between partners involving inserting the penis into the vagina or anal intercourse.

IUD: A contraceptive apparatus inserted into the uterus by a physician to prevent pregnancy.

Intravenous Drugs: Drugs like heroine which are taken by injection, a particular dangerous method if the needle is not clean.

Kaposi's Sarcoma (KS): An AIDS defining illness consisting of individual cancerous lesions caused by an overgrowth of blood vessels. KS frequently occurs in immuno-compromised patients, such as those with AIDS.

Labia: The "lips" of a female's vulva which cover the opening to the vagina.

Lesbian: A term for women who have sex with women.

Lesion: A very general term denoting any abnormality on the surface of the body, whether on the skin or elsewhere.

Malignant: A cancerous growth that can spread to other parts of the body.

Mammogram: An x-ray of the breast and is used to detect breast cancer.

Masturbation: Stimulating one's genitals for pleasure.

Menopause: The time in a women's life when menstrual periods stop, also called the "change of life."

Menstruation: The periodic discharge of bloody fluid from the uterus occurring at more or less regular intervals during the life of a woman from the age of puberty to menopause.

Metastasis: The spread of cancer cells from one part of the body to another. Cells that have metastasized are like those in the original; tumor.

Mons: A small round mound of tissue covered with hair in adults just above the adult sex organs.

Mycosis: Any disease caused by a fungus.

Myopathy: Progressive muscle weakness. Myopathy may arise as a toxic reaction to AZT or as a consequence of HIV infection itself.

Nancy Boy: An English term (slang) for a homosexual.

Nymphophilia: Adult male's sexual desire for sexual intercourse with female children.

Obstetrics: The branch of medicine that involves care of woman during pregnancy, labor, delivery, and following childbirth.

Ocular Herpes: A herpes infection in the eyes.

Onanism: Uncompleted coitus: masturbation.

Oncologist: A doctor who specializes in treating cancer.

Orgasm: A response arrived at from stimulating the body sexually. The male shows a release of semen through the head of the penis; the female does not emit semen as the male does.

Ovaries: The pair of female reproductive glands in which the ova or eggs are formed. The ovaries are located in the lower abdomen, one on each side of the uterus.

Ovulation: The moment during a woman's menstrual cycle when the ovum ruptures through the ovary wall and begins its journey to the fallopian tube.

Ovum: The egg produced by the female. If this egg is fertilized by the male it develops into a baby.

Pap Smear: (Papanicolaou Test). A test to detect cancerous or precancerous cells of the cervix allowing for early diagnosis of cancer.

Parathenophilia: Sexual desire for virgins.

Pederast: A man who practices pederasty; a lover of boys.

Pedophilia: A sexual desire for children, of both sexes.

Pelvic Inflammatory Disease (PID): A gynecological condition caused by an infection usually sexually transmitted that spreads from the vagina to the upper parts of a women's reproductive tract in the pelvic cavity. Severe cases may even spread to the liver and kidneys causing dangerous internal bleeding, lung failure and death.

Pelvis: The lower part of the abdomen between the hip bones.

Penis: The male organ through which the urine and semen passes. Slang: prick, tool, cock, dick, etc.

Petting: To engage in amorous embracing caressing and kissing.

Precancerous: Not cancerous, but may become cancerous with time.

Prostitute: A male of female who sells sexual services.

Prevention: No having sex (abstinence) is the best way to prevent STDs.

Prognosis: The probable outcome or future course of disease in a patient; the chance of recovery.

Puberty: The time in life when the sex organs become capable or reproducing.

Queer: Slang for homosexual.

Rape: Forcing a man or woman into sexual acts against his or her will, sometimes resulting in death or physical harm.

Rectum: The last 6-8 inches of the large intestine. The rectum stores sold waste until it leaves the body through the anus.

Risk Factor: Anything that increases the probability of developing a disease.

Rubber: A slang term for a condom.

Scrotum: The sac below and behind the penis that contains the testes.

Semen: (Seminal fluid). A milk-colored fluid usually ejected from the penis by males during orgasm. (coming, climax)

Serology: A test that identifies the antibodies in serum.

Sexual Intercourse: The male placing his erect penis into the vagina of the female.

Shingles: A skin condition caused by reactivation of a Varicella zoster virus infection, usually acquired in childhood (when it appears as chicken pox). It consists of painful, inflammatory blisters on the skin that follow the path of individual peripheral nerves. The blisters generally dry and scab, leaving minor scarring.

Sperm: A male cell that must unite with an ovum for reproduction to occur; it is ejected from the penis in the seminal fluid.

Sodomy: Carnal copulation with a member of the same sex or with an animal.

STD: Sexually transmitted disease, any disease that is acquired through sexual contact in a substantial number of cases.

Sterilization: A procedure which makes a male or female unable to produce a baby.

Straight: A slang term for a heterosexual person.

Syphilis: A dangerous sexually transmitted disease. There are an estimated 120,000 new cases of syphilis each year in the U.S. If left untreated can in the late stages result in mental illness, blindness, heart disease and death.

TB: (Tuberculosis) A lung infection that occurs often in people with weakened immune systems. TB can be easily passed to others and can lead to death if not treated.

Teens: Some three million teenagers are affected with an STD annually. Behavioral factors that place teens at high risk include early age of first intercourse and multiple partners.

Testes: Glands in the male located in the scrotum which produce male hormones and sperm.

Tomboy: A girl with boyish behavior.

Transmission: The spread of disease, including a sexually transmitted disease, from one person to another.

Transvestite: One who habitually dresses like the opposite sex.

Tumor: An abnormal mass of tissue. Can be cancerous or benign.

Ureters: The tubes that carry urine from each kidney to the bladder.

Urethritis: Inflammation of the urethra. STDs, if they are symptomatic, often cause Urethritis.

Uterus: (Womb) The female organ which sheds its lining monthly as menstrual flow, and is capable of expanding to the vulva.

Vaccine: A suspension of infectious agents or some part of them, given for the purpose of establishing resistance to an infectious disease.

Vagina: (Birth canal) the muscular canal between the uterus and the outside of the body.

Vaginitis: Inflammation of the female vagina.

Vasectomy: A surgical procedure in which a man's sperm ducts are cut, causing sterility.

Venereal Disease: Sexually transmitted disease. Viral STDs including genital herpes, human papillomavirus (HPV), hepatitis B, and HIV (the cause of AIDS) are as yet incurable.

Virgin: A person who has not had sexual intercourse.

Vulva: The external sex organs of the female.

Wart: A raised growth on the surface of the skin or other organ.

Womb: The uterus.

Wrestler's Herpes: The presence of herpes lesions on the boy caused by HSV infection that is usually transmitted through the abrasion of skin during a contact sport, such as wrestling. Also known as herpes gladitorum.

Bibliography

Adkins, Lisa, & Merchant, Vicki, Eds. *Sexualizing the Social Power and the Organization of Sexuality*. New York: St. Martin's Press, 1996.

Antonio, Gene. *The Aids Cover-Up?* San Francisco: Ignatius Press, 1987.

Bass, Ellen and Kaufman, Kate. *Free Your Mind*. New York: HarperCollins, 1996.

Bell, David and Binnie, Jon. *The Sexual Citizen, Queer Politics and Beyond*. Cambridge: Polity Press, 2000.

Boone, Pat. *Coming Out*. Van Nuys, CA: Bible Voice, Inc. 1978.

Boswell, John. *Christianity, Social Tolerance and Homosexuality*. Chicago & London: The University of Chicago Press, 1981.

Boswell, John. *Same-Sex Unions in Premodern Europe*. New York: Vintage Books, 1995.

Brown, Peter. *The Body and Society*. New York: Columbia University Press, 1988.

Burtoft, Larry Ph.D. *Setting the Record Straight*. Focus on the Family, Public Policy Division, 1994.

Cole, William Graham. *Sex in Christianity and Psychoanalysis*. New York: Oxford University Press, 1955.

Cooke, Jean, Kramer, Ann, Rowland-Entwistle, Theodore. *History's Timeline*. New York: Crescent Books, 1981.

Cosby, Michael R.,. *Sex in the Bible*. New Jersey: Prentice-Hall, Inc., 1984.

Dallas, Joe. *A Strong Delusion, Confronting the "Gay Christian" Movement*. Eugene, OR: Harvest House Publishers, 1996.

Dannemeyer, William. *Shadow in the Land Homosexuality in America*. San Francisco: Ignatius Press, 1989.

318

Davidson, Alex. *The Returns of Love*. Downers Grove, IL: Inter-Varsity Press, 1977.

de Beauvoir, Simone. *The Second Sex*. New York: Vintage Books, 1952.

Dixon, Dr. Patrick. *The Whole Truth About AIDS*. Nashville: Thomas Nelson Publishers, 1989.

Edwards, Allen &Masters R.E.L. *The Cradle of Erotica*. New York: Bell Publishing Co., 1992.

Edwards, Jakii, Kurrack, Nancy. *Like Mother Like Daughter*. Vienna, VA: Xulon Press 2001.

Ellison, Bryan J. & Duesberg, Peter H. *Why We Will Never Win the War on AIDS*. El Cerrito, CA: Inside Story Communications, 1994.

Fowler, Richard A., & House, H Wayne. *The Christian Confronts His Culture*. Chicago: Moody Press, 1983.

Fradenburg, Louise, and Freccero, Carla, eds. *Premodern Sexualities*. New York, London: Routledge, 1996.

Gangel, Kenneth. *The Gospel and the Gay*. Nashville: Thomas Nelson Inc., 1978.

Geis, Gilbert, Ph.D. *One Eyed Justice*. New York: Drake Publishers Inc., 1974.

Gies, Frances and Joseph. *Marriage and the Family in the Middle Ages*. New York: Harper & Row, 1987.

Hadleigh, Boze. *Hollywood Gays*. New York: Barricade Books, 1996.

Harvey, John F. O.S.F.S., and Bradley, Gerald V. *Same-Sex Attraction*. South Bend, IN: St. Augustine's Press, 2003.

Harvey, John F. O.S.F.S. *The Homosexual Person*. San Francisco: Ignatius Press, 1987.

_____ *The Truth About Homosexuality, The Cry of the Faithful*. San Francisco: Ignatius Press, 1996.

Herm, Gerhard, The Celts. *The People Who Came Out of the Darkness*. New York: St. Martin's Press, 1976.

Keysor, Charles W., ed. *What You Should Know About Homosexuality*. Grand Rapids, MI: Zondervan Corporation, 1979.

Kirk, Jerry R.. *The Homosexual Crisis in the Mainline Church*. New York: Thomas Nelson Inc., 1978.

Jay, Karla, and Young, Allen. *Out of the Closets*, New York: A Jove/ HBJ Book, 1977.

Jonas, Doris, and Jonas, David. *Sex and Status*. New York: Stein and Day Publishers, 1975.

Jones, Stanton L., and Yarhouse, Mark A. *Homosexuality, The Use of Scientific Research in the Church's Morale Debate*. Downers Grove, IL: InterVarsity Press, 2000.

Karlsen, Carol F. *The Devil in the Shape of a Woman*. New York: W.W. Norton & Company, 1987.

Kiefer, Otto. *Sexual Life in Ancient Rome*. New York: Dorset Press, 1993.

Honrad, Jeff. *You Don't Have to Be Gay*. Hilo, HI: Pacific Publishing House, 2000.

LaHaye, Tim. *The Unhappy Gays*. Wheaton, IL: Tyndale House Publishers, Inc., 1978.

_____ *What Everyone Should Know About Homosexuality*. Wheaton, IL: Tyndale House Publishers, 1985.

Larue, Gerald. *Sex and the Bibl.*, New York: Prometheus Books, 1983.

Licata, Salvatore J, Ph.D., and Petersen, Robert P. *Historical Perspective on Homosexuality*. New York: The Haworth Press, 1980.

Licht, Hans. *Sexual Life in Ancient Greece*. New York: Dorset Press, 1993.

Lovelace, Richard F. *Homosexuality and the Church, Crisis, Conflict, Compassion*. Old Tappan, NJ: Fleming H. Company, 1978.

Madsen, Axel. *The Sewing Circle*. New York: Kensington Books, 1995.

Magnuson, Roger J. *Are Gay Rights Right?* Portland, OR: Multnomah, 1990.

Masters, William H., Johnson, Virginia E., and Kolodny, Robert C. *Masters and Johnson on Sex and Human Loving*. Boston, Toronto: Little Brown and Company, 1986.

McKeever, Dr. James, Ph.D. *The Aids Plague*. Medford, OR: Omega Publications, 1986.

McNeill, John J. S.J. *The Church and the Homosexual*. New York: Pocket Books, 1976.

Michael, Robert T., Gagnon, John H., Laumann, Edward O., and Kolata, Gina. *Sex in America A Definite Survey*. Boston, New York, Toronto, London: Little, Brown and Company, 1994.

Morris, Paul D. Ph.D. *Shadow of Sodom*. Wheaton, IL: Tyndale House, 1978.

Nicolosi, Joseph, Ph.D. *A Parent's Guide to Preventing Homosexuality*. Downers Grove, IL: InterVarsity Press, 2002.

Nicolosi, Joseph, Ph.D. *Reparative Therapy of Male Homosexuality*. Northvale, NJ, London: Jason Aronson Inc., 1997.

Pablos, Julia Tunon. *Women in Mexico: A Past Unveiled*. Austin: Texas Press, 1987.

Paulk, Anne. Restoring *Sexual Identity*. Eugene, OR: Harvest House Publishers, 2003.

Paulk, John and Anne. *Love Won Out*. Wheaton, IL: Tyndale, 1999.

Philpott, Kent. *The Gay Theology*. New Jersey: Logos International, 1977.

_____*The Third Sex*. Plainfield, New Jersey: Logos International, 1975.

Podles, Leon J. *The Church Impotent*. Dallas: Spence Publishing Co., 1999.

Rowe, Dr. Ed. *Homosexual Politics Road to Ruin for America*. Washington D.C.: Church League of America Capitol Hill Office, 1984.

Satinover, Jeffrey M.D. *Homosexuality and the Politics of Truth*. Grand Rapids, MI: Baker Books, 1996.

Scanzoni, Letha and Mollenkott, Virginia Ramey. *Is the Homosexual My Neighbor*. New York: Harper & Row, 1978.

Schlager, Neil, Ed. *Gay & Lesbian Almanac*. Detroit, New York: St. James Press, 1998.

Singer, June. *Androgyny*. New York: Anchor Press, 1977.

Skoglund, Elizabeth R. *Life on the Line*. Minneapolis, MN.: World Wide Publications, 1989.

Smith, Kenneth G. *Learning to Be a Man*. Downers Grove, IL: InterVarsity Press, 1976.

Socarides, Charles W., M.D. *Homosexuality a Freedom Too Far*. Phoenix, AZ: Adam Margrave Books, 1995.

Twiss, Harold L. ed. *Homosexuality and the Christian Faith, A Symposium*. Valley Forge: Judson Press, 1978.

Willhoite, Michael. *Daddy's Roommate*. England: GMP Publishers, 1990.

Williams, Don. *The Bond That Breaks: Will Homosexuality Split the Church?* Los Angeles, CA: BIM, Inc., 1978.

Wittschiebe, Charles. *God Invented Sex*. Nashville, TN: Southern Publishing Association, 1974.

Wooding, Dan. *He Intends Victory*. Irvine, CA: Village Books Publishing, 2003.

Woods, Gregory. *A History of Gay Literature*. New Haven and London: Yale University, 1999.

Wyden, Peter & Barbara. *Growing Up Straight*. New York: Stein and Day, 1968.

About the Author

Peggy Kirk, a northwest marriage and family counselor, musician, award-winning artist and writer, graduated from Northwest College with a B.A. in Counseling and a Masters Degree in Biblical Literature. Currently teaching for Grays Harbor College and Adult Education at Faith Community, she also accepts clients for Marriage and Family Counseling. Her weekly Counseling Column is published in the *Ocean Shores Journal*. She sits on several boards including the State Board for the Christian Coalition in the State of Washington. She is "on-call" as a counselor for Heart and Hands Pregnancy Center and serves on the Professional Resources Council of Celebrate Life Inc.

Ms. Kirk is winner of the 1990 King County Written Arts Award, the Golden Poet Award in 1989, and the Medford Mail Tribune Poet Award. She has written columns for the *Church Musician*, "The Pitching Corner," and for the *Church Journal*, "What Is the Question?" and has published articles in several magazines. Her previous book is *You Aren't Alone: The Voices of Abortion* (Blue Dolphin Publishing, 2003).

Mrs. Kirk has won many prestigious art awards. She has illustrated magazine covers and booklets, and has paintings hanging in the Galleria d'Arce, Venice, Italy, Waterloobay, Bredon Teewkesbury Glos., England. A watercolor painting was chosen by the Bellevue Chamber of Commerce to be presented to His Excellency, Gustav Petriccioli, Ambassador of Mexico in 1991.

You Aren't Alone
The Voices of Abortion

Peggy Kirk

ISBN: 1-57733-113-3, 220, pp., 6x9, paper, $16.95

If you are considering an abortion, this book is for you. Read the stories of women and girls who have had abortions. Read about their lives and decisions. You may find a story similar to your own.

The intention is not to put a guilt trip on you, or hit you over the head with religion, or pass judgment on you. This book was written because of and for women who are in difficult situations.

The women who shared their stories are very brave. As you read about their lives you will laugh, cry, even get angry. Most of all, in reading these stories you may be better able to decide what is right for you. An abortion is a big step with life-long consequences.

In the author's experience as a marriage and family counselor, the loss of a baby in abortion causes post-abortion trauma in nearly every case. Abortion causes a permanent loss. It is because of that loss that serious problems begin to affect the lives of women who have had abortions.

There are alternatives to abortion. Thousands of loving couples who can't give birth themselves are praying daily for a woman to care enough to share her blessing of birth with them.

Others have been where you are at this moment.
You are not alone.

Orders: 1-800-643-0765 • www.bluedolphinpublishing.com

OTHER TITLES
FROM BLUE DOLPHIN PUBLISHING

Awakening Love: *The Universal Mission: Spiritual Healing in Psychology and Medicine* by Nicholas Demetry and Edwin Clonts
ISBN: 1-57733-075-7, 240 pp., 6x9, paper, $14.95

Becoming the Husband Your Wife Thought She Married: *It's Your Life, Too, Man* by James A. Schaller, M.D.
ISBN: 1-57733-059-5, 308 pp., 6x9, paper, $16.95

Coming to Life: *The Emergence of Self in the Human Life Cycle* by James Doak
ISBN: 0-931892-11-2, 160 pp., 5.5 x 8.5, paper, $9.95

Edgework: *Exploring the Psychology of Disease: A Manual for Healing Beyond Diet and Fitness* by Ronald L. Peters, M.D.
ISBN: 1-57733-116-8, 284 pp., 6x9, paperback, $17.95

Freeing the Human Spirit: *A Psychiatrist's Journal* by Louis B. Fierman, M.D.
ISBN: 1-57733-100-1, 240 pp., 5.69 x 8.75, hardcover, $24.95

Improving Relationships: *A Guide for Enhancing Personalities using Nine Personality Types* by Albert Heid
ISBN: 1-57733-117-6, 168 pp., 5x8, paper, $12.95

Johnson's Emotional First Aid: *How to Increase Your Happiness, Peace, and Joy* by Victoria Ann Johnson, M.A.
ISBN: 1-57733-015-3, 72 pp., color illus., 7.75 x 10, paper, $15.95

The Little Book of Big Feared Truths: *Overcoming the Main Obstacle to Healthy Self-Esteem* by Herbert S. Demmin, Ph.D.
ISBN: 1-57733-101-X, 128 pp., 5x8, paper, $12.95

Points: *The Most Practical Program Ever to Improve Your Self-Image* by David A. Gustafson
ISBN: 0-931892-74-0, 192 pp., 5.5 x 8.5, paper, $12.95

Orders: 1-800-643-0765 • www.bluedolphinpublishing.com

Printed in the United States
20167LVS00007B/166